A Radical Dissonance Theory

A Radical Dissonance Theory

Jean-Léon Beauvois
and
Robert-Vincent Joule

Taylor & Francis
Publishers since 1798

UK   Taylor & Francis Ltd, 1 Gunpowder Square, London EC4A 3DE

USA   Taylor & Francis Inc., 1900 Frost Road, Suite 101, Bristol, PA 19007

First published 1996

A catalogue record for this book is available from the British Library

ISBN 0–7484–0472–4 (hbk)
ISBN 0–7484–0473–2 (pbk)

Library of Congress Cataloging-in-Publication Data are available on request

Cover design by Amanda Barragry

Typeset by RGM, The Mews, Birkdale Village, Southport

Printed in Great Britain by SRP, Exeter.

Contents

In memory of Leon Festinger

Introduction

Festinger's theory of cognitive dissonance

The 1950s perspective of rationality

In experimental social psychology, the late 1940s and the early 1950s saw the great tide of human relations studies reach its high point with the work of Kurt Lewin, Bales and their followers. It was only after a considerable lapse of time that the study of small group functioning — of the processes of social influence, social climates and interpersonal communications — which was inspired by, if not inherent in, Elton Mayo's discoveries at Western Electric, was to re-emerge following the appearance of the 'great works' of the period: those of Lewin and Bales, and also those of Asch, Schachter and Festinger (Festinger, 1950).

The possibility of allying the concerns awakened by the discovery of informal structures and social motivations to the spirit and methods of behaviourism allowed Human Relations to achieve maturity, respectability and success in a mere 20 years. The individual (in fact, the worker) was essentially viewed as a being situated within groups and relation networks, directed by social motivations that he or she is able to satisfy to a greater or lesser degree by establishing interpersonal relations and constructing beliefs within the framework of small groups.

The 1950s was to see the development of a new conception of the human being, more in accordance with the nascent or, perhaps, re-emergent cognitivist approach. Within this perspective, individuals are considered to be rational beings: rational in their choices, their behaviour and their theories. Like the perspective that preceded it, this new conception was in no way independent of the prevailing understanding of the human being at work. In addition, the principle of rationality (albeit a limited rationality) was to be impressively reaffirmed in 1958 by March and Simon's highly influential theory of organizational behaviour. However, on this occasion social psychologists were in no mood to play follow-my-leader. In their insistence on subordinating action to knowledge they shared much of the responsibility for promoting what we might term 'the 1950s perspective of rationality'.

The strategist, the statistician, the scientist and the logician

Clearly, when they rediscovered that thought could constitute an important object of research, social psychologists had to look elsewhere for models. At the same time, the normative character of the 1950s perspective of rationality could not be shrugged off. In fact, social psychologists started by adapting theories and models originally elaborated to be prescriptive but that were considered to be, at least in certain situations, descriptive.

This can be clearly observed in the use made of game theory. Popularized by the work of Von Neumann and Morgenstern (1944), this theory[1] deals with the behaviour of rational decision-makers who wish to maximize the benefits to themselves in situations where the behaviour of someone else is the main source of uncertitude. As a normative theory, it is superbly adapted for use by a businessman or army officer seeking to apply rules of optimization. The gamble taken by psychologists, and social psychologists in particular, was to think that the theory could also furnish them with a descriptive model of certain social interactions. The success of game situations in the experiments conducted by social psychologists, in particular after 1957, is well known (see the reviews proposed by Rapoport and Orwart, 1962, and Apfelbaum, 1966).

The same observation is true of the statistical models borrowed by social psychologists to serve as models of human judgement and predictive activity. In an important work which appeared in 1954 (*The Foundations of Statistics*), Savage proposes 'a highly idealized theory of the behaviour of a "rational" person' (p. 7) whose opinions change with the availability of new facts. While it is clear that this theory might serve as a guide for certain professionals, businessmen or medical diagnosticians,[2] the idea that it might account for everyday anticipations and judgements represented a further gamble. This gamble lies at the origin of a long tradition of research in which regression models (from 1955, by Hammond) and Bayesian models were applied to the activities of judgement and prediction (see the review by Slovic and Lichtenstein, 1973).

We find the same attitude in the use of the scientific model of knowledge production. During the 1950s, some of the leading theorists viewed the human being as a spontaneous scientist (naïve or intuitive), a perspective that was to become a key axiom in the development of cognitive social psychology. This is clearly evident in the case of Fritz Heider (1958), whose analyses of naïve psychology and attribution processes were to become so influential. However, we might also include the probabilistic functionalism of Egon Brunswik (see his work of 1956, published by his pupils after his death) and Kelly's (1955) theory of personal constructs. In all three cases, human beings are considered to know the world, know themselves and know others within a perspective of rational action and effective control. Rationality is thus to be found both in knowledge (quasi- or pre-scientific) and in the production of action (based on knowledge).

Finally, we observe the same phenomenon when we turn to borrowings of logical concepts. It is well known that the 1950s saw the birth of the paradigms of the great theories of cognitive consistency. All these theories are based on the hypothesis that there exists a preferred state of the individual's cognitive universe in which the relations between cognitions are maintained in a way that confers optimum coherence (of 'symmetry' for Newcomb, 1953; of 'congruence' for Osgood and Tannenbaum, 1955; of 'consonance' for Festinger, 1957a and of 'balance' for Heider, 1958). In these theories the cognitive dynamic derives from an explicit conception of the nature of this preferred state of coherence. This concept of a preferred state of the cognitive universe, the idea of consistency — in short, the non-contradiction of the propositions of the system — is in no way at variance with the presuppositions of the principal theories borrowed from the field of logic. While certain theorists (Abelson and Rosenberg, 1958) were keen to emphasize the psycho-logical character of the relations between cognitions and, therefore, of the state of consistency, others did not hesitate to borrow their model directly from the field of logic. Thus McGuire (1960) advanced a syllogistic conception of the state of consistency based on the salience of the implications between certain cognitions considered as major or minor and the conclusion of potential syllogisms. It is true that McGuire's theory is somewhat peripheral to the core of cognitive consistency theory. However, we may well imagine that to its advocates cognitive coherence was in every respect a form of rationality (even if this is a 'psycho-logical' rationality) and that in borrowing the term 'consistency' from logic they were reflecting a new conception of the human being that social psychologists were to promote and that, through them or independently of them, was rapidly to find expression within the social sciences and theories of organization.

Cognitive dissonance theory as a theory of consistency

This is how human subjects, as viewed by the social psychologists of the 1960s, might be described. While their cognitive universe is undoubtedly too complex to be simply 'logical', they nevertheless conform to the principles of psycho-logical consistency. They build their social reality in a deterministic or probabilistic way using quasi-scientific procedures and constructs. If their opinions and judgements change, it is because the facts themselves have changed in a statistically apprehensible way. They adapt their decisions and behaviour to what they know about events and objects and to the uncertitudes of the situation (in particular to uncertitudes associated with the behaviour of others) in a way that will maximize the benefits and usefulness to themselves. It is a type of decision-making strategy based on statistics, logic and knowledge.

Such a description would certainly represent a reaction to the concept of the 'nice guy' directed by group standards and social reinforcements; that is to say, the type of description that would certainly have been proposed by a theorist of the 1940s influenced by the great Human Relations movement, and perhaps even by

Introduction

Festinger himself at the end of the 1940s.[3] However, neither the unavoidably caricatural nature of this brief summary nor the evocation of what we know today about the results of later research should be allowed to obscure the fact that rationality, in the various guises described above, was a key concept of social psychology in the 1950s.

Seen from this viewpoint, the theory of cognitive dissonance when presented as a theory of consistency — as, indeed, it was presented by Festinger in 1957 — would seem to sit perfectly within this historical context from which it draws most of its metatheoretical presuppositions. The key idea of the psychological implication between two cognitions can easily be considered as a complex form of the psycho-logical relationship, of which logical implication is only a single case that happens to be simpler than the others. Thus, McGuire's original theory can be entirely rewritten using two or three concepts taken from Festinger. Festinger himself, and others after him, were to insist that cognitive dissonance theory was related to other cognitive consistency theories, and in particular to Heider's theory: 'These were proposed under various names but had in common the notion that the person tends to behave in ways that minimize the internal inconsistency among his interpersonal relations, among his intrapersonal cognitions, or among his beliefs, feelings and actions' (McGuire, 1966, p. 1). 'Each theorist, it would seem, needs a pair of polar adjectives and a paradigm . . . Each pair of words contains one adjective that describes cognitions that fit together consistently, while the other describes cognitions that are inconsistent with one another. The basic paradigm is simply that inconsistency motivates people to alter their cognitive system in such a way that it will become consistent' (Singer, 1966, pp. 47–48). Dissonance theory might therefore have been united or developed in unison with other theories of rationality or, at the very least, with other theories of consistency. However, this was not to happen.

The development of the 1950s perspective of rationality

The various trends growing from the 1950s perspective of rationality were to develop differently in the field of social psychology. An examination of their diverse evolutions exceeds the scope of this work. For this reason we shall restrict ourselves to a few observations of a global nature.

> It took only a few years of research to show that game theory is unable to describe ongoing decisions taken in those situations which are of most interest to a social psychologist, and in particular in so-called 'mixed motivation' situations such as the famous prisoner's dilemma (Apfelbaum, 1966, Plon, 1967). As a result, the experimental study of games has subsequently focused on other objectives (for example, the factors determining the choice of a cooperative or competitive strategy).

Today, few researchers view human beings as spontaneous statisticians. Instead, the famous research conducted by Kahneman and Tversky (1973) has made it possible to enumerate all the rules and laws that subjects apply only with extreme parsimony or that they apply, for example, only because it has been suggested to them in the form of implicit instructions (as we believe to be the case with the work of Kruglanski, Friedland and Farkash, 1984) or when the formal statistical problem that they have been set can be construed in a way that permits a causal analysis (Ajzen, 1977). However, most of the time statistical inference is supplanted by the use of a heuristic.

The axiom that holds that human beings are spontaneous scientists has certainly shown more resistance and may nowadays still be accepted implicitly by the majority of social psychologists. We have no choice but to accept that human beings produce, acquire, remember and manage knowledge. If this knowledge is not at least 'scientific' in tendency, what else can it be? Since most social psychologists hold a monistic conception of knowledge,[4] they must accept the idea that human beings are spontaneous scientists. However, since the 1980s, this axiom seems to have lost some of its heuristic virtues, which related to the conception of the processes of inference and thus to the production of knowledge. This conception had been borrowed from science in a most impressive fashion by the theorist Kelley (1967: analysis of covariation plus analysis of variance). If human beings are indeed spontaneous scientists, it is now only because they articulate knowledge which may tend to be true or tend to be false, in exactly the same way as a scientist. However, they are unfortunately often too biased or too economical with their cognitive resources when required to produce knowledge, with the result that scientific activity cannot be proposed as a universal model of human knowledge.

While the concept of cognitive consistency appears to have lasted well, it arouses little interest nowadays. McGuire, who borrowed an excessively powerful (or excessively simple) model, has since proved to be an excellent self-critic (McGuire, 1968). However, despite the failure of syllogistic consistency and corrected logic, other models of consistency have never been subjected to any decisive theoretical criticism or experimental reverses. Few articles appearing nowadays call on the principles of congruence and/or balance. This disaffection can clearly be traced to the emergence of the information-processing paradigm and the increasing concern of researchers with the analysis of cognitive organization and with the effects associated with this organization. However, this is probably no more than a question of fashion: despite their elegance, 'cognitivist' reformulations of the balance described by Heider in terms of implicational molecules (Abelson and Reich, 1969) have failed to breathe new life into balance theory. As we know, Heider's descriptions of the processes of causal attribution have otherwise survived more successfully. It is probably more correct to explain researchers' relative uninterest in cognitive consistency by the fact that its advocates were able neither to get beyond the original hypotheses of the theory, which finally proved to be relatively trivial, nor to revive the experimental practices which these hypotheses had originally stimulated (Osgood and Tannenbaum, 1955, for congruence theory; Jordan, 1953, for balance theory). In fact, the body of experimental work relating to the principles of congruence and balance has developed little since Zajonc's excellent synthesis (1968).

The specificity of dissonance theory

Rationality or rationalization?

When we turn to the body of experimental work relating to Festinger's cognitive dissonance theory things are very different. It is now commonplace to recall that, despite Festinger's reticence in defending his ideas, cognitive dissonance theory has marked the theoretical and experimental work of the 1960s and 1970s (a review by Cooper and Croyle showed that more than 1000 articles had appeared by 1984). It is yet another commonplace to point out that few theories have given rise to so many debates and so much controversy, or, indeed, have been subjected to so many reformulations. We should remember that the last major reformulation of dissonance theory is barely more than 10 years old (*A New Look at Dissonance Theory*: Cooper and Fazio, 1984). It has thus had a very different history from other theories of consistency, which have all been rapidly swept, largely unmissed, from the forefront of psychosocial research.

These observations led us to formulate the key focus of the current work and of our own conception of dissonance theory (Beauvois and Joule, 1981, Joule, 1986b): if this theory has enjoyed so different a history from that of other contemporaneous theories, it is because it owes relatively little to the 1950s perspective of rationality, despite Festinger's claims to the contrary. It is therefore neither a theory of rationality nor *a fortiori* a theory of cognitive consistency.

1 It is not a theory of rationality, since the dissonance reduction process it describes, while clearly cognitive in nature, is also post-behavioural and consequently incapable of preparing rational action.
2 It is not a theory of consistency, since the function of this post-behavioural dissonance reduction process is not to eliminate cognitive inconsistencies (as we shall see, it can even produce them) but to rationalize behaviour.

If dissonance theory is so much at variance with the theoretical climate of the 1950s, why have we insisted on recalling this climate and commencing this work with a review of the 1950s perspective of rationality? There are at least two reasons.

First, because it is always useful to approach a theory safe in the knowledge of what it is not. The subject described by cognitive dissonance theory does not correspond to the description of human beings which might have been presented by a theorist, even a theorist in the field of cognitive consistency, towards the end of the 1960s.

Second, because first Festinger himself and then his followers took great pains to integrate dissonance theory into the prevailing theoretical climate by presenting it at the metatheoretical level as a simple theory of cognitive consistency. In doing this, they ignored at least two crucial characteristics of the theoretical and experimental practices of dissonance theory, characteristics that were confirmed by the subsequent development of social psychology.

1 Of the theories said to relate to cognitive consistency, dissonance theory is the only one to have produced rigorously counterintuitive hypotheses. This is clearly what provoked the controversies and debates that the theories of balance and congruence have managed to avoid, not without reason.

2 In the experimental situations where these hypotheses have been applied, subjects are first led to produce a behaviour that the theory predicts without being able to account for it: in some cases, subjects must make a choice (decision paradigm), while, in others, they must produce a problematic behaviour, that is to say one that runs counter to their attitudes or motivations (forced compliance paradigm). In brief, the theory, at least in the form it takes in experimental work, necessitates some preliminary behaviour on the part of the subject which the experimenter may know how to elicit without always being able to provide a theoretical explanation for it.

Forced compliance

This perspective requires that we accord a special status to the vast body of experimental work conducted in situations of forced compliance. Although it has been possible to attack dissonance theory on the grounds of the other paradigm in which it has excelled, that of decision (Mills and O'Neil, 1971, O'Neil, 1971), it is the situations of forced compliance that have aroused the most intense, and without doubt the most fruitful, theoretical debates. In such situations, subjects are induced to satisfy a request that the experimenter knows will be problematic for them because it is either counterattitudinal or countermotivational. They may be asked to give a speech counter to their own private opinions as in the two original experiments conducted by Festinger and Carlsmith (1959) and Cohen (1959, described in Brehm and Cohen, 1962). Alternatively, they may be required to perform a boring or unpleasant task (eating grilled grasshoppers), a painful task (receiving a blast of air in the eye), or even a task that contradicts their moral values, as proposed by Glass (1964) for example when he asked students to punish a colleague with electric shocks shortly after they had declared themselves to be against such practices. Finally, the task may simply require subjects to refrain from a particular behaviour, (as in the famous 'forbidden toy' situation first staged by Aronson and Carlsmith in 1963) or to deprive themselves of something (deprivation of food, drink, tobacco, see Brehm and Crocker, 1962, Brehm, 1962, Joule, 1986).

The distinguishing characteristic of the forced compliance paradigm is that, in each case, dissonance theory makes it possible to predict the cognitive effects of a problematic behaviour required by the experimenter and generally accepted by the subjects. It will surprise no one if we assert that, in the wake of Festinger's work, it is the effects of forced compliance that have attracted the most important theoretical work and spawned the most significant revisions to the theory. This is why in the current work we shall remain within the framework set by this experimental paradigm. It also seems to us to be perfectly representative of the situations for which dissonance theory appears to have been developed, in that it studies subjects who are more compliant than rational in their behaviour and whose cognitive task (dissonance reduction) lies precisely in restoring value to behaviour that may have been somewhat lacking in worth when the subjects first agreed to undertake it.

To persuade ourselves of this, let us return briefly to Glass' (1964) experiment. As we have already mentioned, the subjects had previously declared themselves to be against the use of electric shocks in experiments on human subjects. These subjects were then asked to punish a colleague who had made errors in a learning task using 100-volt electric shocks. To make it clear that these were fairly violent shocks, the subjects themselves received an electric shock of 40 volts. Yet, in the so-called 'free choice' situation, none of the subjects refused to comply with the experimenter's request. Can we speak in terms of rational decisions when faced with such an acceptance? It seems to us that the principle of economy is far better satisfied by an explanation in terms of compliant behaviour in the face of a social actor who is endowed with a certain power. As far as the cognitive work tested by Glass is concerned (the devaluing of the victim), it is certainly possible to consider it as a process of restoring the coherence between ideas or even (which would agree better with Glass' views) as a process of restoring the self-concept. However, whichever interpretation we choose, the first task is to restore the value of the behaviour; that is to rationalize the behaviour, and this is all that is predicted by dissonance theory.

Of course, dissonance theory can also function as a theory of consistency and thus as a virtual theory of human rationality. However, even the most cursory examination of its history reveals that this is not how it has worked, inspired and survived during the course of its various reformulations and revisions. It is possible to see these reformulations as originating in the coincidence of two circumstances. On the one hand, it has not been possible for researchers working in the field of dissonance theory, and for the most part within the forced compliance paradigm, to avoid noticing the specificity of this theory when compared with other theories of consistency. Since, however, they had not in our view satisfactorily established all the implications of the original theory, they considered that a new theory was necessary to explain this specificity. What we shall attempt to show here is that this specificity is intrinsically bound up with Festinger's initial formulations, which we intend to present in the following.

The fundamentals of the 1957 theory

In his work, Festinger presents the theory of cognitive dissonance together with the major paradigms within which the theory is operative. Nevertheless, he accompanies this presentation with a number of metatheoretical considerations that seem to us to obscure the theory itself. Our intention here is to recall the fundamental theoretical propositions, that is those that have proved indispensable for the production and interpretation of experimental effects, while ignoring considerations of a metatheoretical nature. For example, when Festinger states 'that dissonance is a motivating factor in its own right' (p. 3), he is formulating a theoretical proposition that underlies experiments constructed precisely in order to validate this proposition. Similarly, when he suggests that 'the strength of the pressures to reduce the dissonance is a function of the magnitude of the dissonance' (p. 18), he is formulating a principle on which every prediction derived from dissonance theory is based.

In contrast, when he writes that 'if one replaces the word "balanced" with "consonant" and "imbalance" with "dissonance", many statements by Heider can be seen to indicate the same process with which our discussion up to now has dealt' (p. 8), he is beginning to examine his own theory. This examination is thus metatheoretical and has no effective consequences at the experimental level.

This metatheoretical examination does little more than reflect Festinger's own judgements and opinions concerning his theory and its position within the broad family of consistency theories. At various stages we shall see that Festinger's metatheory is not always compatible with his own theoretical statements and that it may have led him to commit some unfortunate inaccuracies. For this reason, we consider it necessary to concentrate exclusively on the small number of fundamental propositions that we have termed the core of the 1957 theory. These propositions concern both cognitive organization and cognitive dynamics. There are very few of them.

Consonance and dissonance relations

Cognitive organization, as understood by cognitive dissonance theory, implies only three basic concepts: the concept of cognition (knowledge elements) and two concepts that make it possible to define the relations that may obtain between cognitions taken two at a time: implication and incompatibility. As these are the primitive concepts of the theory we might expect them to possess a minimal definition. Thus Festinger understands cognition or a knowledge element to be 'any knowledge, opinion, or belief about the environment, about oneself, or about one's behaviour' (p. 3). This is therefore an extremely extensive concept which may encompass very abstract representations such as 'the New Haven police should not interfere on the campus' as well as everyday representations such as 'I'm thirsty', 'I've been paid $20' and so on. As for the implication between two cognitions,[5] this is little more than the idea that two cognitions fit together well. The concept receives no systematic definition and is illustrated solely by examples. It can be reduced to the following: the presence of cognition A in a subject's cognitive field must be accompanied by the presence of cognition B. Here again, the type of implication may be extremely varied, from the logical implications that were to be the object of McGuire's theory (1960) to more normative, psychological or even contingent implications which associate the knowledge subjects have of their thirst (cognition A) with the knowledge that they are about to drink (cognition B). It is on this latter type of implication that dissonance theorists have concentrated. When we turn to the concept of incompatibility,[6] we find that it, too, goes practically undefined. It relates to the idea that a cognition may be confronted with another cognition which is contradictory to it ('the obverse'). Thus the cognition 'I have decided not to drink' is the obverse of the cognition 'I am going to drink'.

Once these three primitive concepts are accepted, we can define three possible relations between two cognitions A and B that are effectively present in a subject's cognitive field. If the two cognitions are linked by an implication, we can say they are in a relation of consonance. If one is contradictory to what would be implied by the other, we can say that they are in a relation of dissonance. If no implication is possible between the two cognitions or, alternatively, between one and the obverse of the other, then the two cognitions are in a state of irrelevance (or neutrality). Thus cognition A: 'I am thirsty' and cognition B: 'I am going to have a drink' are, when linked by a psychological implication, in a relation of consonance. In contrast, cognition A: 'I am thirsty' and cognition C: 'I have decided not to drink' are in a relation of dissonance, where A would have implied B which is the obverse of C. Finally, cognition A: 'I am thirsty' and cognition D: 'I have bought a car', where A implies neither D nor its obverse, are in a relation of irrelevance. Clearly, dissonance theory is concerned only with consonant or dissonant, that is to say relevant, relations.

At this point, it is important to note that the definitions given above relate only to pairs of cognitions and take no account of any relation that either might have to other cognitions. Thus, the A–C pair above can be thought of as designating a dissonance relation quite independently of the fact that C might be consonant with other cognitions F: 'I am being paid for it', G: 'I am helping the experimenter'. Thus, cognitive dissonance theory does not allow us to speak of relations of consonance or dissonance for entities other than pairs of cognitions.

The state of dissonance

This concludes our discussion of what the theory has to say about cognitive organization. Unfortunately, Festinger uses the same word, dissonant, to qualify the psychological state of an individual whose mind contains one or more dissonant relations. This is rather surprising, considering that, of the theorists of cognitive consistency, among whom he counts himself, Festinger is the one who insists most fully on the specificity of this psychological state which he calls 'noxious' and which he views as a drive state. However, this is more than just surprising. It is also misleading, since this polysemy of the word 'dissonance' in Festinger's presentation of the theory might lead one to believe that a 'dissonance relation' always generates a 'dissonant psychological state' and that there is a sort of theoretical equivalence between the presence of dissonance relations in a subject's cognitive universe and the drive state which can lead to their elimination or reduction. We shall see that this is not the case. It would thus have been preferable to use different terms to designate the relations between cognitions which do not fit together well and the psychological state which some of these relations can generate under certain circumstances.

Festinger thus sees this state as one of motivational tension and, like any other tension, it needs to be reduced. It is this specific state of dissonance which then orients the cognitive dynamic which has the reduction of the tension as its objective: 'cognitive dissonance can be seen as an antecedent condition which leads to activity oriented toward dissonance reduction just as hunger leads to activity oriented toward hunger reduction' (p. 3). It should therefore be possible to observe cognitive changes that have the effect of minimizing the noxious state of dissonance. Thus, provided that the situation is such as to provoke the feeling of dissonance, individuals who have been induced to deprive themselves of drink might well feel their thirst less in a way that minimizes this state (dissonance reduction). The cognition 'I am thirsty' (which is incompatible with the cognition 'I am depriving myself of drink') is probably critical in the state of dissonance experienced by these individuals. Festinger suggests that the resources available for dissonance reduction are proportional to the tension experienced. In other words, the greater the tension, the more cognitive changes we should see aimed at reducing the state of dissonance. It can be seen that this motivational conception of the state of dissonance requires quantification. Festinger is thus led to propose a measure of dissonance.

The dissonance ratio

If we consider the global context of consonance and dissonance with respect to a particular cognition, then, for Festinger, the total amount of dissonance will depend on the proportion of dissonant cognitions in the set of relevant cognitions. If D represents the sum of all the dissonances involving a particular cognition and C the sum of all the consonances, then the level of dissonance is given by the ratio $D/D + C$.

This is a key element of the theory. We shall see that this ratio contains almost all the specificity of cognitive dissonance theory. Shortly before Festinger decided to quantify the state of dissonance in this way, structural balance theorists had proposed a measure of the imbalance of a structure (Cartwright and Harary, 1956) which derived from a fundamentally different conception. In conformity with the formalization used in structural balance theory, this measure is given by the ratio of the unbalanced triads to the total number of triads implied by the structure (see Flament, 1968).

This was therefore a measure relating to the whole of the structure under consideration and which accorded no particular status to any of the cognitions involved. This type of measure was in perfect conformity with Heiderian premises that viewed the cognitive universe as a sort of scene which is contemplated by the perceiver and which satisfies to a greater or lesser degree his or her preference for balanced structures. Festinger, who advances no arguments for his choice, was to opt for a different approach. In effect, for him the evaluation of the total amount of dissonance requires the analysis of a special element which makes it possible to assign the status of consonant or dissonant to the other cognitions. Therefore, to a certain extent, this measure is oriented by a special cognition whose status will be discussed later. For the moment, suffice it to remember that C cognitions are, by definition, those that imply this special cognition, while D cognitions are those that imply its obverse. The cognitive universe is thus referred to this particular cognition, and this cognition alone, as a measure of the state of dissonance.

In supplying the theory with dependent and independent variables, this measure of the state of dissonance has two types of consequence for experimental predictions. First, when we consider the dependent variables, it may indicate empirically realizable ways of reducing the state of tension. These must always result in a quantitative diminution of the ratio. For the subject, this reduction may be obtained either by suppressing or diminishing the importance of the dissonant cognitions, or by adding consonant cognitions or, finally, by increasing the importance of existing consonant cognitions. Therefore we need only know the cognitions that are susceptible to modifications of this type in order to establish relevant dependent variables. Second, this measure of the state of dissonance provides the principle underlying experimental manipulations, that is, it provides the independent variables: if we know that the subjects in group X possess one dissonant cognition more (or one consonant cognition less) than the subjects in group Y, then we may expect to observe more cognitive change on the part of the subjects of the first group than in those of the second group (the reason being that because the work involved in reducing a tension is proportional to the magnitude of the tension, the cognitive work of dissonance reduction will be proportional to the total amount of dissonance).

To conclude, let us illustrate the functioning of these core propositions by recalling the reasoning of Festinger and Carlsmith (1959) when predicting the famous effect of reward in a situation of forced compliance. A subject who has a particular private opinion (cognition A: 'I find this task boring') receives a certain sum of money ($1 or $20) to defend the contrary opinion in public (cognition B: 'I have said that this task was interesting'). Following this lie, the subject is asked to evaluate the task in question. The subject may feel dissonance in so far as cognition A implies the obverse of cognition B. However, subjects can reduce the dissonance generated by the lie by finding the task interesting since this brings their opinions into conformity with what they have told others about the task. The question is whether this change is greater in a subject who is paid $1 or in one who receives $20. Let us calculate the total amount of dissonance. The particular cognition on which Festinger and Carlsmith chose to base their calculation corresponded to the public statement of interest in the task (cognition B). C is the cognition relating to the reward (C1: $1 and C2: $20). This cognition is consonant with reference to B since we can suppose that C implies B. Finally, we should remember that A is dissonant with reference to B. All other things being equal, the total amount of dissonance will be higher when the value of the reward is low: $D/D + C1 > D/D + C2$. We should therefore observe more marked dissonance reduction work (that is a change towards a more favourable evaluation of the task) in the subjects who received the smallest reward. As we know, Festinger and Carlsmith's results confirmed this prediction.

We are now familiar with the various components forming the core of the 1957 dissonance theory with which, it seems to us, all dissonance theorists should be in agreement. All the predictions permitted by this theory have been directly and exclusively based on what we have set out above.

It can be seen that this core is simultaneously rigorous and flexible.

It is rigorous in that it provides a solid theoretical basis for the key notion of the state of dissonance: this is a state of motivational tension that is induced by the existence of certain relations of dissonance between cognitions and that is oriented towards its reduction, that is the elimination of these relations and the production of consistent, new relations. It is also rigorous in that it provides an unambiguous definition of the measure of this state (dissonance ratio).

It is flexible on at least two counts. First, because it contains no propositions constraining the conditions that have to be fulfilled if the theory is to function. It was not until the 1960s that such conditions were specified. However, it is also flexible because it contains few instructions relating to the operationalization of the main concepts. It is for this reason that writers have so often insisted on the role of intuition in the application of dissonance theory (see Pepitone, 1966, Zajonc, 1968). However, it is important to note that this appeal to intuition relates to the preliminary analysis of the situation (what are the psychological implications? which cognitions are present and relevant?) rather than to the actual functioning of the theory itself. In all but the undoubtedly important question of the conditions necessary for its functioning, the 1957 theory is self-sufficient.

In the following we shall retain all the propositions drawn from this fundamental core and will demonstrate that there is no need to introduce new propositions to account for the specificity of dissonance theory among the other theories of consistency and to formulate hypotheses that are incompatible with its main competitors. However, before turning our attention to this task we shall briefly recall how Festinger's successors felt obliged to amend this theory. We shall see that such modifications are actually based on a procedure which confuses the theory's conditions of functioning with the theory itself, that is a procedure that modifies the fundamental core of the theory by integrating new concepts drawn from a study of its conditions of functioning. Our claim is not only that this was unnecessary, but also that it was incompatible with the original propositions of the theory.

The revisions to the original theory

Since this original statement by Festinger (1957a), cognitive dissonance theory has been the object of numerous revisions. The best known are those proposed by Brehm and Cohen (1962 and after), Aronson (1968, 1969), Wicklund and Brehm (1976) and, most recently, Cooper and Fazio (1984). These were in no way minor revisions and, indeed, we might ask ourselves today what is left of the original premisses. It would appear that the most important premiss to have been retained is that dissonance is a drive state aroused by the juxtaposition of two cognitive elements x and y which do not fit together. For example, in Festinger and Carlsmith's initial experiment (1959), the cognition 'I believe the task is dull' does not fit with the cognition 'I said the task was interesting.' Why? It is in their answer to this question that we discover the difference between the various revisions. As we shall discuss later, whether used explicitly or not the concept of commitment and, it must be admitted, the anthropomorphic intuitions that it can inspire, provide us with the key to these revisions.

The concepts of commitment and volition

In the first work to attempt a synthesis of dissonance studies, Brehm and Cohen (1962) made use of two new concepts: commitment and volition. For these authors, commitment must be considered as a necessary condition for the arousal of dissonance. Its role is considered to be: '. . . first, to aid the specification of psychological implication and hence the determination of what is consonant and what is dissonant and, second, to aid in the specification of the ways in which a person may try to reduce dissonance' (p. 9). However, they fail to provide any really convincing definition of commitment, being content to assert that: '. . . a person is committed when he has decided to do or not do a certain thing, when he has chosen one (or more) alternatives and thereby rejected one (or more) alternatives, when he actively engages in a given behaviour or has engaged in a given behaviour' (p. 7). Moreover, in their attempt to define the concept of commitment, Brehm and Cohen introduce the concept of volition. This concept refers to the feeling of responsibility, control and choice experienced by the individual on making a decision: 'Volition implies not only initiation and selection of behaviour but also responsibility for consequences. What we wish to suggest is that volition provides another source of psychological implication' (pp. 201–2).

The self-concept

It is undoubtedly Aronson's revision that diverges most from Festinger's original version. While Brehm and Cohen were content to subject the conditions preceding the arousal of dissonance to psychological analysis, Aronson (1968, 1969) was to situate dissonance in the discrepancies that may exist between individuals' behaviour and the idea that they have of themselves. More precisely, for this author dissonance is aroused whenever the self-concept is challenged and, in particular, in conditions in which the self-concept is threatened. In his analysis of Festinger and Carlsmith's famous experiment, he proposes that: 'the important aspect of dissonance . . . is not that the cognition "I said X" is dissonant with the cognition "I believe not X". Rather the crucial fact is that I have misled people: The cognition "I have said something I don't believe and it could have bad consequences for people" is dissonant with my self-concept; that is, it is dissonant with my cognition that "I am a decent, reasonable, truthful person"' (Aronson, 1992, p. 202).

The concept of personal responsibility

In the most important work of synthesis devoted to Festinger's theory, Wicklund and Brehm (1976) have incorporated the two earlier revisions in terms of the concept of personal responsibility. According to them, without personal responsibility the dissonant events are psychologically irrelevant for the individual. More precisely, dissonance reduction: 'takes place only when the dissonant elements have been brought together through the personal responsibility of the individual who experiences dissonance' (p. 7). They use two criteria to define responsibility: choice and the foreseeability of undesired consequences. In other words, the individual must have the possibility of choosing to do or not to do what is requested by the experimenter and, moreover, must be in a position to foresee the consequences of the behaviour.

While Wicklund and Brehm differ from Aronson in making no direct appeal to the idea of the self-concept, their use of the concept of responsibility again places the dissonance reduction process at the service of ego defence. As Greenwald and Ronis (1978) have rightly emphasized, to insist on the individual's responsibility for undesired consequences is, like Aronson, to situate dissonance in the discrepancy that may exist between the undesired consequences of the action and the idea that individuals might have of themselves. For example, in the Festinger and Carlsmith experiment the pair of cognitions studied would come down to the cognition: 'I cause undesired consequence' and the self-concept cognition: 'I am a good (or reasonable, or intelligent) person.' Thus, Greenwald and Ronis (1978) are right when they state that the basic character of the theory has changed from revision to revision.

> The theory seems now to be focused on cognitive changes occurring in the service of ego defense, or self-esteem maintenance, rather than in the interest of preserving psychological consistency. Indeed, contemporary dissonance bears a striking resemblance to theoretical statements about ego-related cognitive processes that existed well before Festinger's (1957a) statement. (Greenwald and Ronis, 1978, p. 55)

The 'new look' of Cooper and Fazio

In their work, Cooper and Fazio (1984) were to take over the key elements of Wicklund and Brehm's (1976) revision. In particular, they retained the central notions of personal responsibility, freedom and foreseeability. Cooper and Fazio also agree that cognitive dissonance is not simply brought about by the perception of inconsistency among cognitions, but rather by the perception of having brought about an aversive event. For the fathers of the 'new look', the attitude change ultimately serves less to establish coherence between attitudes and behaviour than to induce a more comfortable perception of the consequences of aversive events.

However, the Cooper and Fazio revision is far more complex than those that preceded it, with dissonance reduction being envisaged as the final phase of a multistage attribution process. In effect, not only must individuals attribute the responsibility for aversive consequences to themselves, but the dissonance arousal resulting from this initial attribution must be negatively labelled and must be assumed by the individual (second attribution of responsibility) if it is to lead to dissonance motivation. It is then this dissonance motivation, and not dissonance arousal, that triggers the attitude change. Thus, Cooper and Fazio (1984) distinguish between two very specific moments: that of dissonance arousal and that of dissonance motivation. Dissonance arousal is a general and undifferentiated state of arousal which can only be labelled positively or negatively. Dissonance motivation only occurs when individuals label their state of arousal negatively and attribute that arousal to their having freely produced an aversive consequence (p. 256).

At a schematic level we can summarize Cooper and Fazio's 'new look' as follows. Once individuals have performed a counterattitudinal behaviour, they attempt to attribute the responsibility for it. They may or may not be able to attribute this responsibility to an outside agent. If they cannot, they attribute the personal responsibility for the act to themselves and consequently enter a state of dissonance arousal. It is at this point that a new attribution takes place, similar to that described in the theory of emotions (see Schachter, 1964, and, above all, Schachter and Singer, 1962; see also Chapter 7 of this book). If this state of dissonance arousal is to result in attitude change, individuals must now:

1 interpret the state negatively; and
2 correctly attribute it to their behaviour.

We might therefore join Clémence (1991, p. 65, Deschamps and Clémence, 1990, p. 93) in asking whether such a revision is not ultimately an extension of the attribution theories in which the phenomenon of dissonance is no more than one particular aspect of the inferential activities of individuals.

To summarize, we can see that, from revision to revision, Festinger's dissonance theory has been transformed gradually into a theory of the ego which is accorded an increasingly large role in the process of self-attribution. The very least that can be said is that the revisions proposed by Festinger's successors borrow extensively from the dominant explanatory models (self theory, attribution theory) and are, in the final analysis, fundamentally different from Festinger's original statement.

Greenwald and Ronis (1978, p. 56) conclude their analysis of 20 years of cognitive dissonance with the extremely relevant question: 'But has it ever really been proven wrong?' More recently, Berkowitz and Devine (1989) rightly suggested that the decreased attention paid to dissonance theory in present-day social psychology can be explained by extratheoretical considerations that influence acceptance of a formulation in the scientific community. The authors suggest that dissonance theory has received less attention because, in particular, its motivational emphases lie outside the core assumptions in the research tradition of the now-dominant cognitive orientation. They conclude their article by writing: 'Perhaps we should more frequently visit our old uncles and aunts as we attempt to explore the full meaning of our theories' (p. 502). This is sensible advice which we would do well to follow more often. For our part, we have repeatedly insisted on the benefits to be gained from returning to Festinger's original statement (see, in particular, Beauvois and Joule, 1981, Joule, 1986a,b).

In the following chapters we shall present our own conception of cognitive dissonance theory. The reader will soon appreciate that this represents more a return to the fundamental core of Festinger's theory than yet another revision to add to those that have gone before.

Notes

1   In fact, the essential principles of the theory had been put forward by Von Neumann in 1928.

2   In fact, Savage's theory was very soon advanced as a norm for businessmen (Schlaifer, 1959) and medical diagnosticians (Ledley and Lusted, 1959).

3   Festinger came to Iowa City in 1939 to work with Kurt Lewin. At that time he was more fascinated by Lewin's conceptual system than by social psychology (see De Visscher, 1991).

4   By monistic conception we mean the (dominant) conception that there can only be one form of knowledge of objects, which can be evaluated in accordance with the criterion of truth value and which has been perfectly realized by science. For a dualistic conception (descriptive knowledge vs. evaluative knowledge), see Beauvois, 1990, and Beauvois and Dubois, 1991.

5   It soon became the custom to speak in terms of 'psychological' implication (see Brehm and Cohen, 1962) and we shall adopt the same terminology here.

6   For a discussion of the 'primitive' character of the 'obverse of' relation, referred to here as the incompatibility relation, see in particular Pepitone, 1966.

Part 1
The Radical Theory of Dissonance

Given our acceptance of all the propositions of the fundamental core of the 1957 theory which we presented in the last section, we shall now proceed to identify a number of consequences which seem to have been neglected by dissonance theorists and use this as a basis for our presentation of a 'radical' conception of the theory of cognitive dissonance.

Why should we consider this conception to be 'radical' (rather than lax)? We believe the term to be justified for two reasons.

First, in establishing this conception, we have been determined to accept Festinger's theoretical statements at face value. Let us give a single example here. In his writings of 1957 (Festinger, 1957a and b), Festinger speaks only of the *binary relations* between the salient cognitions of the cognitive universe. These relations are fully defined by the psychological implication: 'A implies B' and by the 'obverse of' relation: 'A excludes (or is the obverse of) B'. Therefore, in this work, we shall avoid making use of any form of relation between cognitions apart from the binary relations presented here. We shall avoid three-term relations of the type 'A→B if C' on which certain reformulations of cognitive dissonance theory are based. Further examples of our concern to take Festinger's initial formulations at face value will appear shortly.

Second, this conception is radical because it makes common sense and anthropomorphic intuition responsible for no more than the (undoubtedly important) role of defining the relevant cognitions and their virtual implication or contradiction prior to the derivation of hypotheses. It is, of course, common sense that leads us to posit that the fact of receiving a reward for performing a task implies that we perform this task (nothing else being considered, since the theory deals only with binary relations). It is again our common sense that tells us that the fact that we hate a meal implies that we will not eat it. These are the normative psychological implications which cognitive dissonance theory prefers to deal with, leaving more 'logical' implications for consistency theory (McGuire, 1960). However, once common sense has helped us to establish this preliminary definition of the cognitive situation, the process of deriving hypotheses must be as mechanical as possible, being based solely on the algebraic properties of the dissonance ratio $D/D + C$ and on the supposed proportionality between the intensity of the cognitive work and the value of the dissonance ratio.

For at least these two reasons, our radical conception differs from the various revisions of Festinger's theory. As we shall illustrate later, these revisions have ultimately done no more than insert common sense statements (statements that Festinger was able to avoid in his purely theoretical propositions) into the theory of dissonance, while explicitly maintaining that the consistent or inconsistent nature of the relation between two cognitions (for example, a behaviour and its consequences) is linked to a third, most frequently the initial attitude of the subject (see our introductory description of the use of the self-concept by Aronson, 1968, 1969, and of aversive consequences by Cooper and Fazio, 1984).

It will become apparent that the consequences of the fundamental core of 1957 to which we shall adhere in this first section are for the most part the consequences of the form given by Festinger to the calculation of the total amount of dissonance (dissonance ratio: $D/D + C$). For this reason, this section could equally well have been entitled: 'The implications of the dissonance ratio'. In our review of the fundamental core of the 1957 theory, we insisted on the importance of the quantification of the state of dissonance in the form of the ratio of the dissonant cognitions to the whole set of relevant cognitions. This importance is reflected in the fact that the first great hypotheses, those that all but definitively determined the paradigmatic scope of the theory, are based on this quantification. We have seen it applied to the effect of reward in the experiment conducted by Festinger and Carlsmith (1959) which, together with those of Brehm (1959) and Cohen (1959, reported in Brehm and Cohen, 1962), were to initiate experimental research into forced compliance.

In the same vein, quantifying the state of dissonance makes it possible to specify the effect of a threat in the 'forbidden toy' situation (Aronson and Carlsmith, 1963): the subjects who were severely threatened possessed an additional consonant cognition (the threat effectively implies obedience) which increases the denominator and consequently reduces the dissonance ratio. The prediction of evaluative changes in the decision paradigm is performed using the dissonance ratio in a similar way to the situation analysis. Thus, when subjects are able to choose between globally positive alternatives, it is self-evident that the ratio of the number of dissonant cognitions associated with the final choice made to the number of relevant cognitions increases with the number of alternatives proposed. Evaluative change (upgrading of the selected alternative and/or downgrading of the rejected alternatives) must therefore become greater as the number of alternatives increases. This was very soon demonstrated by Festinger himself (1957), as well as by Cohen, Brehm and Latané (1959). It is therefore not surprising that the first researchers to enquire into dissonance effects were exceedingly fond of this ratio. Thus, Brehm and Cohen considered it to be 'the basis of much of what is "nonobvious" in the theory' (p. 301).

However, it should be noted that in the most paradigmatic experiments it is possible to formulate the hypotheses without necessarily comparing the ratios associated with each experimental condition. It is sufficient to observe that in a particular condition the subjects possess one consonant cognition more or one dissonant cognition less to hypothesize that these subjects will have less dissonance to reduce and that, in consequence, they will exhibit less attitude change. For example, in Festinger and Carlsmith's experiment it would be possible to limit oneself to the observation that the reward was consonant and that the higher the reward, the greater the consonance. We would then expect to find less change in the best rewarded subjects. The same reasoning can be applied to threat in the forbidden toy situation: the simple observation that the threat is consonant with obedience would be sufficient for us to expect less change in those children who had been most severely threatened. Finally, in the decision paradigm we might expect that, as the number of positive alternatives grows, there will be more dissonance following the selection of any one of them. As a result, a greater degree of evaluative change would be expected. In this way, we could produce hypotheses identical to those derived from the calculation of the total amount of dissonance.

As we can see, although the dissonance ratio lies at the heart of Festinger's theory, it is not always indispensable in paradigmatic situations for the production of the classic hypotheses which rapidly established the success of cognitive dissonance theory. Intuitions about consonant and dissonant cognitions may appear to be satisfactory. This is undoubtedly the reason why it is rare to see the dissonance ratio invoked explicitly in experimental articles. It is also the reason why many authors have considered dissonance theory to be one of the theories of consistency. Does this mean that we can do without this quantification of the state of dissonance? We do not think so. We shall soon see that situations exist in which it is necessary to calculate the dissonance ratio obtaining in the different experimental conditions. These are precisely the decisive situations in which the predictions made on the basis of Festinger's theory are clearly distinguished from those which could be made using self-perception theory or a theory of self-affirmation (self-presentation theory, impression management theory . . .). We shall also see that an analysis of the most direct implications of the dissonance ratio, as proposed by Festinger, allows us to identify what it is that underlies the specificity of dissonance theory and distinguishes it from the theories of cognitive consistency.

Chapter 1

The generative cognition

One of the reasons justifying the theoretical importance we ascribe to the dissonance ratio is that it is based firmly on the rightful distinction between dissonant relations (between two cognitions) and the psychological state of dissonance. Calculating the dissonance ratio means using the former in order to quantify the latter. We have already pointed out the ambiguities of the polysemous term 'dissonance' in the work of Festinger and the theorists of dissonance. It seems to us to be useful for theoretical reasoning to use different terms to denote different constructs. Thus, we intend to use the terms *consistency* and *inconsistency* when speaking of the *relation between two cognitions* where one implies the other or one implies the obverse of the other. We shall reserve the term dissonance to express the *psychological state (drive)* which may, under certain conditions, result from the inconsistency between two cognitions.

Theoretical standpoint

If we are to calculate the dissonance ratio, then we must choose the cognition with reference to which the others are to be judged either consistent (consonant) or inconsistent (dissonant). We shall refer to this cognition as the generative cognition. In dissonance theory this cognition has a special status which has no equivalent in the consistency theories. It is not one of the consistent or inconsistent cognitions which forms part of the numerator and/or denominator of the ratio. However, it is with reference to this cognition that the other cognitions are individually judged to be consistent or inconsistent (we should remember that dissonance theory only deals with binary relations between cognitions). To illustrate this point, let us return one last time to the experiment conducted by Festinger and Carlsmith (1959). The relevant cognitions are as follows:

— R, the cognition relating to the reward (I have received $x for saying the task is interesting)
— A, the cognition relating to private attitude (I found the task dull)

> — X, the cognition (or set of cognitions) relating to the reasons which induced the subject to accede to the experimenter's request (for example: I like to take part in experiments, I want to help the experimenter . . .)
> — G, the cognition relating to the counterattitudinal behaviour (I said that the task was interesting).

We have termed the cognition relating to the counterattitudinal behaviour G (for generative), since Festinger and Carlsmith took this cognition as the basis for determining what was consistent or inconsistent within the situation that they had constructed. Thus, if we assume that R implies G, then R will be considered to be a consistent cognition. Similarly, since we might assume that A would imply the obverse of G (that is a declaration that the task is dull), A will be considered to be an inconsistent cognition. We have now determined that:

> — A is an inconsistent cognition
> — R and X are consistent cognitions.

The dissonance ratio calculated with reference to the generative cognition G is therefore:

$$T_{(G)} = A / A + R + X$$

In most traditional research the choice of the generative cognition is self-evident. Since this cognition is usually considered to be most resistant to change (see, in particular, Brehm and Cohen, 1962, Wicklund and Brehm, 1976), the choice of the behaviour performed by the subject seems to be obvious. Indeed, this is the way researchers have reasoned when making predictions in a given experimental situation. Moreover, since it is usually possible to produce hypotheses without deriving them from the dissonance ratio, as we have seen, the question may go unasked and may therefore escape discussion. However, we think it is of crucial importance for the correct understanding of dissonance theory. In fact, the analysis of the functioning of dissonance theory in the paradigmatic situations in which it has been so successful (in particular in situations of forced compliance) shows that this generative cognition is always the representation of the subject's behaviour. This indicates that it is always in terms of this behaviour that the relevant cognitive elements (consistent and inconsistent) must be defined and the orientation of the cognitive work of dissonance reduction formulated. However, the majority of theorists seem to have neglected the status of the behaviour which turns dissonance reduction into a fundamentally postbehavioural cognitive process.[1] Some (Wicklund and Brehm, 1976) explicitly reject this interpretation, arguing 'that dissonance reduction is organized around the cognition that is most resistant to change, whether or not that cognition has its bases in a behaviour commitment' (p. 5). However, it should be noted that the authors base this idea on anecdotal examples of 'good sense' and not on an analysis of the experimental data.

In contrast, the theories of others, who do not necessarily discuss the status of the behaviour, proceed as if the work of dissonance reduction were oriented by the private attitude of the subject. This is true, for example, of Cooper and Fazio (1984), for whom the relevant cognitions ultimately only acquire a status with reference to this private attitude. It is superfluous to point out that in their 'new look' revision Cooper and Fazio totally omit the use of the dissonance ratio.

The reluctance of theorists to take account of the behavioural status of the generative cognition may indeed be comprehensible. First of all, the ability to make predictions without necessarily resorting to the use of dissonance ratios makes it possible to consider the relation of psychological implication (fit together) as a symmetrical relation in which the behavioural cognition has no special status. On this basis, it is equally possible to ascribe a privileged status to attitude and analyse dissonance with respect to it. However, apart from this ambiguity, there is a second reason. This relates to the incorrect equating of any relation of inconsistency between the cognitions with the psychological state of dissonance. This process consists of a surreptitious appeal to one of the theories of consistency, or even to a theory of rational decision every time it appears that two cognitive elements do not fit together. While doing this, authors continue to use Festinger's terms, thus creating the impression that Festinger's theory is still at work, even where this theory has no further role to play, as is the case when behavioural predictions have to be made.

Let us take the anecdotal example used by Wicklund and Brehm (p. 5). An individual buys a sports car and then realizes that this car has road-holding problems which he had not previously suspected. According to Wicklund and Brehm:

> If the individual is unable to convince himself that he really likes to drive the car, then his dissonance will persist and indeed will be salient every time the car is driven. Under these conditions, dissonance reduction may more easily be accomplished by changing the cognition about the behaviour ... (he will) come to believe that buying it was a mistake and to sell it. In this case, the resistance to change of the behavioural cognitive element is less than that of the cognitions with which it is dissonant, and dissonance reduction is accomplished by changing the behavioural element.

In this type of example, authors use at least two theories. Dissonance theory makes it possible to understand that a person who has made this type of purchase feels psychological tension (state of dissonance) which has to be reduced in one way or another. Using this type of theory we may hypothesize that the individual will find, for example, that his new car is so beautiful, that it lets him show off in front of the ladies, that he really does need a sports car .... In such a case, the process of dissonance reduction does not necessarily have to comprise a negation of evident road-holding problems. There is nothing in the fundamental core of dissonance theory that allows us to predict that he will change his car after becoming aware of its faults. To make this prediction it is necessary to resort to a different theory and this is what Wicklund and Brehm tacitly do. This new theory, which envisages a logical sequence of information processing behaviours, is closer to a theory of rational decision, precisely the type of theory approved by Bruner in his criticism of Festinger (see note 1), than it is to dissonance theory.

To summarize, even if the experimental field of dissonance theory offers no truly conclusive answer to the question, it does at least seem to suggest that the cognitive work of dissonance reduction is oriented by a generative cognition which is behavioural in nature. Unfortunately, nothing in the fundamental core of the theory allows us to state that the generative cognition is necessarily behavioural. However, it seems to us that it is of fundamental importance to adopt such a position.

That is why in the following we shall present a number of experiments that allow us to elaborate two types of hypothesis: one in which the behavioural cognition is generative and one where this role is fulfilled by a different cognition (this time an attitudinal cognition). As we shall see, all the results indicate that the generative cognition is provided by the representation of behaviour and thus demonstrate that behaviour possesses a special status in establishing the total amount of dissonance and, in consequence, in dissonance theory itself.

Experimental evidence

Let us frame the theoretical problem in a way that can be tackled experimentally. There are three subjects. The first has, for reasons X, produced behaviour B which is inconsistent with his attitude A. The second has done the same, again for reasons X, but possesses an additional cognition C, which is inconsistent with behaviour B but consistent with attitude A. The third has again done the same thing, again for the same reasons X, but possesses cognition C′ which is consistent with behaviour B and inconsistent with attitude A. Which of these three subjects has the greatest total amount of dissonance? If the generative cognition is indeed the representation of the behaviour, then it can only be the second. This subject has a cognition C, which is inconsistent with behaviour B and which the others do not possess. If, in contrast, the generative cognition is that relating to attitude, then the third subject is the one we are looking for. This subject possesses a cognition C′, which is inconsistent with his attitude A and which the others do not possess. This theoretical example is all the more interesting since, in both cases, if C or C′ is inconsistent with the supposedly generative cognition, then it is consistent with the cognition which is not considered to be generative. The dissonance ratios for each of the subjects can be formulated as follows for the two hypotheses:

if the generative cognition is behaviour
subject 1: $T1(G) = A/A + X$
subject 2: $T2(G) = A + C/A + C + X$
subject 3: $T3(G) = A/A + C' + X$

here $T2(G) > T1(G) > T3(G)$

if the generative cognition is attitude
subject 1: $T1(G) = B/B$ (while X reasons imply the behaviour, nothing is consistent with the attitude A)
subject 2: $T2(G) = B/B + C$
subject 3: $T3(G) = B + C'/B + C'$

here $T3(G) = T1(G) > T2(G)$

As a comparison of the dissonance ratios reveals, the choice of behaviour B as the generative cognition makes it possible to differentiate between the three situations: we should observe most cognitive change in subject 2, with subject 3 producing the least and an intermediary level observable in subject 1. Things are very different if we take attitude A as the generative cognition. It is probable that theorists who attribute a privileged status to attitude would be proud of their intuitions and would not consider it important to calculate such dissonance ratios. Moreover, as we have just seen, it is impossible to differentiate between two of the subjects since, in both cases, the dissonance ratio is equal to 1. It is clear that this theoretical equality does not correspond to the intuition which attributes so much importance to attitude. In fact, subject 3 possesses a cognition that is inconsistent with his attitude and that is not present in subject 1. We would therefore intuitively expect more dissonance in this subject and consequently a higher level of cognitive change. Therefore we arrive at opposed predictions depending on whether we take behaviour or attitude as the generative cognition. Five experiments will allow us to come to a decision.

The effect of arbitrary feedback

Experiments 1, 2 and 3 all focus on the change of evaluation of a boring task which had just been performed by the subject and which was followed by arbitrary feedback (positive or negative) from the experimenter concerning the quality of performance. This type of situation illustrates the possible theoretical alternatives that we have presented above. For reasons X, subjects have accepted (behaviour B) to perform a task that they know to be particularly uninteresting (attitude A) and that requires no special skill. In conformity with the notion of psychological implication, the fact of knowing that a task is dull (attitudinal cognition A) psychologically implies the obverse of the behavioural cognition B: 'I have freely accepted to perform this task.' The free acceptance of a boring task therefore implies the generation of a state of dissonance, as would the acceptance of eating a worm on the part of someone who hated that particular type of food. At the end of the task, subjects may hear that their performance was very mediocre (cognition C), which is inconsistent with behaviour B but consistent with attitude A, that is to say the knowledge they have concerning the boring nature of the task. In contrast, they may be told that their performance has been excellent (cognition C') which is consistent with behaviour B but inconsistent with attitude A.

Experiment 1. The effect of negative feed-back concerning performance on attitude towards a task

Experiment 1 (Beauvois and Joule, 1982, experiment 1) was performed using final-year, high-school students aged about 17 years. The experiment was presented to them as investigating the effects of tiredness on visual discrimination. The task consisted of spending half-an-hour copying shapes that were very similar to one another. The subjects had to copy as many of these shapes as they could, while making as few mistakes as possible. In the free-choice condition, the experimenter insisted that, if they did not want to, the subjects need not perform the requested task. In the no-choice condition, the subjects were told the opposite, namely that they were expected to perform the task, which was presented as a genuine piece of schoolwork. After 30 minutes, the experimenter stopped the subjects and collected their sheets of paper, examining them while he did so. In the negative-feedback condition, he then said: 'I've just had a look at your work and, on the whole, you've produced some very mediocre copies. To tell the truth, I'm very surprised because we've already used this type of test with more than 100 people and you're the first to have copied so few of the signs... I'm not even sure that we're going to be able to use your work. We might even have to repeat the experiment using different people.' In the no-feedback condition the experimenter gave the subjects no information. Then, in all the conditions, he asked the subjects to provide a rating of between 0 (completely uninteresting) and 20 (exceptionally interesting) in order to measure their attitude towards the task. Only in the free choice condition is it possible to apply dissonance theory. In this condition, if we accept that the generative cognition is indeed behaviour, that is agreeing to spend half-an-hour performing a boring task that one is not obliged to perform, then we can understand that the negative information supplies an additional inconsistent cognition C. In fact, given that the accomplishment of the task requires no particular skill and that performance can be seen as the simple investment of time, receiving a poor grading is inconsistent with having freely agreed to perform the task. The subjects who feel the most dissonance should be those who reduce this dissonance the most. They should thus show the highest level of attitude change and find the task the most interesting. In contrast, if we consider the generative cognition to be attitude A, we arrive at the opposite hypothesis. In this case, knowing that one has performed badly in a task is consistent with the knowledge that the task is boring. Thus the subjects who have the additional consonant cognition should feel the least dissonance and therefore undergo the least attitude change.

In the no-choice condition, dissonance theory is no longer predictive and it is no longer possible to expect that without some attempt at reinforcement subjects will find the task any more interesting than following negative feedback.

The results (see Table 1.1) unambiguously confirm that in the dissonant condition (free choice), the correct hypothesis is the one in which behaviour is selected as the generative cognition. Moreover, we find the expected reinforcement effect we expected in the no-choice condition.

Table 1.1. The effect of negative feedback concerning performance on attitude towards a task.

	without feedback	negative feedback
Dissonant condition (free choice)	6·7	10·5
Non-dissonant condition (no choice)	5·9	3·8

Notes: The larger the number, the more positive the attitude towards the task. $n = 20$ subjects in each situation. Interaction is statistically significant ($F = 9·54$, $p < 0·05$), as is the simple effect of feedback on the condition of dissonance.

Experiment 2. The effect of positive feedback concerning performance on attitude towards a task

Experiment 2 (Beauvois and Joule, 1982, experiment 2) was designed to be symmetrical to the preceding one. Both the task and the manipulation of the free choice condition (as opposed to the no-choice condition) were, in all respects, identical to those used in experiment 1. However, this time, the no-feedback condition was contrasted with a positive-feedback condition in which the subject's work was praised by the examiner, who said: 'I'm pleasantly surprised because, on the whole, you've produced exceptionally good work. Since we've been using this type of test, and we've already tested more than 100 people, you have copied far more of the signs in half-an-hour than anybody else . . . . This is certainly going to help us modify our original conclusions. It's really very good.'

In this new experiment, the subjects who received the positive feedback possess a cognition C′ which is consistent with their behaviour (and which is also likely to sustain the integrity of the self). If it is the behaviour that corresponds to the generative cognition, then these subjects should feel less dissonance than the others. As a result, they should reduce this dissonance less and should consequently find the task *less* interesting. In contrast, if we reason on the basis of the subject's private attitude (cognition A: 'this task is boring'), then such positive feedback might be thought to induce a cognition that is actually inconsistent with the subject's knowledge of the dull nature of the task. A subject who had received this sort of feedback should therefore feel more dissonance and, as a result, should find the task *more* interesting. The results (see Table 1.2) are only compatible with the first of these hypotheses; the one that views the behaviour as the generative cognition. In the no-choice condition we observe a reinforcement effect, with the subjects finding the task more interesting after receiving positive feedback.

Table 1.2. The effect of positive feedback concerning performance on attitude towards a task.

	without feedback	negative feedback
Dissonant condition (free choice)	6·5	5·15
Non-dissonant condition (no choice)	2·4	4·9

Notes: The larger the number, the more positive the attitude towards the task. $n = 20$ subjects in each situation. Interaction is statistically significant ($F = 15$, $p < 0.01$). The simple effect of feedback in the dissonant situation is only marginally significant ($p < 0.10$).

Taken together, these two experiments indicate that the cognition against which the dissonance ratio should be measured is, indeed, behaviour. Predictions based on this cognition are fairly well confirmed[2] (entirely so in experiment 1) whereas the predictions formulated with attitude as the generative cognition are in flagrant contradiction with the results. However, these two experiments have their limits. First, the fact that we have introduced positive and negative feedback in two separate experiments makes it impossible to compare them. Second, the fact that our subject groups were drawn from an educational institute means that we might have ignored cognitions relating to the significance of the task and even of the feedback. Finally, although marginally significant, the effect of positive feedback was not proved. The interaction observed in experiment 2 may have been due simply to the reinforcement effect noted in the non-dissonant condition. These were the reasons for performing experiment 3 (Beauvois and Rainis, 1993a).

Experiment 3. Effect of feedback concerning the quality of performance on the attitude towards a task

The subjects of experiment 3, sociology students, were individually invited to the laboratory. First, the task was described to them. The task consisted of spending 20 minutes sticking very small paper squares on to certain letters of a long text (this task had been evaluated very negatively by the subjects of a control group). Before starting to work, all the subjects were told that they were free to participate or not in the experiment (zero refusals). All the subjects were therefore in a state of dissonance. The subjects were stopped after working for 20 minutes. They were then asked to read a text that had no reference to the experiment to allow the experimenter time to simulate a correction. After five minutes, the arbitrary feedback variable was manipulated, just as in experiments 1 and 2 (three conditions: no feedback, positive feedback, negative feedback). The experimenter then investigated the subjects' post-experimental attitude towards the task by asking them to rate it on an 11-point scale. The results relating to the attitude towards the task are presented in Table 1.3.

Table 1.3. *Effects of arbitrary feedback on the evaluation of a boring task in a situation of cognitive dissonance.*

no feedback	negative feedback	positive feedback	control
4·59	7·78	4·27	2.35

Notes: The higher the figure, the more positive the evaluation of the task. $n = 22$ subjects in each experimental situation and 20 subjects in control situation. The effect of feedback is statistically significant ($F = 32·198$, $p < 0·0001$). The three experimental groups differed significantly from the control group. Among the experimental groups, the group receiving negative feedback differed significantly from the other two.

Despite the provision of a very different type of training, the results of experiment 3 confirm those of experiments 1 and 2. That the situation induced considerable dissonance is shown by a comparison between the subjects of the control group, to whom the task was simply described, and those of the no-feedback experimental group who had to perform the task. The latter found the task more interesting than the subjects of the control group. The finding that negative feedback increases dissonance is only predictable if we adopt the cognition representing the behaviour as the generative cognition. In fact, even if this feedback is consistent with the private attitude of the subjects, it is clearly inconsistent with the behaviour cognition B: 'I have freely accepted to do this work.' Finally, we again find that the subjects in the positive-feedback condition seem to experience no less dissonance than those in the no-feedback condition (comparison of the no-feedback group and the positive-feedback group). We shall return later to the interpretation of this negative result, which seems to indicate that quality of performance forms part of the experimenter's request, that is it is part of the contract of forced compliance accepted by the subjects, with the result that positive-feedback does not constitute a separate item of information for them, even though it may have positive implications for their self-concept.

Effect of argument time and success on a persuasion attempt

Experiments 1, 2 and 3 took the form of forced compliance situations involving the performance of a dull task. Thus, the subjects' private attitude related to an experimental task which, though undoubtedly boring, was at least unusual (crossing out signs, sticking tape on letters) and extremely rare in their everyday life (we might say that the tasks were of an extremely low existential significance). We could therefore argue that this is simply a minimal attitude which has a very low resistance to change, can be easily revised and whose modification has no immediately perceivable consequences since the subjects are unlikely to expect ever again to be involved in a similar task. We might therefore lay ourselves open to the criticism that we have created conditions extremely favourable to our position and that, given such conditions, any dissonance theorist would have joined us in arguing that the private attitude cannot be the generative cognition.

One might also point out that in the experimental situations described above, the cognitions C or C′ which are implied by our theoretico-experimental reasoning were unequally related to the behaviour on the one hand and to the subjects' private attitude on the other. For example, the negative-feedback contributes a cognition that is glaringly inconsistent with the behaviour. Agreeing to perform a task for someone implies that we do it for them as well as we can. However, although this negative-feedback might fit with the subjects' privately held negative attitude towards the task (we perform tasks we dislike less well), it cannot be considered to be as powerfully implied by this attitude as the behaviour is implied by the agreement to cooperate with the experimenter.

To summarize, while the results presented above clearly demonstrate that in the forced compliance situation that we used (performance of a boring task) the generative cognition can be based on nothing other than the behaviour, this might not have been the case in a situation in which:

1   the private attitude relates to objects which are of greater importance in the everyday life of the subjects; and
2   the additional cognitions C and C′ (or their obverse) which we use in our reasoning are implied equally strongly by the attitude as by the behaviour.

Experiments 4 and 5, which we present below (Beauvois, Ghiglione and Joule, 1976, experiments 1 and 2), make use of a different forced compliance situation (counterattitudinal role-playing) which seems to us to take account of these two considerations. As we shall see, these experiments again confirm that the generative cognition is the one that corresponds to the behaviour.

Experiment 4. Effect of a successful (versus unsuccessful) counterattitudinal persuasion attempt on attitude

Experiment 4 was presented to the subjects as a piece of research into persuasion. In reality it also formed part of a more complex experiment investigating attitude change. Shortly after declaring that they did not believe in the existence of extra-terrestrial beings, the subjects (high-school students of an average age of 17 years) were nominally recruited to convince their equally unbelieving classmates that extra-terrestrial beings regularly visit our planet. The subjects were clearly convinced that they were merely cooperating with the experimenter, exactly like Festinger and Carlsmith's subjects (1959). They were also provided with the arguments they were to use during the persuasion stage of the experiment. The recipients of the persuasion were also completely unaware of the true nature of the experiment. Following the persuasion attempt, all were required to indicate on a 21-point scale their agreement with the statement 'Today there can be no doubt that extra-terrestrial beings regularly visit our planet in their spacecraft.'

In fact, these 'collaborators' were the true subjects of the experiment, which measured their own change of opinion (measurements taken before and after the experiment) as a function of the success or failure of the persuasion attempt which they had freely undertaken. This success or failure was determined post-experimentally by the recorded attitude of the targets of the persuasion attempt. If private attitude is the generative cognition, then successful persuasion provides an additional inconsistent cognition, while failure, in contrast, provides an explicitly consistent cognition. The fact of not believing in the existence of extra-terrestrial beings implies that we do not convince a classmate that they exist. In consequence, the subjects who failed to convince their classmates should experience the least dissonance and should therefore exhibit the least attitude change. The situation is very different if we consider the behavioural cognition to be the generative cognition. If this is the case, then successful persuasion results in a cognition which is manifestly consistent with behaviour. The fact that we agree to convince a person of belief Y implies that this person should ultimately be persuaded by our arguments. In contrast, failure to persuade the target results in an inconsistent cognition. In this case, we would expect to see more attitude change in favour of the proposed argument in the subjects who failed to convince their classmates.

Table 1.4 shows the average attitude change (before/after) exhibited by subjects as a function of whether or not they were successful in persuading their classmates.

Table 1.4. The effect of a successful (versus unsuccessful) counterattitudinal persuasion attempt on attitude.

	Successful persuasion ($n=12$)	Unsuccessful persuasion ($n=8$)
Before–after difference in targets	14·08	3·00
Before–after difference in subjects ('collaborators')	2·66	11·00

Notes: The higher the number, the greater the change of attitude in favour of the defended position. The change observed in the subjects in the two conditions differs at the threshold value $p < 0·05$ (Mann-Whitney U).

The table shows that the subjects who failed to convince their target (low before–after difference: 3) exhibited the greatest attitude change in favour of the position they were defending (before–after difference: 11). In contrast, the subjects who argued most persuasively (before–after difference in targets: 14.08) did not come to accept the position they were defending (before–after difference: 2.66). Once more, these results show that the dissonance ratio should be calculated on the basis of the behavioural generative cognition B: 'I have freely agreed to convince X of the existence of extra-terrestrial beings.' The success of the persuasion attempt provided the subjects with a cognition that is manifestly consistent with their behaviour and, in this case, completely inconsistent with their private attitude A: 'I do not believe in the existence of extra-terrestrial beings.' It is clear that success reduced the dissonance experienced by the subjects, with the successful subjects showing no change in their attitude relating to the existence of extra-terrestrial beings (the difference of 2·66 is not statistically significant).

It is important to note that both subject groups were in a state of considerable commitment. Whether they were successful or not in persuading their classmates, all the subjects had the explicit aim of convincing, and their task could not be reduced to an inconsequential role-playing activity consisting solely of presenting a counterattitudinal argument. All the subjects had freely agreed to attempt to persuade the target and the success of this attempt was fully implied by their agreement. Moreover, the persuasion attempt was addressed to a classmate whom they met every day and to whom they would later have to explain themselves. Thus, in this experiment, the consequences of the subjects' action were particularly salient. This particularity of the experimental situation doubtlessly goes some way to explaining the apparent contradiction between these results and those obtained by Cooper and Worchel (1970) and by Cooper, Zanna and Goethals (1974) in situations similar to those used by Festinger and Carlsmith. In both these studies we might ask whether the fact of having to convince a colleague was really implied by the acceptance of a counterattitudinal role and whether the subjects who failed to convince their targets were truly committed to the counter-attitudinal behaviour. We shall return to these results later.

In the four experiments we have described so far, the critical cognitions C or C' were, to a certain extent, external cognitions produced by the situation, that is by the experimenter or by a colleague, without forming an integral part of the contract of forced compliance. Moreover, they emerged only after the performance of the counterattitudinal act, as if they provided some sort of justification for it. An observation made by Rabbie, Brehm and Cohen (1959) inspired us to manipulate a new type of critical cognition C'. These authors had noted that, under certain conditions, the attitude change manifested by subjects involved in a counterattitudinal role-playing situation was reduced in the individuals who had produced the most arguments. Festinger and Carlsmith (1959) themselves also observed a greater degree of attitude change in the subjects who had been the least expansive in the presentation of their lie. If subjects have agreed to present position Y, then finding arguments in favour of position Y seems fully consistent with having entered into the agreement. The more arguments the subjects find, the more cognitions they possess that are consistent with their behaviour. These cognitions, however, are clearly inconsistent with their private attitude, which corresponds to the completely opposed position and which should therefore lead them to propose completely opposed arguments. Thus, in our theoretical situation, the adoption of the counterattitudinal position possesses the status of the critical cognition C'. It is consistent with behaviour while being inconsistent with the initial private attitude which would have implied an argument in favour of the opposite standpoint. The *post hoc* observations of Festinger and Carlsmith and Rabbie, Brehm and Cohen therefore suggest that the production of arguments reduces the total amount of dissonance and support the view that the generative cognition is behavioural in nature. Experiment 5 (Beauvois, Ghiglione and Joule, 1976, experiment 2) provides a more direct test of this point of view.

Experiment 5. The effect of counterattitudinal advocacy on attitude (group pass)

Experiment 5 involved psychology students, divided into six supervised groups, who were asked to write a text fiercely opposing time wasted by students on leisure activities that are not directly connected with their studies. Some of the subjects (dissonance condition) were told that they were free to participate or not. The commitment of these subjects was reinforced by asking them to sign their essay and telling them that a local paper was interested in the research and that some of the essays might be published. Others (non-dissonant condition), who were told that the essay was part of their course work, had no choice whether or not to perform the required task. The second independent variable related to the time of presentation of a 21-point scale designed to record the subjects' attitude towards the position for which they were required to argue. In the first condition the scale was presented before the subjects started their counterattitudinal essay. In the second condition the subjects were stopped after 7 minutes and asked to fill in the rating scale. In the third condition the scale was presented 35 minutes into the essay. In the last two conditions subsequent analysis of the content revealed the number of arguments proposed by the subjects at the point at which the measurement of attitude was taken.

The assumption of the generative nature of behaviour led us to expect the level of dissonance (and thus attitude change) would fall the more time the subjects had to find arguments in favour of the counterattitudinal position for which they were arguing. It is self-evident that taking private attitude as the generative cognition would force us to the opposite expectation, with subjects experiencing more dissonance the more time they had to find arguments opposed to their private attitude. The results are presented in Table 1.5. As one would expect, the number of arguments discovered by the subjects varies as a function of argument time. In the dissonant condition the results unequivocally confirm the findings of Festinger and Carlsmith and Rabbie, Brehm and Cohen concerning the existence of an inverse relation between the verbalization of a counterattitudinal opinion and attitude change in the direction of this opinion. No such relation is found in the non-dissonant condition despite the fact that the production of arguments is in all points comparable to performance in the dissonant condition.

Table 1.5. The effect of counterattitudinal advocacy on attitude (group pass).

	Dissonant condition			Non-dissonant condition		
	0 min	7 min	35 min	0 min	7 min	35 min
Number of arguments	0	3·54	7·31	0	4·23	7·66
Attitude	8·00	5·56	1·40	3·38	1·85	4·40

Notes: The greater the number, the more closely the measured attitude conforms to the counterattitudinal activity. $n = 14$ subjects in each situation. Interaction is statistically significant for the dependent variable 'attitude' ($F = 7·3$, $p < 0·05$).

Experiment 6. The effect of counterattitudinal advocacy on attitude (individual pass)

Experiment 5 shows that it is the students who develop the most arguments opposing student leisure activities who remain most committed to these activities. This observation appears to be entirely incompatible with the hypothesis of a generative attitudinal cognition and demonstrates once more that the state of dissonance has to be measured with respect to the behavioural cognition. We should note that, unlike experiments 1, 2 and 3, the attitude mobilized in this experiment is far from being of a low existential significance. In contrast, this experiment recorded attitudes that were probably readily available to the subjects concerning objects of great significance in their everyday lives (cinema, sport, cultural activities . . .). Nevertheless, since experiment 5 was conducted using groups of subjects (supervised groups) and not individually as is usually the case in dissonance experiments, we considered an individual-pass replication of the experiment indispensable. This replication was conducted recently (Joule and Lévèque, 1994). As we shall see, the results provide us with unambiguous confirmation of those presented above.

In this experiment the subjects (humanities students at the Université de Provence, Aix-en-Provence) were individually invited to the laboratory. They then learned, either in a free-choice or no-choice condition (independent variable 1), that they had to write as persuasive an essay as possible defending the counter-attitudinal position 'leisure activities are a waste of time for students.' In one condition of independent variable 2, the subjects were told that they would be expected to work for 5 minutes and they were asked to express their attitude before starting to write. The attitude was measured on a 21-point scale, where 0 represented complete disagreement and 20 corresponded to complete agreement. In the second condition, the subjects performed the required task for 5 minutes before expressing their attitude. In the third condition 20 minutes were allowed for the essay and attitude measurement took place after completion of the essay. The results concerning the subjects' attitude towards the position they had just defended, or were just about to defend, are presented in Table 1.6. We again note that the subjects who exhibited most attitude change in the free-choice condition were those who had not yet presented any arguments in favour of the counter-attitudinal position. This time, an opposite pattern can be observed in the no choice condition.

Table 1.6. Effects of counterattitudinal advocacy on attitude (individual pass).

	Dissonant condition			Non-dissonant condition		
	0 min	5 min	20 min	0 min	5 min	20 min
Attitude	6·2	3·4	2·5	1·3	2·95	8·05

Notes: The higher the number, the more closely the measured attitude conforms to the counterattitudinal act which has just been, or is about to be, performed. In a control group, the measured attitude had the value 2·6. $n = 20$ subjects in each experimental situation. Interaction is statistically significant ($F = 33·03$; $p < 0·0001$).

Thus, the results of all the experiments we have described in this chapter support the view that the behavioural cognition functions as the generative cognition in the evaluation of the total amount of dissonance.

Finally, in support of this position we should like to present an argument which is both formal and experimental in nature and which leads us to conclude either that the dissonance ratio is an error on Festinger's part or that attitude cannot be a generative cognition of interest to researchers. This argument takes as its basis the fact that the generative cognition is not one of the relevant cognitions forming part of the numerator or denominator of the dissonance ratio $D/D + C$. Although it is with respect to the generative cognition that the other cognitions are judged to be relevant or not, this cognition does not itself appear in the dissonance ratio.

However, while a major modification of the generative cognition (a denial of the behaviour, for example) may possibly eliminate the dissonance, it cannot result in its partial reduction. This is because a reduction can only be performed by decreasing the numerator or increasing the denominator of the ratio. We cannot consider the expressions 'to reduce the experienced dissonance' and 'not to experience dissonance' to be theoretically equivalent. Now, all the research indicating the validity of dissonance theory reveals a change of *attitude*, thus proving that, in this research, attitude corresponds to a cognition that must be included in the dissonance ratio unless, that is, we are to abandon the use of the dissonance ratio. This reasoning was also proposed by the first dissonance theorists, including Festinger himself, who considered the dissonance ratio to be a necessary frame of reference for making predictions. In consequence, if we consider that attitude can be modified in order to reduce dissonance, then we must consider it to be a relevant cognition which, in consequence, forms part of the ratio. It cannot therefore be the generative cognition.

While it is true that this argument is based on considerations of a relatively formal nature, it in no way implies that attitude cannot correspond to a cognition which is highly resistant to change. It is clear that it can be very resistant to change and is probably particularly salient at the very moment when the experimenter makes his or her request, or at the point when the dissonance reduction process is thought to commence. We know that under conditions where the initial attitude is salient (Bem and McConnell, 1970) subjects do not modify this attitude. In such cases, the rationalization process seems to prevent subjects from forming a re-presentation of their own change of opinion or belief. Indeed, if subjects were to form such a representation of their own change of opinion, this would no doubt take the form of a defensive reaction to the situation (Beauvois, Ghiglione and Joule, 1976). In cases where the initial attitude is salient, other procedures are probably employed for the cognitive management of the counterattitudinal request. One might conclude that in such cases subjects who have nevertheless agreed to the request devalue their counterattitudinal behaviour and consequently experience less dissonance. This is what we have sometimes observed in experiments which have been left unpublished since they did not give rise to the expected attitude change. Such cases always involve attitudes which are deeply rooted in social or political debate (an anti-apartheid attitude, for example, see Channouf, 1990). This type of attitude is probably implied by important antecedent behaviour which is itself difficult to downgrade or revise. This is very likely also the case in some pieces of published research that address attitudes which are particularly salient for the subjects. An example is the research by Cooper and Mackie (1983), who asked their politically active subjects to give a speech attacking their party's candidate. Another example is provided by Clémence and Deschamps (1989), who asked teachers to defend a pupil assessment model which was patently at odds with their professional practices. It seems likely that in such cases[3] the subjects downgraded their counterattitudinal behaviour and consequently experienced no dissonance. Later, we shall discuss the precise theoretical significance of this 'downgrading of the behaviour' which eliminates dissonance and makes its reduction by the classic method of decreasing the dissonance ratio unnecessary. However, this does not change the fact that in the vast field of forced compliance experiments, observations reveal a more or less systematic change in the attitudinal cognition. Thus, in practice, researchers have implicitly admitted that the generative cognition corresponds to behaviour,[4] even if they have refused to say so in their theoretical statements. From now on we shall consider this to be an essential characteristic of cognitive dissonance theory and express it below as an initial conclusion together with its consequence.

Conclusion 1 *The dissonance ratio, the reduction of which corresponds to the dissonance reduction process, is defined with reference to one and only one cognition. This cognition appears in neither the numerator nor the denominator of the ratio. It is the representation of the subject's behaviour.*
Consequence *When the initial attitude is particularly salient dissonance can be eliminated by downgrading the behaviour.*

Notes

1   Moreover, it was at this postbehavioural aspect of the dissonance reduction process that one of the first major criticisms of Festinger's theory was aimed. At a conference held just before the appearance of Festinger's book in 1957, Bruner (1957) maintained that it was regrettable to focus on the cognitive repercussions of behaviour rather than concentrate on its cognitive antecedents. Evidently, Bruner preferred a conception of prebehavioural processes, one inspired by theories of economic decisions, which was much closer to the 1950s perspective of rationality than Festinger's theory.
2   The dissonance reduction observed in the positive-feedback situation shows that, here, to use the terminology of self-affirmation (Steele and Liu, 1983, Steele, 1988), restoring the integrity of the self is not sufficient to reduce the tension implied by the inconsistency.
3   This is doubtlessly also the case when a piece of experimental equipment (a mirror, for example, see Scheier and Carver, 1980) causes subjects to focus on their private attitudes.
4   Rajecki's (1990) excellent book provides an exemplary illustration of the difficulty a number of theorists experience in acknowledging the behavioural nature of the generative cognition. This author proposes a ratio that is envisaged as a variant of

Festinger's dissonance ratio. This ratio represents a person's thinking about *an attitudinal object* (p. 223) and not the cognitions which are relevant with reference to another given cognition. This is therefore less a dissonance ratio than a sort of index of cognitive coherence in the evaluation of an object which is perfectly compatible with a theory of attitude consistence (what is good about the object is entered in the denominator and what is bad about it is entered in the numerator; the ratio consequently becomes a bad/good ratio). This does not prevent Rajecki from providing an excellent description of the functioning of Festinger's theory in its major experimental paradigms. However, in his work Rajecki modifies the very nature of the proposed ratio: the subject's behaviour becomes, as if by magic, the attitudinal object.

Chapter 2

Rationalization or cognitive consistency?

Long-term inconsistencies

The experiments presented in the last chapter show that the dissonance ratio must be calculated with reference to a generative cognition which is, as the experimental practice of dissonance theory leads us to expect, the representation of behaviour. However, these experiments also reveal a second implication of the way Festinger proposed calculating the total amount of dissonance. In the calculation of the ratio, that is in the definition of the state of dissonance, the cognitions under investigation acquire a status only by virtue of the relation of consistency or inconsistency which each of them has to the generative cognition. It is because the private attitude would have implied the obverse of the generative cognition (which represents the behaviour) that it appears in the dissonance ratio and that is the only reason for its appearance. In short, in the definition of the state of dissonance only those binary relations of consistency or inconsistency which involve the generative cognition are taken into account.

Does this mean that the other cognitions are unable to stand in any relation, in particular a binary-type relation, to one another? There is no a priori reason to believe so. Festinger's theory in no way excludes the possibility that the cognitions entered in the numerator or denominator of the ratio may be linked by relations of consistency or inconsistency quite independently of their relation to the generative cognition. However, while such relations may obtain, they are not taken into account in the quantification of the state of dissonance. Since the dissonance reduction process operates exclusively through the reduction of the dissonance ratio, it implies nothing about the effect on these other relations. In other words, *it is possible that relations of consistency or inconsistency between cognitions exist which remain unchanged by the dissonance reduction process*. It is even possible that the process causes existing inconsistencies to become salient; indeed, it might even lead to the production of new inconsistencies. In short, the dissonance reduction process is not necessarily oriented towards the production of harmony between cognitions: it only bears on the binary relations in which the generative cognition is involved.

Arguing from a theoretico-experimental perspective, we might formulate the problem in terms similar to those used in our discussion of the generative cognition. Let us assume that two subjects each possess two relevant cognitions, one of which, X, is in conformity with the subject's behaviour B (X implies B), while the other, for example an attitudinal cognition A, contradicts this same behaviour B (A implies the obverse of B). If, during the experimental pass, one of the subjects is provided with a third, critical, cognition C which is in conformity with B but contradicts A, then this cognition will reduce the dissonance ratio. By reducing the dissonance ratio this cognition also reduces the necessity to change cognition A to which it is nevertheless opposed. This implies the retention of an internal inconsistency that was not present before the appearance of C. Thus, the subject who will exhibit the least change of attitude A will be the one who has acquired a new relation of inconsistency between this attitude and the critical cognition C. This subject will therefore leave the laboratory with a new relation of inconsistency between his or her cognitions (in this case between C and A).

There is nothing fanciful about this theoretical case. Its occurrence can be observed in the experiments described in the last chapter, most demonstratively so in experiments 4 and 5, in which the very nature of the experimental situation made the advent of the critical cognition C likely. As we saw in experiment 4, the least attitude change was exhibited by the subjects who successfully convinced their classmates that the earth was visited by extra-terrestrial beings. It is even probable that these subjects underwent no attitude change whatsoever. However, it is precisely these subjects who leave the experiment with a new relation of inconsistency which can be expressed as follows: 'I have succeeded in persuading my friend of thesis T in which I do not myself believe.' If these subjects have not changed their attitudes, it is because they feel less dissonance, thereby proving that the dissonance calculation ignores certain relations of inconsistency between cognitions. In contrast, the subjects who exhibit the greatest attitude change are those whose cognitions in the numerator and denominator of the dissonance ratio are in a relation of consistency: 'I have not persuaded my friend of a thesis T in which I do not myself believe.' If they have exhibited such a great degree of attitude change, it is because they experience most dissonance, demonstrating this time that the dissonance calculation ignores certain relations of consistency between cognitions.

We could draw the same conclusions from the results of experiment 5. The subjects who changed their initial attitudes the least were those who found most arguments opposing extra-curricular activities, that is the subjects who were at leisure to produce for themselves cognitions which stood in a relation of inconsistency to their initial attitude. The subjects who modified their attitude towards extra-curricular activities the most were the ones who did not have the time to produce arguments running contrary to their beliefs. As in experiment 4, it is when the situation generates relations of inconsistency between the cognitions in the numerator and denominator of the dissonance ratio that the subjects feel the least need to reduce dissonance.

The reader may well now understand why we have asserted, perhaps rather provocatively, that dissonance theory is not a theory of cognitive consistency. In effect, it is difficult to see how a theory of consistency or cognitive coherence could account for the fact that the subjects who change the least are those whom the situation invests with additional inconsistent relations. The reader may now also understand why we have insisted so vigorously on the misleading nature of the polysemy of the term 'dissonance' in Festinger's theory. This polysemy can lead the observer to speak of a state of dissonance each time any relation of inconsistency between cognitions is noted. This tendency can be clearly observed in Quattrone's (1985) summary of dissonance theory: 'According to the theory of cognitive dissonance, an individual who holds two or more cognitions (i.e. beliefs or evaluations) that are psychologically inconsistent will experience an uncomfortable state of arousal called dissonance. The individual will then be driven to reduce dissonance, usually by changing one or more of the cognitions so that they are no longer inconsistent' (p. 4). In our previous work (Beauvois and Joule, 1981, 1982, Joule, 1986a) we have described such approaches which reduce Festinger's theory to some type of consistency theory as 'lax'. This is because they fail to follow the implications of the theory through to their logical conclusion. It now seems clear:

1   that the state of dissonance cannot be equated with the simple presence of relations of inconsistency between cognitions; and
2   that the aim of the dissonance reduction process is not the elimination of all the inconsistent relations. Some of these relations are affected while others are not. The only ones affected are those that stand in a relation of relevance to the generative cognition.

Given these premises we can now state our conception of the dissonance reduction process with greater precision. We have just demonstrated that its function is not to reduce all the subject's cognitive inconsistencies but only those which involve the generative cognition, that is the representation of the subject's behaviour. Thus, the dissonance reduction process consists of modifying the subject's cognitive universe in a way that eliminates cognitions which might have implied a different behaviour or which causes the emergence of new cognitions which imply the subject's actual behaviour. Its function thus appears to be to restore the cognitive quality, or better, the value of the behaviour. We have termed this process 'rationalization' (Beauvois and Joule, 1981). Dissonance reduction can thus be thought of not as an attempt to bring about internal consistency, but as a process aimed at the rationalization of a behaviour that was produced to satisfy a request made by the experimenter but that from the outset was not justified by the subject's convictions, motivations or beliefs. We shall return to this question when we come to discuss the status of compliance in cognitive dissonance theory. We are now able to put forward a second conclusion drawn from our analysis of the implications of the dissonance ratio:

Conclusion 2 The aim of the dissonance reduction process is not the production of cognitive coherence but the rationalization of behaviour.
Consequence Dissonance reduction may result in greater inconsistency between private cognitions.

The nature of attitude change

Before analysing the other implications of the dissonance ratio, we must examine some of the consequences of the conclusions we have already drawn. The vast body of experimental work produced by dissonance theorists is almost exclusively restricted to the study of changes in assessments measured on a limited number of rating scales or, more generally, to the study of evaluative changes.[1] Subjects who have just given a speech advocating enhanced university rights modify their attitude in a way that aligns them more closely with the position they have been defending. They feel that it is good to improve university rights. Similarly, subjects who have just agreed to go without tobacco find that they have less desire to smoke than subjects who have not agreed to this privation. Children who have agreed to refrain from playing with a wonderful robot find the robot less compelling than before, and so on. This is the type of change that has generally been studied and observed by researchers. It corresponds to a modification of the known cognition which, by psychological implication, would have led us to expect the obverse of the subject's effective behaviour.

However, a true theorist of consistency should expect other changes. It is known (Katz and Stotland, 1959, Rosenberg, 1960) that the various components of an attitude towards an object, in particular the evaluative and cognitive components, interact and tend to move into alignment. Thus, a medical student who has just been defending public healthcare should, from the strict point of view of cognitive consistency, not only find public healthcare valuable (which can be measured) but should also modify his or her beliefs concerning private medicine, the price of drugs, the effects of negotiations between doctor and patient, and so on. Curiously enough, dissonance theorists have shown little interest in the study of the spread of systematically observed evaluative changes through the attitudinal universe of subjects in forced compliance situations.[2] Should we conclude from this that the negative results obtained have excluded such a study from the field of scientific discourse?

In the foregoing we have argued that dissonance theory is not a theory of cognitive consistency. Our analysis can equally well be applied to attitude consistency. There is nothing in dissonance theory that leads us to expect changes other than those limited modifications that restore the value of the behaviour. Should such changes arise, we would be forced to assert that they result from something other than the dissonance reduction process. After all, once dissonance has been reduced — and rationalization performed — there is no reason why a new process, this time one of attitude consistency, should not commence and result in changes different from those predicted by Festinger's core theory. However, we may question whether the type of change that is implied by the idea of attitude consistency really occurs in forced compliance situations.

Four recent experiments (experiment 7: Pavin, 1991a, experiment 8: Pavin, 1991b, experiment 9: Pavin, 1992, 1993, experiment 10: Channouf, 1990) suggest to us that the answer to this question must be a qualified, if not a negative, one.

Experiments 7, 8 and 9 were conducted using 8- to 10-year-old school-children, all of whom had stated in a preliminary questionnaire that the summer holidays were too short. In all three experimental cases the counterattitudinal act consisted of writing to the education minister to persuade him that the summer holidays are far too long. The letter was said to form part of a major nationwide inquiry into schoolchildren's opinions. The independent variable 'commitment' was manipulated in the three experiments (obligation and anonymity: non-commitment vs. free choice and signing the letter: commitment). The interval between the counterattitudinal act and the final measurement was manipulated in all three experiments (measurement immediately after the children had finished writing vs. measurements delayed for between 5 minutes and 4 weeks).

Experiment 7. Stability of the attitude acquired in the forced compliance situation and memory of the counterattitudinal arguments

In experiment 7 the experimenter provided subjects with a number of arguments which they could use in their letters (model arguments) and asked them to think of others themselves (personal arguments). The experimenter then measured both the post-experimental attitude of the subjects towards the length of the summer holidays and the number of arguments recalled by subjects. The results of the delayed measurements are presented in Table 2.1 (between subjects variable; immediate measurements having previously been taken for all subjects).

Table 2.1. Stability of the attitude acquired in the forced compliance situation and reproduction of the counterattitudinal arguments.

	Attitude	Model arguments	Personal arguments
Free choice (commitment)			
Pre-exp measurement	4·70		
5-minute interval	10·21	0·63	0·80
1-week interval	10·55	0·36	0·56
4-week interval	10·08	0·37	0·57
Obligation (no commitment)			
Pre-exp measurement	4·30		
5-minute interval	5·73	0·74	0·77
1-week interval	5·62	0·31	0·57
4-week interval	7·03	0·37	0·59

Notes: Attitude was measured on a 24-point scale. The higher the number, the more closely attitude conforms to the counterattitudinal position (the holidays are too long). $n = 36$ or 38 in each cell. The results relating to the reproduction of arguments are given as the average frequency of recall. Commitment effect on attitude: $F = 67·13$; $p > 0·001$. Delay effect on attitude: NS.

The results reveal a massive change of attitude in the commitment situation and indicate further that this change is still observable after a week and even after a month. This result is particularly interesting in view of the fact that we possess relatively few data concerning the effects of counterattitudinal role-playing in children and because it relates to an attitude which is of considerable importance in the life of pupils. At the same time, we note that in the counterattitudinal letters, neither the model arguments nor the personal arguments were reproduced any more frequently by committed subjects who underwent substantial attitude change than by uncommitted subjects who manifested no attitude change.[3] It thus seems that the attitude which is acquired in the forced compliance situation and which persists after 4 weeks, in spite of the existential significance of the object, in no way affects the memory of cognitive elements which are consistent with this newly acquired attitude and which are capable of producing an advantageous (that is a consistent) modification of its cognitive component. In other words, everything in experiment 7 suggests that the attitude change resulting from dissonance reduction represents a sort of quasi-hermetic 'cognitive pocket' which makes it possible to rationalize the compliant behaviour exhibited towards the experimenter but which fails to penetrate deeply into the universe of the subject's private attitudes. This suggestion is clearly confirmed by experiment 8.

Experiment 8. Stability of the attitude acquired in the forced compliance situation and attitude consistency

This new experiment (Pavin, 1991b) was conducted like the preceding one, with the counterattitudinal act again consisting of writing to the education minister to persuade him to shorten the summer holidays. The children's commitment was manipulated in an identical way. The interval between the act and the attitude measurement was either 5 minutes or 5 weeks. One month before the experiment the children had completed a long questionnaire concerning holidays and school life (pre-experimental measurements). This questionnaire dealt with extremely varied aspects of the two topics (holiday friends, holiday homework, the pleasure of going to school, the opportunity to stay up late during the holidays, getting bored during the holidays . . .), with the importance attached to these matters by the child (for example: is it important for you to have friends during the holidays?) as well as with the children's representation of the opinion of their classmates. The questionnaire also contained the critical question relating to the length of the summer holidays (main dependent variable).

The same questionnaire was used to provide the dependent measures after the children had performed the counterattitudinal behaviour (after an interval of either 5 minutes or 5 weeks). Pavin clearly expected to observe both the reproduction of the dissonance effect and the stability of the newly acquired attitude. Application of the concept of attitude consistency would also have led him to expect any changes to spread to other elements in the subjects' cognitive universe which were closely related to the question of summer holidays.

The questionnaire contained 20 items, each of which was the object of three questions. Table 2.2 presents only a representative selection of the results obtained.

Table 2.2. Stability of the attitude acquired in the forced compliance situation and attitude consistency: post-test/pre-test differences.

	Interval	
	5 minutes	5 weeks
Paradigmatic item (holidays too long)		
committed subjects	6·41	6·49
uncommitted subjects	0·95	0·05
Other items:		
holiday friends		
committed subjects	1·22	−2·20
uncommitted subjects	0·61	−1·62
holiday homework		
committed subjects	1·70	−1·47
uncommitted subjects	1·38	−0.56
pleasure of going to school		
committed subjects	0·49	−0.28
uncommitted subjects	0·41	−0·16
staying up late		
committed subjects	−0·33	−1·04
uncommitted subjects	−1·82	0·25
boredom		
committed subjects	−0·01	−1·52
uncommitted subjects	−0·84	−0·66
doing what you want		
committed subjects	0·27	−0·77
uncommitted subjects	−0·45	−1·27

Notes: All the measurements (pre- and post-test) were made on a 24-point scale. The consistency hypothesis would predict positive differences, as is the case with the paradigmatic item. The few significant, time-related differences (5 minutes vs. 5 weeks), are difficult to interpret.

The results of this experiment are particularly striking: there are no statistically significant differences between the pre- and post-experimental measurements except in the attitude towards the length of the summer holidays. This difference appears only in the free-choice subjects, irrespective of whether the measurement was taken 5 minutes or 5 weeks after the counterattitudinal act. As in experiment 7, we again witness a major change in the cognition, which is inconsistent with the behaviour. This change persists over time without provoking an enhancement of the consistency of other cognitive elements, even after 5 weeks have elapsed. This change does not even affect the children's representation of the opinion of their classmates. The questionnaire was constructed so that the children had to provide their own opinion and the opinion which they attributed to their classmates in their response to each item. Pavin noted that the new attitude held by the subjects entailed no revision of the attitude attributed to their friends. As a result, the pupils who took part in experiment 8 left the experiment with a new inconsistent relation which can be expressed as follows: 'I do not think about the question of summer holidays in the same way as the other members of my group (class).' This is precisely the point that Pavin explores in experiment 8.

Experiment 8. The stability of the attitude acquired in the forced compliance situation and the subject/classmates difference

This follow-up experiment was conducted in the same way as the preceding one using the same pre-experimental questionnaire and the same manipulation of the intervals between the counterattitudinal act and the post-experimental measurements (in this experiment, 5 minutes and 2 weeks). In contrast, all the subjects in experiment 8 were committed (free choice, signing of letter to minister).

Despite this, a new independent variable was introduced, namely the salience of the self/group difference in attitude towards the summer holidays. When taking the immediate measurements (taken, we should recall, as soon as the child had finished the letter), the experimenter said to 50 per cent of the subjects whose new attitude differed from the one they attributed to their classmates (this was, in fact, the case for nearly all the subjects), 'Well, I see that you don't think the same way as your friends about the summer holidays!' The remaining 50 per cent did not receive this comment. The delayed measurements were taken either 5 minutes or 15 days later (2×2 design). Once more a major attitude change was observed and this again persisted in the delayed measurements, both 5 minutes and 15 days after the problematic behaviour (see also Table 2.3). The attitude attributed to the subjects' classmates remained unaffected. Under no condition did it differ from the attribution made in the pre-test questionnaire. The salience of the subject/group difference had only a long-term effect. Fifteen days after manipulation a significant, although very slight, attenuation of the subjects' personal attitude concerning the summer holidays was observed, principally among the subjects who had been made aware of the difference by the experimenter. In contrast, this attenuation is not significant in the other subjects (who had not been exposed to the experimenter's manipulation of this salience). It is important to note that this attenuation neither eliminates nor changes either the subjects' attitude or the subject/group difference which results from the attitude change. It simply reduces their magnitude.

Table 2.3. The stability of the attitude acquired in the forced compliance situation and the subject/classmates difference.

	Interval: 5 minutes	Interval: 15 days
Difference made salient by experimenter	6·74	4·93
Difference not made salient by experimenter	7·02	5·55

Notes: The higher the number, the greater the difference between the attitude of the subject and that attributed to the subject's classmates. $n = 20$ subjects in each cell. In the pre-test questionnaire the mean attitude of the subjects was 1·14. The mean attitude attributed to the peer group was 2·90.

Thus, the research conducted by Pavin (for a complete account, see Pavin, 1992) reveals no effect of attitude consistency consequent on the evaluative change which is induced by the counterattitudinal act. However, this evaluative change occurs systematically and persists well beyond the experimental situation, for a period of at least 4 weeks, despite the fact that it relates to an object which is of considerable existential importance to the subjects. Clearly, such a set of negative results is not sufficient to allow us to reject piecemeal the hypothesis of an alignment of cognitions following the change induced by the forced compliance situation. However, it does provide further arguments in support of our claim: dissonance reduction presupposes only the modification of cognitions which imply the obverse of the generative cognition. Its purpose is not to establish consistency between cognitions.

Experiment 10. The effect of a counterattitudinal essay on the evaluative, cognitive and behavioural components of attitude

Experiment 10 (Channouf, 1990) provides us with clues about a number of conditions under which the evaluative change may spread to affect adjacent cognitions in the subject's attitude universe. The subjects were students who had to write a counterattitudinal essay defending a selection procedure for university admission. Some time beforehand they had completed two questionnaires designed to allow the experimenter to manipulate two independent variables. First, they filled in a long opinion-oriented questionnaire (independent variable 'item type') relating in part to their opinions concerning certain aspects of selection (items said to be 'directly linked' to the critical item which measures their attitude towards selection). This questionnaire also dealt with other matters of opinion (for example, the recourse to private-sector funding of university budgets) which are habitually associated with the question of selection in the French political debate on university education (these items are said to be 'indirectly linked' to the critical item). The subjects also completed a questionnaire which assessed the degree to which they considered internal effects to provide a causal explanation of reinforcement and behaviour (independent variable 'explanatory model'). This second questionnaire made it possible to select 12 students whose convictions regarding the causal explanation of psychological events, behaviour and reinforcements were extremely external in nature (see Beauvois and Dubois, 1988) and to juxtapose them with 13 students who preferred an explanation in terms of internal mechanisms.

The experimenter started the forced compliance session by activating the subjects' explanatory model. To do this he presented the results of the questionnaire and then presented a brief summary of internality to one group and of externality to the other.[4] Thus the experimenter told the first group: 'The questionnaire shows that you're an internal type of person, that is someone who thinks that what he does and what happens to him has its roots in himself and not in situations or circumstances.' To the second group he said: 'The questionnaire shows that you're an external type of person, that is someone who thinks that what he does and what happens to him has its roots in situations or circumstances rather than in himself.' Then, having made the free-choice nature of the task clear, he asked the subjects to write a counterattitudinal essay in support of a selection procedure for university admission. When the essays had been written, the experimenter claimed that it was necessary to revise the questionnaire of opinions which the subjects had already completed and presented them with a new questionnaire (new response format, new fillers...) in which certain items were drawn from the earlier questionnaire. Some of the items expressed opinions directly linked to the idea of selection (for example, studies proceed better when selection has been applied); others expressed opinions that were indirectly linked to the idea of selection but were associated with the concept in the student's belief system (the value of using private-sector funds in the university budget). It was these items that were to provide the cognitive measures. Finally, the experimenter invited the subjects to sign a petition supporting selection and then to take part in a demonstration in front of the Education Office in support of the same cause (behavioural measures). Thus, the dependent variables related not only to the traditional evaluative item of the forced compliance paradigm but also to the cognitive, and even the behavioural, components of the attitude object.

The results (Table 2.4) demonstrate the recurrence of the dissonance effect, with both subject groups exhibiting a highly significant attitude change on the critical item in favour of selection for university admission (F(before/after) = $59 \cdot 24$, $p < 0 \cdot 0001$). There is no difference between internal and external subjects on the item which makes an assessment of the dissonance reduction work possible. If we consider the items that are directly and indirectly linked to the critical item, we observe a change consistent with the attitude change only in the internal subjects and then only in connection with the items that are *directly* linked to the critical item. The vast majority of subjects, both internal and external, refused to make the requested behavioural commitment (petition, demonstration) to the cause of university selection.

Table 2.4. The effect of a counterattitudinal essay on cognitive and behavioural components of attitude.

	Attitude towards selection*	Direct items	Indirect items
Internal ($n=13$)	$-2 \cdot 33$	$-0 \cdot 85$	$-0 \cdot 05$
External ($n=12$)	$-1 \cdot 69$	$-0 \cdot 00$	$-0 \cdot 33$
Behavioural commitment**		petition (%)	demonstration (%)
Internal ($n=13$)		38	8
External ($n=12$)		8	8

Notes: *Before–after difference
      **Percentage of subjects who agreed to the behaviour. None of these percentages differs significantly from the others. In both groups the attitude towards selection changed significantly in favour of the counterattitudinal position defended by the subjects (F = $59 \cdot 24$, $p < 0 \cdot 0001$). However, there was no difference between the two groups. The before–after difference for the direct and indirect items is significant only in the case of the direct items and then only in the internal subjects (F = $10 \cdot 41$, $p < 0 \cdot 004$).

Experiment 10 thus provides an excellent reproduction of the dissonance effect in both groups of subjects. Weak, although very significant, changes relating to the opinion items directly linked to the attitudinal cognition which one might suppose to be produced by the work of dissonance reduction are observed only in the internal subjects. Why should this be the case? We shall return to the problems raised by the role of causal explanation processes in forced compliance situations at a later point. For the moment, we shall limit ourselves to presenting a highly plausible explanation which has been proposed by Channouf. We now know that internal beliefs are more normative than external ones and the existence of a norm of internality in western cultures has been amply documented (Jellison and Green, 1981, Beauvois, 1984a, 1994, Beauvois and Le Poultier, 1986, Dubois, 1987, 1994, Beauvois and Dubois, 1988). We might therefore suppose that the internal subjects are also the most normative. However, we might also suppose that this tendency is not confined to the causal explanation of psychological events and that such subjects are equally sensitive to other normative phenomena. If this is the case, and given that attitude consistency is itself normative,[5] we might well imagine that internal subjects would attempt to modify their beliefs in a way that produces attitude consistency to a greater extent, or at least earlier, than the other subjects. Furthermore, this modification would occur either *independently of the dissonance reduction process itself* or following this process. This explanation at least possesses the quality of simplicity and, for us, this is its essential quality. At the point we have reached in our argument, it does not require us to modify our conception of the dissonance reduction process in a way that admits the presence of processes of causal explanation.[6]

Taken as a whole, these four experiments ultimately provide little support for the hypothesis that cognitive changes take place in accordance with a principle of attitude consistency in forced compliance situations. The observed changes certainly affect the attitudinal cognition (a cognition which is entered in the numerator of the dissonance ratio because it would have implied the opposite behaviour to that actually obtained from the subject), sometimes in an extensive and persistent way. However, the process of reducing the psychological state of dissonance seems to go no further. Other conditions appear to be necessary if this change is to spread to other adjacent conditions of the attitude universe, for example the specific upgrading of the idea of consistency which undoubtedly occurred in Channouf's internal subjects (1990). If these conditions are not fulfilled, then the only work performed is that of dissonance reduction and this affects only a very limited number of cognitions — namely those which make it possible to rationalize behaviour.

Notes

1   As Steele (1988) has correctly pointed out, this practice often makes it difficult to investigate alternative hypotheses since the available rationalization procedures seem to be in some way predetermined for the subjects.

2   Here, it is only for the sake of convenience that we base ourselves on the old tripartite model of attitude structure. Our argument is equally valid for any conception of attitude which holds that this cannot be reduced to the simple evaluation of the object. For example, it is applicable to the sociocognitive model of attitude (Pratkanis and Greenwald, 1989), which requires not only an evaluative summary of the object but also a knowledge structure *supporting that evaluation* (p. 249). To adopt the terms used by these authors, it is difficult to imagine that the heuristic function of attitude can be modified unless the schematic function is also modified.

3   In the 'no commitment' condition only the subjects in the 'reproduction after 4 weeks' situation exhibit a very curious change of attitude in favour of the counterattitudinal position. It would appear reasonable to interpret this in terms of the sleeper effect, with the arguments which had not been forgotten somehow working in memory independently of the counterattitudinal essay. This interpretation can do nothing but enhance the theoretical interest of Pavin's observation that there is a similarity between the memory work of subjects who change their attitude and that of subjects who undergo no change.

4   Prior research (Channouf, 1991) had shown that this is a good way to activate the explanatory models, with 'activated' subjects outperforming 'unactivated' subjects in their recall of phrases associated with their explanatory model (internal vs. external) taken from a narrative text which had been presented as a memory task.

5   The existence of a norm of consistency is implicitly accepted by many theorists (see Poitou, 1974), and in particular by the advocates of self-affirmation or self-presentation processes which imply that one makes a good impression if one shows oneself to be consistent.

6   This explanation, which implies a higher degree of consistency in internal subjects, finds support in another experiment described by Channouf. In this experiment, the subjects argued in favour of their private attitude (against university selection) and should therefore have experienced no dissonance. In this instance, only the internal subjects, whether committed or not (whether or not the free-choice nature of the task had been made clear), exhibited a polarization of attitude in line with the position they were defending. Following the pro-attitudinal essay, it was again only the internal subjects who agreed to take part in the demonstration.

Chapter 3

The status of cognitions of commitment

Since 1962, Brehm and Cohen have insisted on the necessity of what they call the volition of the subject if a state of dissonance is to be induced. Thus, these authors necessarily accept the idea that the simple presence of relations of inconsistency between cognitions is not a sufficient condition for the arousal of this drive state. In fact, the 1960s were to prove a rich source of experiments showing that the primary effect of 'dissonance' in forced compliance situations, that is a more marked change of attitude or evaluation in favour of the problematic behaviour in poorly rewarded than in well rewarded subjects, is observed only if the subjects are allowed to choose whether or not to perform the requested act. When subjects do not have this choice the dissonance effect is replaced by a reinforcement effect (Linder, Cooper and Jones, 1967, Holmes and Strickland, 1970).

If research had halted at this point, then the idea of volition proposed by Brehm and Cohen would undoubtedly have been considered sufficient, with subjects only feeling dissonance if they believed that they wanted to undertake the behaviour which they had performed. However, at the same time as the critical importance of 'free choice' was being demonstrated, the same authors, as well as other researchers, were revealing the significance of other cognitions relating to the public or anonymous nature of the problematic behaviour (Carlsmith, Collins and Helmreich, 1966), the irrevocable or reversible nature of the act (Helmreich and Collins, 1968) and, above all, the role of cognitions concerning its consequences (Cooper and Worchel, 1970, Calder, Ross and Insko, 1973). Like free choice, such cognitions seem to function as more or less necessary conditions for dissonance arousal. In our view, the idea of commitment, in the form proposed by Kiesler in 1971, provides the best conceptual synthesis of this rich research tradition and allows us to hypothesize that the induction of a state of dissonance in a forced compliance situation requires the subject's commitment to the problematic behaviour. In fact, Kiesler treats all the cognitions that have been studied as preconditions for dissonance effects (free choice, public nature of the behaviour, irrevocability, consequences and so on) as variables affecting the individual's level of commitment to the behaviour. However, while Kiesler locates the idea of commitment within the tradition of research into the conditions necessary if the state of dissonance is to arise, he considers that dissonance theorists have mishandled the concept and have denied it the status it deserves: 'However, to say that one is then committed to the decision is, to my mind, simply another way of saying that one has decided. And this is one reason why I think that this usage of the term makes commitment a "throwaway" concept. One is using it redundantly' (Kiesler, 1971, p. 47). We know that, since 1971, a number of dissonance theorists have placed at least two of the conditions of commitment (free choice and consequences) at the heart of their formulations and that this has sometimes led them to revise Festinger's original theory, turning it into a theory of 'personal responsibility' (Wicklund and Brehm, 1976) or a theory of the cognitive management of the consequences of behaviour (Cooper and Fazio, 1984). It is clear that for these researchers the subject's commitment to the behaviour, or at least the conceptual equivalent of this commitment, forms a key element of the revised theory. However, we shall attempt to show that these revisions have failed to invest commitment with its correct theoretical status within dissonance theory. Furthermore, we shall attempt to demonstrate that, despite the absence of any theoretical or experimental necessity, these revisions have distorted the fundamental core of the theory. To illustrate our point of view better we shall start by looking at the way in which the variable 'reward' was treated by the first dissonance theorists.

The theoretical status of rewards

Let us take the example of a person who agrees to perform an act which is slightly immoral in that it consists of telling a colleague the opposite of the truth. This is the situation in which Festinger and Carlsmith's subjects (1959) found themselves. To reward them for their assistance the experimenter offered these subjects a monetary payment which, in some cases, was far from negligible.

We may recall that Festinger and Carlsmith's reasoning was based on an implicit psychological implication which holds that the fact that we are paid to do something implies that we will do it and will refrain from doing the opposite. It is this psychological implication that justifies the appearance of the reward as a consistent cognition in the denominator of the dissonance ratio. Thus Festinger and Carlsmith, like Cohen in 1959, avoid any recourse to the subject's private attitude in deciding what status the reward might have with reference to the counterattitudinal behaviour. They are content to accept the existence of a psychological implication, in reality totally normative, in terms of which the subject's behaviour can be viewed as an implication of the reward he or she is to receive. For them this implication was the only possible theoretical basis for the hypothesis which holds that dissonance is reduced as the size of the reward increases. As we know, the results agree perfectly with this line of reasoning: the reward does indeed function as a cognition which is consistent with the behaviour.

However, their very use of the term 'lie' might well have led theorists to a rather different type of analysis. Is it moral to be rewarded for saying the opposite of what one believes? If we pursue this idea we might be tempted to say that the relation (of consistency or inconsistency) between the reward and the behaviour cannot be defined without taking the subject's private attitude into account. To be rewarded for saying what we believe is not the same as being rewarded for saying the opposite of what we believe. In the first instance the reward is totally consistent with the behaviour (the fact that I receive a reward implies that I will say what I am asked to say), whereas in the second it may give rise to an additional immorality (not only have I said the opposite of what I believe but I am also being paid for it). Our argument is not new: it is exactly the same as that advanced by Rosenberg (1966) when he claimed to be able to account for the dissonance effect in terms of evaluation apprehension. This type of reasoning consists of attributing to the reward–behaviour relation a significance which is dictated by the subject's private attitude. Why was this argumentation, which makes the relation between two cognitions dependent on a third, not adopted by the first theorists of dissonance? Quite simply because it makes use of what we might term a 'phantom' concept, one that does not exist in the initial theory: the ternary relation. As we have insisted in our presentation of the 'fundamental core' of 1957, this theory applies the concept of psychological implication exclusively to binary relations between cognitions and proposes no mechanism for handling the type of ternary relation which is implied by the reasoning outlined above. The consequence of reasoning in this way would be to suppose that the relation between two cognitions (the knowledge subjects have about their behaviour and their knowledge concerning the reward they are to receive) may be dependent on a third (their private attitude). As we know, the experimental results confirm the reasoning proposed both by Festinger and Carlsmith and by Cohen and invalidate the alternative reasoning which we have presented above: as far as we know, no experimental result exists to support the hypothesis that the reward may give rise to an inconsistent cognition.

Why, then, have we expounded an argument which we know to be unsupported by the data and which has never been advanced (or, at least, published) by a dissonance theorist? We have done so because we believe that it is precisely this type of reasoning that has led, for example, to the concept of the 'aversive consequences of behaviour' (Cooper and Fazio, 1984), to the likening of dissonance to guilt (Stice, 1992) and, more generally, to the major revisions of dissonance theory. Given that this reasoning is incorrect when applied to the question of reward, why should it be considered correct when applied to free choice or the consequences of behaviour?

The status of cognitions of commitment

Let us label the cognitions in question as follows:

cognition F: I was given the choice whether or not to do what I finally did
                 (F for free choice)
cognition P: what I have done will be known by people other than the
                 experimenter (P for public nature of the behaviour)
cognition C: there will be consequences to what I have done (C for
                 consequences)
cognition I: I cannot undo what I am currently doing (I for irrevocability).

These four cognitions have been shown, either individually or in combination, to
be necessary for the production of dissonance effects. These cognitions
undoubtedly raise a theoretical problem which cannot be treated in the
fundamental core of the 1957 theory. Does this constitute a reason to change the
fundamental core? We do not think so.

These cognitions clearly have the status of relevant cognitions since they are
critical to the production of dissonance effects. For example, free choice is so
critical that it is usual to consider the expressions 'free-choice condition' and
'dissonant condition' as synonyms. However, the core theory of 1957 provides for
only two types of relevant cognitions: those that stand in a relation of consistency
to the generative cognition and those that stand in a relation of inconsistency to
this cognition. As we shall see, the cognitions F, P, C and I are, generally speaking,
neither consistent nor inconsistent.[1]

These cognitions cannot be in a relation of consistency with the generative
cognition since they are necessary for dissonance arousal. So much would appear to
be self-evident.

At the same time they cannot be in a relation of dissonance with the
generative cognition G which, as we know, is the representation of the
problematic behaviour. For them to be so within the strict framework of the
fundamental core of the 1957 theory which deals exclusively with binary relations,
we would have to be able to assert that $F \rightarrow not\, G$, $P \rightarrow not\, G$, $C \rightarrow not\, G$ and
$I \rightarrow not\, G$. Consequently, we would have to be justified in making the following
psychological implications:

cognition F: the fact of having the choice to do or not to do something
                 implies that we do not do it
cognition P: the fact that other people know about an act implies that we
                 do not do it
cognition C: the fact that an act has foreseeable consequences implies that
                 we do not do it
cognition I: the fact that we cannot undo an act implies that we do not do
                 it.

At the very least these psychological implications are contranormative since the
prevailing ideology is not conducive to constrained, anonymous, inconsequential
behaviour. We would go so far as to assert that such psychological implications are
meaningless. Here, it is important to remember that, in view of the nature of the

core theory of 1957, these are the only implications which allow us to consider cognitions F, P, C and I to be inconsistent with the generative cognition G. A seemingly 'natural' solution might be to invent a new concept to denote ternary relations in what would then be a revised theory and to affirm that these cognitions are inconsistent with G in view of the subject's private attitude. Thus the subject's freedom would become an intolerable freedom, the consequences of his acts would become 'aversive' consequences and so on. The reader will understand that we do not find this a satisfactory solution. There are a variety of reasons for this:

First, because we have had to reject it when dealing with the question of reward, despite the fact that it could apply to this cognition just as well as to the others. There is no obvious justification for applying a different reasoning to reward from the one we use in connection with free choice or the consequences of behaviour.

Second, because experiments have shown that it is behaviour and not private attitude that orients the cognitive work of dissonance reduction.

Finally, because we already possess a concept, namely commitment, which allows us to avoid this counter-intuitive revision of a theory whose predictive performance has so far proved to be excellent.

In other words, if subjects who have agreed to perform an act are to feel a psychological state of dissonance it is necessary (1) that they are committed to the behaviour and (2) that this behaviour is problematic for them, that is, it can be thought of as the obverse of what their attitudes or motivations would have implied. If these two conditions are satisfied then it will be possible to observe the work of dissonance reduction taking place. We should note that the cognitions that are relevant for these two conditions are not the same. This becomes clear in the following notational formulation of the dissonance ratio which, of course, remains the major theoretical tool in predicting the subject's cognitive work:

$$T(g)F \text{ and/or } C \text{ and/or } P \text{ and/or } I = D/D + C$$

We consider that this notation provides an excellent illustration of the two inseparable faces of a single comprehensive theory of dissonance. The left-hand expression corresponds to the subjects' commitment to their behaviour[2] and implies that we are able to formulate propositions concerning 'the pledging or binding of the individual to his behavioural act' (Kiesler and Sakumura, 1966, p. 349, Kiesler, 1971, p. 30). The right-hand expression corresponds to the orientation of the cognitive work of dissonance reduction and implies the application of the core theory of 1957 which our presentation enables us to retain in its entirety.

Conclusion 3a *The cognitions relating to the free choice, consequences, public nature and irrevocability of the problematic behaviour are cognitions of commitment. In view of this, their theoretical function is to determine the conditions of the psychological state of dissonance.*
Consequence *Since they are neither consistent nor inconsistent with the generative cognition, the cognitions of commitment do not appear in the dissonance ratio.*

However, this presentation does not overcome all the ambiguities. Let us consider, for example, the consequences of the problematic act. The above discussion leads us to consider them to be cognitions of commitment which are therefore neither consistent nor inconsistent with the generative cognition G. No doubt, though, the reader will remember that we earlier treated the consequences of a persuasion attempt as consistent (when the persuasion attempt succeeded) or inconsistent (when it failed). We need to distinguish between two different types of consequence. Certain consequences prove to be direct implications of the act which has been requested of the subject and which this subject has agreed to perform. This was precisely the case in experiment 4, which was presented in chapter 1. In this experiment the subjects agreed to help the experimenter convince their colleagues of the existence of extra-terrestrial beings who regularly visit the earth. In this case, the failure of the persuasion attempt could be equated with a failure to fulfil the requirements of the task and could, in view of the fact that the subject's behaviour had proved to be of no use to the experimenter, be considered as a type of negative feedback. The act which the subject agreed to accomplish thus implied a number of consequences which had the status of goals. We can easily understand that the failure to attain these goals represents a cognition which is inconsistent with the generative cognition which implies precisely the attainment of these goals. 'I have agreed to persuade' does not fit well with 'I have not succeeded in persuading' but instead implies 'I have succeeded in persuading.'

It would have been very different if the experiment had been presented as research into high-school students' opinions of paranormal phenomena or, alternatively, as a pre-test aimed at enhancing the subject's acquaintance with the range of available arguments. Such a presentation would not have created any necessary link between the counterattitudinal behaviour and the success of an attempt to influence a colleague. Any such success would then have appeared as an additional consequence which, although an explicit part of the situation, remained unnegotiated. This is the case, for example, when subjects who have to write a counterattitudinal essay are told that the results of the research may be published in the press and that their arguments may be reused for non-experimental purposes. In such a case the consequences of the act are part of the context; they are included in the circumstances surrounding the act and function as a condition of commitment. They imply neither the act nor its obverse and, similarly, neither they nor their obverse are implied by the act. Their presence simply commits the subject to the act just as their absence may free him from any commitment, to the point where no dissonance reduction is observed. It can be seen that if we are to attribute the correct status to the consequences of an act we must properly understand the significance of the act to the subject. Similarly, the distinction between cognitions of commitment and the consistent or inconsistent cognitions must frequently be based on detailed knowledge of the concrete situation.

What is true for the consequences of an act is equally valid for free choice. We shall dwell for rather longer on this point since our conception of free choice is an important element in the radical theory of dissonance that we are presenting in this work.

The commitment to compliance

Free choice

Of the conditions which must be satisfied by the forced compliance situation if dissonance effects are to be observed, free choice was not only the one to be identified the earliest (see Brehm, 1959) but it is clearly also the most important. Situations in which the condition of free choice is not fulfilled do not give rise to dissonance effects (see Wicklund and Brehm, 1976). In consequence, 'free choice' can be considered as a paradigmatic characteristic of the forced compliance situation.

The classic method of realizing the 'free choice' condition is to announce to the subjects that they are free to agree or refuse to do as the experimenter asks. Here is one of the earliest examples (Brock, 1962) which, nevertheless, remains a prototype for more recent experimental manipulations: 'I would like to emphasize that even though you came over here tonight, there is no obligation at all to write this essay. If you don't want to write it you can get up and walk out if you wish' (p. 266).

If we consider its experimental consequences, we see that this 'free choice instruction' which is addressed to the subjects possesses at least three important features. First, it has relatively little (if any) effect on the actual behaviour of the subjects. It was very soon discovered that there was no notable difference in the number of subjects refusing to perform the counterattitudinal task requested by the experimenter in the 'high choice' and 'low choice' conditions. Indeed, in both conditions this number proved to be very low (Zimbardo, 1969). Second, the few subjects who have so far been asked to express their feeling of freedom in such so-called 'free choice' situations tend rather to evoke a feeling of constraint (Steiner, 1980). Finally, despite these two observations, the free choice instruction is necessary for the arousal of a state of dissonance.

It therefore becomes necessary to reflect more thoroughly on what it is that subjects 'freely' agree to when they receive the free choice instruction. There are two possible answers to this question, both of which have very different theoretical implications.

The first answer consists of arguing that the subjects agree to the experimental situation which is explained to them, that is they agree to a demand made by the experimenter which is problematic for them. They agree in some way to comply with the situation which confronts them.

The alternative holds that the subjects agree to undertake the precise behaviour which is asked of them and no other, for example 'to write persuasive essays in favour of becoming a Catholic' (again Brock, 1962). This time, the subject's choice bears on the counterattitudinal act itself.

To draw a comparison that is not without significance, we might say that the first alternative corresponds to an individual's agreement to work for a given employer. In doing this, he accepts the contract of employment which implies his later obedience to the employer or his representatives and which provides an envelope definition of the types of job he will be asked to undertake. The second alternative corresponds to the acceptance of the particular job this employer asks of him on a given day. 'Today, I'd like you to deal with this tonne of pig iron.' Note that on this occasion our employee could perfectly well say: 'I don't want to give up my first choice of working for you, I really want to work for you but I would rather you gave me a different job from handling this pig iron.' The first choice represents what we shall call *a commitment to compliance or obedience*, the second *a commitment to the counterattitudinal act or activity*.

In fact, the traditional methods of manipulating free choice in forced compliance situations do not make it possible to distinguish between these two choices. However, all the theoretical formulations which are based on the idea of free choice implicitly accept that the second alternative is operative. This is particularly true of all the reinterpretations of dissonance effects in terms of self-perception (Bem, 1967, 1972) to which we shall return in more detail later. If we suppose that subjects have chosen compliance (as opposed to non-compliance), it is difficult to see how, on the basis of this choice, they can attribute to themselves an attitude which conforms to the counterattitudinal act. They might perhaps attribute to themselves an interest in psychological research, a liking for the experimenter, even a gift for masochism, but certainly not a particular fondness for the spinach or grilled grasshoppers which they have to eat as a consequence of their compliance or for the electric shocks which they have agreed to receive. It is only because we think that what the subject has agreed to is the act itself that we can hypothesize that the subject infers an attitude which conforms to this act. This is a theoretical decision justified by an ambiguous manipulation which, as we shall see, is not as 'natural' as might be imagined a priori. It is quite probably erroneous.

Commitment to compliance and commitment to the act

Let us suppose that we have just presented the subject with the two alternative choices described above. The situation should require two preliminary decisions on the part of the subject and could take the following form:

> I am going to ask you to work for me. You will have to do things like eating a plateful of grilled grasshoppers, going without tobacco for a few hours, writing as persuasive an essay as possible in favour of increasing

university rights and similar tasks. What it is that you will actually do will have to be decided later. But first of all you, and you alone, must make a first decision: you are quite free to refuse or to agree to take part in the experiment I'm proposing to you. It's up to you to decide.

This is how the first choice would be put to the subject (thus providing the possibility of a first commitment). This choice is between compliance and non-compliance, with subjects agreeing or refusing to perform for the experimenter an act which they know will be costly in some way, even if they do not know exactly what it is. Such subjects are in a similar situation to the worker in our analogy who must decide whether or not to work for a particular employer, despite having only a general idea of what he might in reality be asked to do.

Let us suppose that the subjects finally decide to comply. This represents a first expression of freedom. The experimenter can himself select the behaviour which the subjects are to perform or ask the subjects to make this decision for themselves. 'Decide for yourself: grilled grasshoppers, no tobacco or the essay in favour of increased university rights.' In this way the subject would be offered a second choice (leading to a commitment to the counterattitudinal act) that relates specifically to the precise act which is to be undertaken. There can be no doubt that this choice is different from the earlier one: the subjects no longer have to decide whether or not they will do something unwelcome for the experimenter. They have already decided that. We may well imagine that they are not indifferent to whether they eat the grilled grasshoppers, go without cigarettes or write the essay. We may further suppose that when this choice is offered to them they will select the act which is least unpleasant for them. Let us suppose that they choose the essay.

As we have said, the classic method of manipulating the free choice condition does not allow us to distinguish between these two possible types of choice. However, once it becomes possible to distinguish between them both conceptually and experimentally, we are bound to conclude that these two expressions of the subjects' freedom do not possess the same theoretical status. Let us first examine the choice of the act itself which, in the situation we have described above, is the second to be made. This choice has all the appearance of a decision since it comes down to deciding, for example, whether to write an essay rather than eating grasshoppers or going without tobacco. As such, we might suppose that it will introduce an additional dissonance. We shall see that this is not, in fact, the case, for two reasons which are specific to the situation of decision within a framework of compliance:

1   unlike in classic decision-making situations, subjects who have just agreed to comply in the performance of some unpleasant act are already virtually in a state of dissonance when this decision is asked of them; and
2   unlike in the majority of classic decision-making situations, none of the alternatives offers a real advantage, each probably only being characterized by its cost to the subjects.

For these reasons, the situation of decision-making within a framework of compliance will possess special properties. This choice, or, more exactly this obligation to decide, will give rise to cognitions which, curiously, prove to be consonant with the behaviour that is finally undertaken. Since this choice is a decision in the classic sense of the word, the subjects will probably choose the alternative which is most advantageous to them. If this is so, then they will be able to justify their behaviour by the fact that it enabled them to avoid the other two alternatives which would probably have been more unpleasant ('I escaped the grasshoppers and I didn't have to go without cigarettes'). This is what is shown by the calculation of the two dissonance ratios which are established with reference to the generative cognition: 'I am going to have to argue in favour of an increase in university rights.' Here Dg(F) is the dissonance ratio established for a subject who was not able to choose to write the essay and D′gF is the ratio established for a subject who chose to write the essay and therefore refused to eat the grasshoppers or refrain from smoking.

$$Dg(F) = U - /U - + R > D'g(F) = U - /U - + R + T + E$$

where

Dg(F): the dissonance created by the generative cognition g when the experimenter states the subject's freedom F

R: cognitions relating to the various reasons leading to compliance and therefore implying the behaviour

U −: cognition relating to the private attitude of the subject towards university rights; this attitude would have implied a different behaviour

T: cognition relating to the desire for tobacco which implies the behaviour 'defend an increase in university rights'

E: cognition relating to the desire not to eat grasshoppers which implies the behaviour 'defend an increase in university rights'.

As we can see, these dissonance ratios clearly show that the choice of the act itself in such a situation of preliminary compliance cannot be considered to be a necessary condition for the arousal of a state of dissonance. On the contrary, it reduces dissonance and, *a fortiori*, the attitude change that corresponds to the reduction of this dissonance. There is therefore no reason to consider this particular choice to be a factor of commitment necessary for the arousal of dissonance in the forced compliance situation we are studying here.

Let us therefore turn our attention to the initial choice in which the subject, in agreeing to comply, accepted the experimental situation. What the subject freely agreed to do was to undertake an unpleasant or problematic act (counter-attitudinal or countermotivational) as part of a situation to be organized by a person of authority, namely the experimenter. Thus, in some way the subject has accepted the contract of forced compliance and a relationship of obedience towards the experimenter. If, of the two choices we have identified within the situation which is habitually referred to as one of 'free choice', there is one that is necessary for the arousal of a state of dissonance, then it can only be this initial choice since, as we have seen, the other choice actually reduces the dissonance which is produced by the counterattitudinal act. The cognition resulting from this preliminary choice should be characterized by the properties of what we earlier defined as a cognition of commitment (unless the dissociation of the two choices eliminates the contractual properties of this 'free choice') with regard to the future generative cognition g (for example, 'I am writing an essay in favour of increasing university rights'). If this is genuinely the case, then this cognition should be deemed relevant since its presence is necessary for the induction of a state of dissonance. However, at the same time, it cannot be considered to be either a consistent cognition (its presence would then reduce the total amount of dissonance) or an inconsistent cognition, since in this situation it is clear that the fact of having agreed to the contract of forced compliance implies that the subject will perform the counterattitudinal act.

Experiments 11 and 12: Commitment to compliance and free choice of the problematic act in a forced compliance situation
Experiments 11 (Beauvois, Bungert, Rainis and Tornior, 1993, exp. 1) and 12 (Beauvois, Bungert and Mariette, 1995) implemented a situation comparable to that described above. The subjects were given the choice of whether or not to take part in a counterattitudinal role-playing situation (variable: commitment to compliance). Before they made their decision or, in the no-choice condition, before they were told to take part, the subjects were told the topics (all counterattitudinal) that they might have to write about (drivers of under 16 no longer to be allowed to drive when accompanied by an adult; shorter holidays; grants to be restricted to pupils achieving an average mark of 14/20 in the preceding year). However, they were not told which of these essays they would ultimately have to produce. Instead, the experimenter insisted that this was something which would be decided later. Some of the subjects were then asked to choose which of the counterattitudinal essays they wanted to write (variable: commitment to the counterattitudinal act), while the others were not. In line with the above analysis, it was expected that commitment to compliance (free agreement to take part in the forced compliance situation) would be a necessary precondition for the observation of dissonance reduction effects and that commitment to the act (choice of the counterattitudinal act performed) would reduce these effects.

Nearly 300 subjects, pupils in their last two school years in Grenoble, participated individually in experiments 11 and 12. In the condition known as commitment to compliance the experimenter insisted that the subjects were entirely free to agree or refuse to take part in the research into the topics which had already been announced to them and asked them to come to their own decision. In contrast, in the opposite condition (no commitment to compliance) the experimenter stated that the research had been requested by the minister and made no mention of the possibility of refusing to take part. None of the subjects assigned to the commitment to compliance condition refused to participate. The variable 'commitment to the counterattitudinal act' was then manipulated. In the condition of commitment the experimenter reformulated the three topics and asked the subject which one he or she would like to write about. In the uncommitted condition the experimenter told the subject to write about 'today's topic' (to establish intergroup parity the topics in this condition were selected to match the selection frequencies of the topics in the committed condition).

Having completed these manipulations, the experimenter gave the subject a pen and paper and emphasized the necessity of writing as 'persuasive an essay as possible' in support of the selected topic. The attitude measurement (taken after the essay was written in experiment 11 and both before and afterwards in experiment 12) was made on a nine-point rating scale relating to the essay topic. We observed a similar pattern of results whether the attitude measure was taken before or after the writing of the counterattitudinal essay. The results of the two experiments confirmed the predictions. In Table 3.1 we reproduce the results of experiment 11 and the measurements taken following the counterattitudinal act in experiment 12. The table reveals a generally similar pattern of results for primary and interaction effects. The non-factorial differences between the two experiments are probably because their performance was separated by an interval of one year and because they were conducted in different schools.

Table 3.1. Commitment to compliance and free choice of the problematic act in a forced compliance situation.

	Experiment 11 Commitment to act		Experiment 12 Commitment to act	
	Commitment	No commitment	Commitment	No commitment
Commitment to compliance				
Commitment	3·44	5·28	5·06	6·62
No commitment	3·32	3·76	2·50	2·43

Notes: The higher the number, the more closely the subject's attitude conforms to the position defended in the selected essay (dissonance effect). In experiment 11, $n = 25$ subjects in each cell. In experiment 12, $n = 25$ subjects in each cell. Commitment to compliance effect: $F = 3·96$ $(p < 0·05)$ in experiment 11 and $F = 132·25$ $(p < 0·0001)$ in experiment 12. Commitment to act: $F = 7·66$ $(p < 0·007)$ in experiment 11 and $F = 6·64$ $(p < 0·01)$ in experiment 12. Interaction: $F = 2·88$ $(p < 0·10)$ in experiment 11 and $F = 9·93$ $(p < 0·002)$ in experiment 12.

Experiment 13: The effect of commitment to an unperformed task on the rationalization of a later counterattitudinal behaviour

One limitation of experiments 11 and 12 is that the subjects' commitment to compliance was manipulated so that they knew the precise type of task they would be required to perform (writing a persuasive essay) even if they did not know which essay would be selected. The two choices proposed to the subjects were not therefore completely differentiated, with the first in a sense prefiguring the second. Thus, we might argue that in these experiments what we have termed commitment to compliance was only effective in so far as the subjects' preliminary agreement related not to compliance itself but to the performance of what, among other things, was finally demanded of them. One way of excluding this possibility is to give the subjects the opportunity to commit themselves to compliance and, following this commitment, to require them to perform a task of a completely different nature. If the commitment effect persists, we will then be able to claim with certainty that commitment to compliance is a necessary precondition for the arousal of dissonance. This situation was introduced in experiment 13 (Beauvois, Bungert and Mariette, 1995, exp. 2).

The subjects were all in their final school year. One of the two conditions implementing a new independent variable (known as the 'paradigmatic' condition) represented a faithful replication of experiments 11 and 12. As expected (see Table 3.2), the results obtained in this condition reproduced those of the earlier experiments. In another condition of this new independent variable (known as the 'non-paradigmatic' condition), the three tasks announced to the subjects as those to which they would have to commit themselves if they agreed to take part in the research (two refusals) were notoriously tedious (copying telephone numbers, crossing out signs, sticking confetti). After manipulating this commitment to compliance (commitment as against non-commitment to compliance: independent variable 2), the experimenter, pretending to have made a mistake, declared unilaterally that the experiment would not involve the previously announced tasks but would require something completely different of the subject, namely the (counterattitudinal) essays presented in experiments 11 and 12 (the topics of holidays, grants and driving were all announced to the subject). At this point the experimenter no longer gave the subject the freedom to agree or refuse to take part in the research. Instead, he passed directly on to the manipulation of the choice (as against no choice: independent variable 3) of the essay topic, as was the case in experiments 11 and 12.

Table 3.2. *Commitment to compliance and free choice of the problematic act in a forced compliance situation.*

| | Paradigmatic | | Non-paradigmatic | |
| | Commitment to act | | Commitment to act | |
	Commitment	No commitment	Commitment	No commitment
Commitment to compliance				
Commitment	5·36	6·63	4·72	4·82
No commitment	3·36	2·59	2·77	2·05

Notes: The higher the number, the more closely the subject's attitude conforms to the position defended in the selected essay (dissonance effect). $n = 22$ subjects in each cell. The primary effect of the variable 'paradigmatic/non-paradigmatic' is significant ($F = 6·69$; $p < 0·02$), with subjects rationalizing more in the first condition than in the second. The effect of commitment to compliance is highly significant ($F = 60·17$; $p < 0·00001$). The interaction of commitment to compliance and commitment to the act is significant ($F = 4·25$; $p < 0·05$), although further analysis shows that this interaction is effective only in the paradigmatic condition. The variable 'commitment to the act' shows no significant effect.

It can be observed that in the 'non-paradigmatic' condition the commitment to compliance continues to function as a necessary condition for the observation of attitude change: *even though the subjects actually committed themselves to a different type of task and were not asked to commit themselves to the essays they were offered*, they reduced dissonance and in consequence exhibited an attitude change which was not observed in the subjects who were not given the freedom to agree or refuse to perform the boring tasks announced to them ($4 \cdot 72$ and $4 \cdot 82$ versus $2 \cdot 77$ and $2 \cdot 05$). Everything would therefore seem to suggest that it is the acceptance of a relationship of obedience towards the experimenter (and not the agreement to the particular counterattitudinal task which is ultimately performed) that acts as a precondition for the state of dissonance. The choice of one counter-attitudinal act out of three (commitment to the act) in the 'non-paradigmatic' condition provokes *no* rationalization if there is no preliminary commitment to compliance (agreement to the boring tasks).[3]

What we have termed commitment to compliance is thus a distinctive feature of the forced compliance situation and is necessary if a state of dissonance is to be aroused. In contrast, the choice of the particular counterattitudinal act is, in itself, totally ineffective (situations of non-commitment to compliance and commitment to the counterattitudinal act). When the subject has made a prior commitment to compliance, the choice of the act reduces the dissonance (in experiment 11 it actually eliminates all the dissonance). To put it another way, the situation that generates the most dissonance, and therefore the most rationalization, is the one in which the individual has 'freely' chosen compliance and is therefore required to perform an act which is not itself negotiable. It should be noted that this is precisely the situation which appears to have the greatest ecological validity. Social life is full of situations into which individuals are declared to be free to enter or not but within which what they have to do is not negotiable (school situations, work situations and so on). The fact remains that what individuals rationalize is not their compliance but the act itself, which they were not free to choose.

Concerning personal responsibility

The idea of commitment to compliance which we have presented in heuristic form above has many implications for our conception of the forced compliance situation.

First, it leads us to emphasize the relationship of authority which binds the subject to the experimenter, a relationship whose importance has been pointed out by a number of authors (see Poitou, 1974, Clémence, 1987) but whose theoretical treatment has previously proved problematic. The idea of commitment to compliance seems to us to be a step towards such treatment and we shall return to this point later.

Most importantly, however, it allows us to formulate serious reservations about revisions to the initial theory which are ultimately based simply on the idea that, in situations of forced compliance, subjects have chosen to do what they do and that it is precisely because they have made this choice that they feel dissonance. This is certainly the case for Brehm and Cohen who in 1962 assumed that the dissonance experienced by subjects was linked to the *volition* they associated with their behaviour. If, instead, we adopt the variable 'commitment to compliance', we observe that, on the contrary , the subjects who chose to do what they did in experiments 11 and 12 experienced less dissonance than those who were unable to choose. The same argument also applies to later revisions of the theory which are based on, or incorporate, the idea of an internal attribution of *personal responsibility* (Wicklund and Brehm, 1976, Cooper and Fazio, 1984). Let us recall that in experiments 11 and 12 and 13, the experimenter emphasized that the second decision was independent of the first ('that will be the object of a second decision which will have to be taken later on . . . but for the moment I want you to decide . . .'). He thus implicitly emphasized his own responsibility in situations where he dictated the behaviour to be undertaken and, correlatively, that of the subject in the situations where he or she was allowed to choose. If we adopt Cooper and Fazio's point of view, for example, then this second choice should have reinforced the subject's perceived freedom and sense of personal responsibility.[4] However, this is far from what is observed in reality: the possibility of an internal attribution which is offered by the second decision and, *a fortiori*, of an internal attribution of the personal responsibility for the consequences of the counterattitudinal act reduces the dissonance aroused by the act. It is, of course, possible (and indeed probable) that in the standard forced compliance situation subjects fail to make the somewhat theoretical distinction between the choice of compliance and the choice of the act (a distinction which we forced them to make in our last three experiments). However, this in no way reduces the significance of the fact that when subjects are compelled to make this distinction, it is not the choice of the act that is important but the choice of compliance. We have seen that the subjects who feel the most dissonance are the ones who can attribute to the experimenter the responsibility for their having to do one thing rather than another[5] (non-commitment to the act) but who at the same time can say 'I got myself into this mess' (commitment to compliance).

The position of a theory of commitment in the forced compliance paradigm

It was therefore not without some justification that we asserted that the cognition of commitment F (free choice) was not an inconsistent cognition similar to those entered in the dissonance ratio. This cognition does not relate to the problematic behaviour itself with reference to which cognitions are judged to be consistent or inconsistent (in the classic situation this act is not negotiable), but to the 'freely' accepted situation in which subjects find themselves when they produce this behaviour. We shall not enter the discussion about whether this freedom is illusory

(Kelley, 1967) or not (Kiesler, 1971). For the purposes of our argument it is enough to know that it does not affect the acceptance or refusal of the situation which is proposed to the subject, even in cases where subjects have declared their dislike of this type of experiment and have explicitly stated that they would never want to take part in one (Glass, 1964). This is why, in the following, we shall not speak of freedom or even of the 'feeling of freedom'[6] but of the *statement of freedom*. The experimenter states (or does not state) that the subject is free to take part or not take part in the experimental situation. We can describe this situation as a situation of compliance since it implies the subject's obedience to an agent (the experimenter) who makes a problematic demand and who possesses a certain degree of authority. Once this situation has been accepted, the behaviour of the subject is and remains at the discretion of the experimenter.

It is probable that the other cognitions of commitment will admit a similar treatment. Neither the irrevocability of the act nor its public nature is negotiable. Both are inherent in the situation as it is presented to the subject. In 20 years of research into forced compliance we have never met a single subject who, having entered into the situation, contested these characteristics and refused, for example, to sign a counterattitudinal essay. The same is true of the virtual consequences of the act. Thus, the properties F, I, C, P and perhaps others form a kind of 'package' which the subject accepts in its entirety as the situational context of his or her act.

A theory of commitment to forced compliance must take account, independently of the dissonance ratio,[7] of the properties of this situational context which determine whether or not subjects are committed to their agreement, whether or not they will therefore feel dissonance as a result of the act which is expected of them and, consequently, whether or not they will rationalize this act. When he presented his 'psychology of commitment' in 1971, Kiesler was modest enough to point out that this was not a theory but a framework programme of research. We should perhaps admit that we have not yet advanced far from this position, being able to state scarcely more than the conclusion and consequence below, whose theoretical basis in any case remains to be established.

Conclusion 3b A number of properties of the forced compliance situation (statement of freedom on the part of the agent who is applying the pressure, salience of the consequences of the counterattitudinal act, irrevocability of this act, public nature of the act) combine to commit or not commit subjects to compliance.
Consequence In situations of commitment, the counterattitudinal act will cause dissonance which the subject will reduce exactly as the core theory of 1957 predicts, and only in this way.

Notes

1 While they may sometimes be consistent or inconsistent, they do not then possess the same status since they have to be included in the calculation of the total amount of dissonance. For example, this is the case when the consequences of the counterattitudinal act form an explicit part of the forced compliance contract binding the subject to the experimenter (see our experiment 4). Moreover, we shall shortly see that decision-making activity within the forced compliance paradigm may result in cognitions which can be classed as relevant.

2 We know that in his writings of 1971, Kiesler discusses the possibility of what he terms an 'internal commitment', which is essentially determined by the importance the behavioural act has for the subject. However, an 'external-type commitment' seems to be far more prevalent in the numerous experiments he reports. This is determined by the circumstances in which individuals are led to perform the act to which they are committed: a statement of the subject's freedom on the part of the experimenter; the salience of the consequences of the act and/or its public nature ensured by the experimenter; the experimenter's request for the subject to repeat the act; a statement of the irrevocability of the act by the experimenter and so on. It is clear that it is this type of external commitment relating to the situation in which the problematic behaviour is performed (and thus the way in which the experimenter has set up this situation) that we are discussing here (see Beauvois and Joule, 1981). In fact, the idea of internal commitment would be a contradiction of our presentation of the 'cognitions of commitment'.

3 Moreover, the fact that the post-experimental measurement of the attitude towards the two topics rejected by the subject ('grants' and 'driving' if the subject wrote about 'holidays') reveals *no* significant effect, either primary or interactive, proves that only the attitude towards the object of the counter-attitudinal essay is affected. This provides us with further proof of the extreme specificity of the rationalization process.

4 Just as it should have resulted in a fresh attack on the integrity of the self.

5 In their discussion of perceived freedom as one of the preconditions of personal responsibility, Cooper and Fazio (1984) suggest that subjects can avoid dissonance if they answer the question 'why did I behave in this way?' by saying 'because the investigator told me to'. This is exactly the reply we might expect from the subjects who experienced the most dissonance in our experiments. We shall shortly return to the question of the status of causal explanations in forced compliance situations and present experimental arguments in support of the idea that an internal attribution of responsibility for the counterattitudinal act may result in a reduction of dissonance.

6 In two experiments reported by Steiner (1980) subjects in a free-choice condition did not express a marked feeling of freedom in the post-experimental controls.

7 In its theory, our model is relatively incompatible with a multiplicative model of dissonance (for example: dissonance × commitment × consequences; see Calder, Ross and Insko, 1973, Rajecki, 1990). It is, however, entirely compatible with the results that have been produced in support of this model. In fact, these results (see, in particular, those of Calder, Ross and Insko, 1973) come from experiments in which commitment (for these authors: choice) and the consequences of the act were manipulated on an all-or-nothing basis. To think of dissonance being multiplied by either is thus a metaphorical step.

Chapter 4

Dissonance, self-perception and causal explanation

While, as we have pointed out, a number of theorists have thought it necessary to revise Festinger's theory, others have clearly considered it possible to invalidate it by reinterpreting the so-called 'dissonance effects' in terms of processes that they believed to be more acceptable than the dissonance reduction process. In order not to overburden our summary we shall simply distinguish between two major reinterpretations of dissonance effects:

Bem's reinterpretation (1967, 1972) which invokes self-perception processes and which we consider to be prototypical of all the reformulations of the dissonance reduction process in terms of self-attribution (which is the tendency exhibited by Jones in his 1990 attempt at synthesis; in his work forced compliance is dealt with in the chapter devoted to self-knowledge).

Reinterpretations that rely on the processes of self-presentation, impression management or the like, whether for the subject this consists of preserving a good self-image or of presenting a good image of the self to somebody else, that is the experimenter (self-affirmation: Steele and Liu, 1983; Steele, 1988; self-presentation; Baumeister, 1982; impression management; Tedeschi, 1981).

All these reinterpretations are based on the idea of an attitude–behaviour consistency which either functions as a basis for self-perceptual inferences or is of value in the maintenance of the integrity of the self. For Bem, the principle of behaviour–attitude consistency is what allows subjects to infer their attitude from their behaviour and from the conditions under which this behaviour was elicited. If there is nothing in the situation that can explain my behaviour (no pressure, no promise of reward and so on), then it must be accounted for by my attitude, that is to say that my attitude is consistent with my behaviour. Moreover, one might well ask how else a self-attributive inference could be made. As for the second type of reinterpretation, these become ineffective as soon as we question the presupposition of an implicit *norm of consistency* which accords a particular value to the consistency between what you do and what you think: you feel that you are a good person if you can manage to be consistent and you present a positive self-image if you can show yourself to be consistent . . .

It is therefore no surprise that the debate between this type of conception and the versions of dissonance theory which we have termed 'lax' should have continued unabated. Steele (1988) was quite right to point out that the main contribution of the 'revisionists' was the claim that dissonance (inconsistency) must wound self-integrity before a rationalization process can be observed: 'revisionists have argued that conditions unrelated to consistency are necessary for dissonance arousal.... Clearly, these conditions have as much to do with ensuring that the dissonant act will threaten one's goodness, competence and worth as with consistency motives' (p. 269).

In this work it is clear that we are not going to draw the same conclusions as Steele. Rather, we shall argue that the revisionist versions of dissonance theory are primarily characterized by the way they equate the state of dissonance to the simple presence of inconsistencies in the subject's cognitive universe, that is by their insistence on attitude–behaviour consistency as an aim of the cognitive dynamic of a committed subject. If we are to believe Jones (1990), Festinger himself would eventually have come to think that there was no significant difference between his theory and the one proposed by Bem. While it may seem presumptuous to say so, we have no doubt that he is wrong. Instead, in view of the fact that our analysis of the implications of the dissonance ratio has led us to propose hypotheses which not only owe nothing to the principle of consistency but also in some cases lead us to expect new inconsistencies, it is likely to prove difficult to reinterpret these hypotheses in terms of self-perception or related theories which are unable to function without the support of this very principle of consistency. In our attempt to demonstrate this we shall focus rather more closely on the self-perception process as a preparation for our discussion of the status of attributive processes in situations of forced compliance.

The limitations of the reinterpretations

The effect of random feedback

Let us briefly recall experiments 1, 2 and 3 (effect of random feedback relating to the quality of performance on the evaluation of a tedious task) and try to put ourselves 'in the shoes' of a subject who, within a context of free choice, has agreed to perform a very boring task. He is told by the experimenter that his work is of such poor quality that it should simply be ignored. Let us suppose first of all that in order to reply to the question concerning his evaluation of the task this subject needs to rely on a self-attributive inference. He will no doubt say to himself: 'If I have freely agreed to take part in this experiment, it is doubtlessly because the task that was described to me was of some interest to me, unless I did it simply in order to help science. However, if I performed so badly then, seeing that the task doesn't call for any particular skills, it can only be because I got bored doing it.' Let us now suppose that this subject's principal motivation is to avoid devaluing himself too much either in his own eyes or in the eyes of the experimenter. Clearly the task rating scale with which he is provided gives him the chance to do this. He will emphasize just how uninteresting he found the task:

'You see, I'm not worthless, I'm not even unwilling. But this task is so uninteresting that I can't work up any enthusiasm for it.' Thus negative feedback should result in a more negative attitude towards the task. It appears that in both cases, whether he infers his attitude from a process of self-perception or whether he is attempting to prove his worth, the subject who has received negative feedback should find the task less interesting than subjects who have not received this feedback. If we now try to imagine ourselves in the position of a subject who has just received positive feedback we may well be tempted to adopt a completely contrary self-attributive reasoning: 'If I've done so well in a task which doesn't require any particular skill, it must be because it ended up by interesting me.' We should thus expect to see a more favourable attitude towards the task. In terms of the theories of self-affirmation we should expect positive feedback to *eliminate* dissonance since it reinvests the self with the worth which might have been called into question by the presence of an inconsistency. We know that these predictions are not fulfilled.

Experiment 14. Interpersonal simulation: attitude attributed by observers to the subjects in experiments 1 and 2

Experiment 14 (Beauvois and Joule, 1982, experiment 3) confirms our interpretation of the situation in terms of self-perception. This experiment consisted of an interpersonal simulation conducted in precisely the same way as those performed by Bem in support of his well-known reinterpretations of the incentive effect. The observer-subjects (students) had to imagine themselves 'in the shoes of' one of the real subjects of experiments 1 and 2.[1] They were provided with a detailed description of the situation in which the genuine subject was placed and they were told all the information which was made available to this subject. They were also informed of the decisions and behaviour of the real subject. Finally, using the rating scale employed in the experiment, the observer-subjects had to guess the response made by the real subjects in their assessment of the task. As Bem postulated, provided that such observer-subjects possess all the information available to the real subjects, they can be considered to provide a good simulation of the self-perception processes which are believed to be at work in the real subjects. The results, which are presented in table 4.1, fully confirm the validity of the predictions suggested by our analysis of experiments 1 and 2 in terms of self-perception: the most positive attitude towards the task is attributed to the subjects who received positive feedback, while the most negative attitude is attributed to subjects who received negative feedback. The difference between the two conditions is highly significant.

Table 4.1. Interpersonal simulation: attitude attributed by observers to the subjects in experiments 1 and 2.

	Negative feedback	Positive feedback	No feedback
Real subjects	10·50	5·50	6·60
Observers	3·80	9·38	5·32

Notes: Only the 'free choice' conditions of experiments 1 and 2 were simulated. Negative vs. positive feedback: $t = 4·89$ ($p < 0·001$).

The results of this interpersonal simulation therefore conform to our interpretation of the effect of feedback relating to the quality of performance, when this interpretation is phrased in terms of self-perception theory. At the same time, they completely contradict the results obtained in experiments 1 and 2 which are derived entirely from cognitive dissonance theory. We should not be surprised by the success of dissonance theory in this type of situation: we have emphasized that in such cases this theory leads to the formulation of hypotheses which do not conform well to intuitions of consistency. Indeed, subjects leave the laboratory with cognitions which, on the one hand, do not fit together well and, on the other, are very unsatisfactory from the point of view of self-integrity ('I like this work' and 'I have done this work very badly'). We may therefore expect reinterpretations of dissonance effects which are formulated in terms of self-perception or self-affirmation and are consequently based on intuitions of consistency to prove to be ineffective in the presence of such inconsistencies while, in contrast, dissonance theory continues to function perfectly. We shall encounter the same phenomenon in connection with the choice of the counterattitudinal act.

The choice of the counterattitudinal act

Let us return once more to experiments 11, 12 and 13 and imagine ourselves in the position of a subject who has agreed take part in a counterattitudinal role-playing situation and who has then himself chosen which of the three possible essays he will write (this is a counterattitudinal essay: for example, in favour of banning accompanied driving for young people of between 16 and 18). He is then asked about his attitude towards this task.

If he infers his attitude from his behaviour, then the choice of one object ahead of the others constitutes the most natural basis for a self-attributive inference. If, in the absence of any particular constraint, he chose one specific essay rather than the alternatives, it is presumably because this essay corresponded most closely to his own ideas. A self-attributive process would therefore again suggest greater behaviour–attitude consistency.

If he wants to affirm his self-worth then we can reproduce the arguments of the advocates of self-attribution or impression management theory. We could, for example, join Steele and Liu (1983) in claiming that this subject may feel that one of his values is threatened by his own behaviour (not only has he agreed to the situation but he has also *chosen* to defend this point of view), which may threaten his self-esteem. He will therefore try to combat this threat by modifying his attitude in a way that makes it conform more closely to his behaviour. Tedeschi's interpretation (1981) follows a similar path: even if he feels no internal discomfort, the subject will want to show the experimenter that he is the type of person who acts in line with his beliefs and that he chose to say what he thought. On the rating scale which is offered to him he will therefore indicate that there is no dramatic discrepancy between his behaviour and what he believes to be true. In both cases, we would expect the choice of one of the three alternative counter-attitudinal acts to result in an increase in the consistency between the post-experimental attitude and the subject's behaviour.

Experiment 15. Interpersonal simulation: the attitude attributed by observers to the subjects in experiments 11 and 12

Experiment 15 (Beauvois, Bungert, Rainis and Tornior, 1993, exp. 3) validates our interpretation of the choice of the counterattitudinal act in terms of self-perception theory. This experiment again consisted of an interpersonal simulation, with the 80 subject-observers (final-year high-school pupils) each having to simulate the functioning of one (and only one) subject in experiment 11 (an experiment, we might recall, that was in every way identical to experiment 12, except that the attitude measurement was performed post-behaviourally). Here again the results are clear (table 4.2): the observers attributed a vastly more favourable attitude towards the object of the essay to the subjects who had agreed to the situation (the subjects who were 'committed to compliance') and, of these, to those subjects who had themselves chosen the essay topic (the subjects who were 'committed to the counterattitudinal act'):

Table 4.2. Interpersonal simulation: the attitude attributed by observers to the subjects in experiment 11.

	Commitment to act	
	yes	no
Commitment to compliance: real subjects (see table 11)		
yes	3·44	5·28
no	3·32	3·76
observers		
yes	8·40	6·50
no	1·20	0·90

Notes: $n = 20$ observers by cell. The two primary effects are significant (compliance: $F = 40,74$, $p < 0\cdot00001$; act: $F = 12,04$, $p < 0\cdot0001$), as is the interaction ($F = 6,35$, $p < 0\cdot01$). Remember that in experiment 11, $F_{(compliance)}$ was $3\cdot96$ ($p < 0\cdot05$), $F_{(act)}$ was $7\cdot60$ ($p < 0\cdot007$), $F_{(interaction)}$ was $2\cdot88$ ($p < 0\cdot10$).

Once again, self-perception theory and the theories of self-affirmation generate the same predictions since they are only able to call on intuitions of consistency, that is precisely those intuitions that are operative in the observer-subjects of our interpersonal simulations. And, once again, these predictions are undermined by the experimental results provided by the real subjects (experiments 11 and 12). In contrast, these results are precisely those which can be derived from dissonance theory (that is to say that they conform to the implications of the dissonance ratio), a theory which is in no way dependent on intuitions of consistency.[2]

We do not intend to weary the reader with a recapitulation of all the other experiments which we have presented in support of our conclusions 1, 2, 3 and 4. In each case (see, in particular, the effect of counterattitudinal argument time on attitude change in experiment 5), the radical theory of dissonance functions well without the support of the intuitions of consistency or common sense which are indispensable to its rivals. In each case, the results argue in its favour. Ultimately, it would appear that if the controversies that have pitted these theories against each other have proved to be insoluble[3] it is because they related to hypotheses which failed to take account of the specificity of dissonance theory. This specificity resides in the fact that dissonance theory is not a consistency theory but a theory of the rationalization of behaviour undertaken under conditions of commitment. When this specificity is admitted and made operative, the rivals of dissonance theory are seen to be incapable of reinterpreting it or even of emulating it.

The status of processes of causal explanation

In our opinion, the failure of self-perception theory to account for the dissonance effects which we have described above has a much more general theoretical significance which relates to the status of causal explanation processes in forced compliance situations. We are certainly not the first researchers to ask what relations might exist between the dissonance reduction process and the processes of causal explanation following an individual's behaviour. Other authors have tackled this question before us and their conclusions seem to us to be perfectly legitimate (Zanna and Cooper, 1976, Fazio, Zanna and Cooper, 1977). To cut a long story short, these conclusions consist of dividing the work between the two processes, the first occurring when the subject has undertaken a discrepant behaviour and the second when the subject produces a consistent behaviour which is more extreme than a previous behaviour. However, before this, hypotheses had already been tested (and validated), which clearly imply more than a simple division of work between the two types of process and point towards a true synergy. For example, Sherman (1973) successfully demonstrated that subjects who had been identified as internal on a locus-of-control scale proved to be more sensitive to the forced compliance situation than external subjects. While it is far from easy to interpret individual differences in the anticipation of reinforcement control (which is what the locus of control concept amounts to) in terms of the causal explanation of an actual behaviour (Beauvois, 1984a, Beauvois and Dubois, 1988), everything suggests, in view of results such as Sherman's, that individuals whose explanations of events tend to accentuate the causal significance of the actor are more likely than others to modify their attitude following a counterattitudinal act. Furthermore, the results obtained by Sherman were recently reproduced by Channouf, Py and Somat (1991) using high-school subjects. These authors used a questionnaire of internality to distinguish between internal and external subjects.

This questionnaire contained items relating to the explanation (internal vs. external) of behaviour as well as of reinforcements (see Beauvois and Dubois, 1988; Dubois, 1987, 1994).

Experiment 16. The effect of inducing an internal vs. external orientation on attitude change

Experiment 16 (Channouf, Le Manio, Py and Somat, 1993), which was conducted using 80 children aged between 10 and 12 years, takes us even further in the same direction. These authors used a procedure for inducing internal or external orientations. The effectiveness of this procedure, which was based on a cognitive empathy principle, had been demonstrated in earlier research (see Beauvois and Dubois, 1991). It consisted simply of showing the subjects a multiple-choice questionnaire of internality which had supposedly been completed by a classmate in a way that was either extremely internal or, in contrast, extremely external. The subjects were then instructed to 'imagine themselves in the place of' this classmate in performing some task in which the researchers expected to observe an effect of the internal/external variable. Thus the subjects used by Channouf, Le Manio, Py and Somat had to imagine themselves to be either an external person or an internal one and perform the experiment (a counterattitudinal essay) in the way it would have been performed by the subject whose internality questionnaire they had read. The variable 'internal/external' thus represented the first independent variable of this research. The second independent variable was the interval between the counterattitudinal behaviour (an essay in favour of shortening the summer holidays; see Pavin's experiments 6, 7 and 8 above) and the post-experimental attitude measurement. This measurement was taken immediately after the discrepant behaviour, then again one week later in a different context and by a different experimenter and, finally, again in a different context and by a different experimenter, one month after the discrepant behaviour.

As in Pavin's experiments, the results obtained by Channouf, Le Manio, Py and Somat (see table 4.3) reveal a strong attitude change effect and confirm the stability of this change) one month after the counterattitudinal essay, the experimental subjects still differed from a control group formed of 115 pupils of the same age at the threshold value $p < 0.005$ (F = 9·08). This result is of particular interest because, unlike in Pavin's experiments, all three post-experimental measurements were taken by a different investigator claiming to be conducting a piece of unrelated research.

The results also point to an effect related to the type of induced orientation. The subjects who had to imagine themselves in the place of a classmate who had supposedly provided internal-type answers to the internality questionnaire were more sensitive to the counterattitudinal role-playing situation and consequently changed their attitude towards summer holidays more than the subjects who had to imagine themselves in the place of a subject who had provided external-type responses. This effect remained significant even when the post-experimental measurements were taken one month after the discrepant behaviour (the interaction between the two variables was not significant).

Table 4.3. *The effect of inducing an internal vs. external orientation on attitude change.*

Orientation	Immediate measurement	Interval 1 week	Interval 1 month
Internal $(n = 40)$	5·47	4·77	5·02
External $(n = 40)$	4·15	3·75	3·12

Notes: The higher the number, the more strongly the subjects felt that the summer holidays were 'too long' (12-point appreciation scale). Control group: $m = 1·98$ $(n = 115)$. The overall set of experimental subjects differs from this control group at the threshold value $p < 0·0001$ ($F = 32·74$). $F_{(internal/external)} = 5·85$ ($p < 0·03$).

Although they are not, in truth, particularly numerous, such results indicate that serious consideration should be paid to the effect of an internal/external variable in attitude change (see also Sogin and Pallack, 1976; Nichols and Duke, 1977). However, from a theoretical viewpoint they are difficult to reconcile with what we know about the dissonance reduction process and the forced compliance situation.

Internality, externality and forced compliance

Of course, a *strictly* self-attributive interpretation of the attitude change which is obtained in situations of forced compliance would make it possible to explain this effect of the internal/external variable by suggesting that internal individuals are probably more inclined to attribute to themselves an attitude which corresponds to their behaviour while, in contrast, external subjects are probably more likely to find the causes of their behaviour in the situation itself rather than in their own characters. The internal subjects will consequently modify their attitudes more, since, unlike the external subjects, they will explain their compliant behaviour in terms of their own characters. Unfortunately, we can only accept this interpretation if we agree to let in through the back door the very processes of self-perception which the weight of experimental research has already obliged us to kick out of the front.

Nevertheless, without adopting this strictly self-perceptual interpretation of attitude change, we might suggest that because they are more prepared than others to attribute the cause of their counterattitudinal behaviour to themselves either makes the internal subjects more sensitive to the discrepancies which underlie dissonance, or makes these discrepancies more salient since they are associated with a behaviour which the internal subjects believe they themselves have produced. Thus, internal subjects would in some way feel more dissonance than external subjects. This interpretation, which is not strictly self-perceptual, retains the hypothesis of a process that is specific to dissonance reduction. It adds to this hypothesis the idea that internal subjects are more dissonant than external subjects because the inconsistency they feel weighs on them more heavily. This is probably the sort of interpretation which would be provided by a 'lax' theorist of dissonance, that is a theorist who conflates inconsistency and dissonance and who, in consequence, omits the calculation of the dissonance ratio. However, our 'radical' perspective leads us to reject this interpretation. The reason, if the dissonance ratio is formulated as we have systematically formulated it in this work (with the expressions to the left and right of the equation), relates to the theoretical evidence itself, even though this appears contrary to common sense; the evocation of any cause (whether internal or external) for the counterattitudinal behaviour should *reduce* dissonance and *a fortiori* the attitude change. Evoking any cause for the counterattitudinal act should result either in the production of a *consistent cognition* (which is most likely when we are dealing with internal causes) or of a *loss of commitment* (the most likely eventuality when we are dealing with any of the numerous external causes).

Why should a cause, in particular if it is internal, produce a consistent cognition? This proposition, even if it appears somewhat counterintuitive, is a consequence of Festinger's notion of psychological implication: every cause implies, and also implies 'psychologically', its effect. The fact that I have a bad temper psychologically implies that I get angry just as, as all dissonance theorists have admitted, the fact that I am thirsty implies that I drink or the fact that I am a supporter of Castro implies that I will speak in favour of Castro rather than against him. If I get angry and, in doing this, tell myself that I am a bad-tempered person, then this reduces any dissonance I might experience because it produces a consistent cognition which psychologically implies the generative cognition 'I am getting angry'. In contrast, it seems that numerous external causes may have the effect of reducing the subjects' commitment to a situation to which they have been committed by an earlier statement of freedom. In effect, our ideological climate leads us to consider only what we think of as external forces to be obstacles to our freedom. Despite much insistence on human potential, we have not learned to consider the forces within ourselves, with the exception of a few rare *biological forces*, as obstacles to our freedom. Although bad-tempered, I remain free to get angry or not. In contrast, the instructions I receive from my employer, or the power supply to my workplace, constrain me and limit my freedom. It is therefore possible that evoking external causes for the behaviour of forced compliance may undermine the effectiveness of the statement of freedom made by the experimenter and therefore reduce the subject's commitment.

If these considerations are justified, then we might think, in view of the ease with which we obtain attitude change in forced compliance situations and the sometimes surprising magnitude of such effects, that the subjects who agree to perform a counterattitudinal task are not inclined to seek causal explanations for their behaviour. If they were to do so — and if our reasoning is correct — then they would undoubtedly change their attitudes less than they actually do. How then can we account for the effect of the 'internal/external' variable predicted and obtained by Sherman and by Channouf et al.? In our opinion, the reason is not to be found in the total amount of dissonance, that is in the right-hand expression of the equation that yields the dissonance ratio. Instead, it is to be sought in the subject's commitment, which is expressed in the left-hand part of this equation. As we have just said, everything suggests that individuals tend not to construct a theory to account for their compliant behaviour and that it is unlikely that under such circumstances they turn to self-attributive inferences. In contrast, we might well accept the idea that internal individuals are more sensitive than external ones to the commitment instructions. There are at least two arguments in support of this idea.

First, we may well imagine that the availability, even if it is subliminal, of a register of internal (as opposed to external) causal explanations affects the way the experimenter's statement of freedom is processed. The internal subjects may attribute more significance to it than the external ones. Internal subjects may therefore be more easily committed and external individuals less easily committed than subjects who are neither truly internal nor truly external (control subjects). This would imply that more of the internal subjects and fewer of the external subjects change their attitude than do the control subjects (who are neither really internal nor really external), given that commitment does not affect the dissonance ratio and therefore the magnitude of the change.

As a second argument, we might imagine that the well known normative nature of internal subjects (Beauvois, 1994; Beauvois and Dubois, 1988; Dubois, 1994) means that, even without turning to a register of causal explanations, they are readier than the others to accept the proposition, which is itself extremely normative, that they are free individuals. In effect, everything suggests that the feeling of freedom possesses a normative character within our cultural environment and that this may lead the more normative subjects to accept a statement which declares them to be free. In consequence, a higher proportion of internal subjects would change their attitude than is observed in the remainder of the population (external and control subjects combined). We are unable to present any research in support of either of these arguments.[4] In contrast, experiment 17 (Beauvois and Rainis, 1993b, see Beauvois, Michel, Py, Rainis and Somat, 1995), which we describe below, provides evidence in favour of our analysis of the place of causal explanations in the forced compliance situation.

Two distinct effects of causal explanations

Experiment 17. Effect on attitude change of the salience of internal vs. external causal explanations of counterattitudinal behaviour
Everything seems to suggest that the salience of causal explanations of the problematic behaviour, whether internal or external in nature, should result in less attitude change since these explanations equate to consistent cognitions. However, we would also expect the two types of explanation to differ in their

impact on the subject's commitment to compliance. More precisely, we expected internal explanations to exhibit commitment properties somewhat similar to those generated by a statement of freedom, while external explanations should tend to release subjects from their commitment in much the same way as a statement of obligation.

The subjects (sociology students) were either.declared or not declared to be free to perform a particularly boring number-copying task (copying the telephone directory). None of the subjects who were told that they were free to perform the task refused to take part. The tedious nature of the task was emphasized in the presentation stage which took the form of a 5-minute video that each of the subjects had to watch. This video showed a 'subject', who was obviously extremely bored, in the process of performing the task. When the subjects had finished the number copying task, the experimenter either took an immediate measurement of their attitude towards the task (11-point scale) or preceded this measurement with a brief questionnaire examining the reasons that had led the subjects to agree to perform the task. The questionnaire was designed in a way which made either 10 internal or 10 external causes salient,[5] with the subjects indicating on a rating scale the extent to which each of the causes had contributed to their decision. Here, we shall report only those results relating to the paradigmatic variable (attitude towards the task) which seem to us to be particularly illustrative of the role of causal explanations in the forced compliance situation (table 4.4).

Table 4.4. Effect on attitude change of the salience of internal vs. external causal explanations of counterattitudinal behaviour.

		attribution	
	none	internal	external
committed subjects	9·17c	3·75b	2.42a
uncommitted subjects	2·17a	4·48b	2·17a

Notes: The more positive is the attitude towards the task, the larger is the number (11-point rating scale). $n = 11$ or 12 subjects by cell. The two primary effects ($F_{commitment} = 39·35$, $p < 0·0001$; $F_{attribution} = 40·15$, $p < 0·0001$) and interaction ($F = 65·53$, $p < 0·0001$) are very significant; simple effects: the means that do not have the same exponent differ at the threshold $p < 0·01$; the means that have the same exponent do not differ.

These results provide us with a number of clues. First, they seem to confirm our claim that evoking either internal or external causes reduces attitude change in forced compliance situations. In effect, we observe that the committed subjects who were given time to reflect on the internal or external causes of their behaviour exhibit a very significantly less favourable attitude towards the task than the subjects of the control group (no attribution). We even observe that evoking external causes totally eliminates any attitude change. The difference in the magnitude of the effect generated by internal and external causal explanations may be because the latter certainly have a double effect in that they not only reduce the dissonance ratio but also diminish commitment. On the one hand, they resemble the internal causes in representing a cognition which is consistent with the generative cognition 'I have agreed to perform this task', which they psychologically imply in Festinger's sense of the term. On the other hand, however, they differ from the internal causes in that, in evoking external pressures, they doubtlessly provide subjects with opportunities to reduce their commitment and this attenuates the impact (or the credibility) of the experimenter's statement of freedom. (Can you think of yourself as being truly free when you are induced to think, for example, that 'you have to help research' or that 'it is the type of situation where you can't really refuse'?). We find this second interpretation all the more plausible because the results show the completely opposite effect for the internal explanations; the uncommitted subjects, but not the committed ones, who were led to consider the possible internal causes of their behaviour exhibited a highly significant attitude change. In contrast, the 'commitment' variable was ineffective in the subjects of the external 'explanation condition'.

Causal explanations thus appear to have a double effect in forced compliance situations. On the one hand, whether they are internal or external in nature, they produce cognitions that are consistent with the generative cognition and in so doing they reduce the dissonance ratio and consequently the requirement for attitude change. On the other hand, however, they affect the extent to which subjects are sensitive to their commitment, and here a difference can be observed between the internal and external causes. External explanations may lead to a loss of commitment on the part of the subject, whereas internal explanations appear to make subjects more sensitive to their commitment. This might provide an explanation of those experimental results which have shown internal subjects to be more sensitive to the situation of forced compliance. However, we are doubtful whether this explanation is sufficient on its own.

Our doubts are based on another implication of the results obtained in experiment 17. In effect, these results show that, in the standard situation, subjects are little inclined to seek causal explanations for their behaviour. The massive attitude change observed in the controlled commitment situation suggests that the subjects in this situation have not spontaneously evoked the possible causes of their acceptance. Had they done so, their attitude towards the task would certainly have been less positive. Doubtlessly, as Channouf (1990) has suggested, the agreement, among a population of students, to a request made by an experimenter forms part of a relational script. Further, the progress of this script enables subjects to avoid recourse to any inferential procedure (Langer, 1978) or, at least, to any inferential procedure concerning the agreement as such, thus freeing cognitive resources for allocation to other requirements of the situation. In truth, we fail to see any reasons for not considering this to be a very general rule. It may be that the specific characteristics of a particular situation may exceptionally provoke causal inferences. Thus, the provision of a questionnaire of internality may lead subjects to make causal inferences and may thereby account for the few results available relating to the internal/external variable. However, it might also be possible to argue that simply because of their more normative nature, internal subjects may, without any recourse to processes of inference, be more sensitive to the desirability of a status of individual freedom. This status is offered to them by the statement of freedom made by the experimenter within a situation where, like the other subjects, they nevertheless agree to the request.

Dissonance reduction and causal explanation in a situation of forced compliance

There are thus a number of theoretically acceptable ways of accounting for the greater sensitivity of internal subjects (or subjects for whom internal-type explanations have been made more salient) to forced compliance situations containing a statement of freedom. As we have seen, these possible explanations allow us to avoid any conception of the attitude change observed in this situation in terms of self-perception or, more generally, attribution theory. Furthermore, this change is perfectly well accounted for by an unrevised, and therefore radical, theory of cognitive dissonance. At this point, we can sum up the development of our argument in a fourth conclusion:

Conclusion 4 *The dissonance reduction process does not originate in a more general process involving the causal explanation of the problematic behaviour.*
Consequence *If this type of behaviour explanation process occurs it can only produce consistent cognitions or cognitions that reduce commitment.*

Does this mean that the general type of forced compliance situation in which attitude change is observed excludes any phenomena involving a causal explanation of events? Most researchers would find an affirmative answer to this question not only provocative but also very strange. We have no doubt in believing that Channouf (1990) is right, and we shall return to this question, in pointing out that the experimenter's request activates a sort of script whose progress allows subjects to avoid having to make many inferences from their behaviour or from the situation within which they have produced this behaviour. If this is, indeed, the case, then the attitude change resulting from dissonance reduction will be maximized (see our experiment 17). However, it is nevertheless possible to accept that certain characteristics of the situation (which remain to be investigated) may provoke the activation of explanatory processes relating to the problematic behaviour. We have seen that in such cases dissonance may be reduced or the commitment of the subject diminished. However, we may also imagine that these or other characteristics of the forced compliance situation may affect and modify the cognitive registers relating to the causal explanation of events, thus also affecting and modifying subsequent cognitive functioning and, more particularly, subsequent attributive inferences. This is a conjecture of considerable theoretical interest.

We are not in a position to provide the reader with the experimental results which would be necessary to confirm hypotheses derived directly from this type of theoretical conjecture. This represents a new field of research into the cognitive effects of forced compliance which we are only just beginning to explore. Instead, to conclude this chapter we shall cite a secondary result of experiment 3 (Beauvois and Rainis, 1993a) which argues in favour: (1) of the existence of this type of effect of the forced compliance situation on the registers of causal explanation; and (2) of the possible orthogonality of the processes related to dissonance reduction and those related to the causal explanation of psychological events (behaviours and outcomes). Let us recall that the subjects who were declared to be free in experiment 3 had agreed to perform an exceedingly tedious task which consisted of masking certain letters in a text (by sticking small paper squares over them). Once they had performed the task, some of them received positive or negative feedback concerning the quality of their performance and the usefulness of their work, while others did not. They were then asked to evaluate the task on a rating scale. We have seen how this feedback from the experimenter dramatically affected evaluation, with subjects who received negative feedback finding the task much more attractive than the others: (table 1.3, pp. 13).

In fact, just after providing their evaluation of the task, the subjects also filled in a relatively long questionnaire investigating their causal theories. This questionnaire, which was adapted from one used by Chandler and Spies (1984), asked subjects to evaluate 10 causal factors (luck, aptitude, help, competence, effort, task, chance, knowledge, skill, mood) on five seven-point scales (general /particular, uncontrollable/controllable, unpredictable/predictable, internal origin/external origin, stable/unstable). A first preliminary study conducted among the subjects who, like those of experiment 13 described above, were induced to put themselves in the position of an internal or external individual (see Beauvois and Dubois, 1991, for the validity of this manipulation) made it possible to derive an externalization index of causal theories. Subjects responding as if they were an external person found the 10 causal factors more general, more un-controllable, more unpredictable, more unstable and, obviously, more external.

Then, in a second preliminary study, the questionnaire was administered to students and professionals. In this control sample, the mean externalization index was 149 (maximum: $10_{factors} \times 5_{scales} \times 7_{points} = 350$). This externalization index of causal theories constituted the second dependent variable of experiment 3. In our view, it does not reflect a stable property of causal theories that subjects have in their permanent memory. Rather, it reflects a transient orientation (internal vs. external) of the causal theories subjects hold in a given situation.

We should remember that the feedback communicated to the subjects was arbitrary in nature, bearing no relationship to their real performance (which was unknown to the experimenter at the time when she manipulated the independent variable 'feedback'). However, the subjects' actual performance was subsequently evaluated (number of letters correctly masked in 20 minutes). This made it possible, *a posteriori*, to establish a second dual-state independent variable: actual performance (better or worse than the mean). It was thus possible to observe that this second independent variable in no way affected the evaluation of the task, an evaluation that we know to be governed by the dissonance reduction process. The fact that subjects have or have not performed better than the mean score does not therefore induce them to find the task more or less interesting, unlike the *arbitrary* feedback provided by the experimenter. However, at the same time, this arbitrary feedback has no effect on the externalization index (F = 1·47). It does not therefore incline the subjects' causal theories towards either internalization or externalization. Thus, learning that their work is of no interest to the experimenter or, in contrast, that it is exceptionally useful (in other words, being informed of the usefulness of the problematic behaviour to the experimenter) does not induce the subjects to modify the internal or external nature of their causal theories. Should we conclude that the externalization index is not a particularly sensitive measure? In fact, the opposite is the case, since this variable is affected dramatically by the independent variable 'actual performance': subjects whose performance was *worse* than the mean score modified their causal theories considerably, the orientation of this modification being towards greater internalization.[6]

Table 4.5. Effects of arbitrary feedback and effective performance on causal theories (externalization index).

| | feed-back | | | |
	negative	positive	no feedback	control
subjects > *m*	149	156	141	
(*n* = 32)				149
subjects < *m*	77	98	94	
(*n* = 34)				

Notes: Externalization index: the higher the figure, the more the causal theories tend towards an external type. Subjects > *m* and < *m* differ significantly (F = 72·52, $p < 0.0001$).

To summarize, while having no effect on subjects' causal theories, arbitrary feedback has a considerable effect ($p < 0.0001$) on their evaluation of the task which they have agreed to perform for the experimenter (see table 1.3). At the same time, the actual performance achieved does not affect this evaluation but determines to a considerable extent the internal or external nature of the causal theories held by the subjects. Thus, as expected, an independent variable (arbitrary feedback) affects the dependent variable which reflects the work involved in reducing the dissonance of the initially inconsistent relevant cognition (evaluation of the task), while another independent variable (actual performance) affects the dependent variable which reflects the internal (vs. external) character of the causal theories activated in the situation. These two sizeable effects are completely independent of one another (no interaction was observed either for the first or for the second dependent variable) and seem therefore to be the product of distinct sociocognitive processes.

As we have seen, the radical theory of dissonance very naturally makes it possible to derive the effect of feedback on task evaluation. It also makes it possible to state that the processes relating to the causal explanation of events and the dissonance reduction process are different in nature and that the variables which affect the former do not necessarily affect the latter and vice versa. However, we lack plausible theoretical explanations for the effect of actual performance on the causal theories mobilized by subjects in such situations. Why should it be that the subjects who have agreed to perform a particularly dull task for an experimenter who has told them that they are free not to participate, and whose poor performance demonstrates that they have clearly made no great personal investment in the task, reduce dissonance in just the same way as the other subjects (no interaction between the two independent variables) while, unlike the subjects who have made a personal investment in the task, they modify their causal theories in the direction of greater internalization?

It might be argued that, for these subjects, the fact of having fulfilled the contract of forced compliance as required, although in some kind of *minimum* way, enables them to feel that they are in some way in control of the situation. This feeling of control would not have been experienced by the subjects who ultimately did no more than obey in acting out the script called forth by the situation and, in particular, by the experimenter's request. The former, but not the latter, may have been able to say something like: 'I agree to do what is asked of me because I see no reason to refuse but, despite this, I manage to control the situation of obedience. Since the work is really very boring I do not make a great personal investment and that is my way of controlling what happens.' Such a feeling of control may then provoke the internalization of the causal theories which the subject is later required to mobilize.

This is, of course, no more than a *post hoc* hypothesis. However, we consider it to be particularly interesting since it enables us to develop our conception of the nature of the forced compliance situation which has been delineated by the preceding experiments.

The radical theory of dissonance

We have now concluded our analysis of the theoretical consequences of the fundamental core of the 1957 theory which formed the object of the first part of this work. We hope that the reader will be satisfied that in this analysis we have remained faithful to the letter (we hesitate to say the spirit since this would lead us to deal with the metatheory) of Festinger's theoretical formulations. However, while a number of researchers who are well acquainted with the field of cognitive dissonance and are equally aware of what we have written are happy to accept what we have termed here the fundamental core of the 1957 theory, they appear to take issue with the consequences we have drawn from it.[7] In reviewing one of our articles, one anonymous expert, whose evaluation was otherwise generally positive, asked why we insisted on speaking in terms of dissonance while, in his view, being so wildly out of step with what he believed dissonance theory to consist of today.

The reason is that the predominant conception of dissonance theory nowadays derives from what we have called 'lax' interpretations. This laxity is nothing new; very early on researchers, seduced by the polysemy of the term 'dissonance' in the 1957 text, forgot the theoretical constraints imposed by the core theory. In his splendid presentation of cognitive theories in social psychology which appeared in 1968, Zajonc, who was involved in none of the 'revisions', advanced nine propositions to summarize dissonance theory. Some of these propositions were already incompatible with the dissonance ratio as Festinger has described it and drew cognitive dissonance theory towards the theories of cognitive consistency.

Let us take proposition 4 as an example: 'the severity or the intensity of cognitive dissonance varies with a) the importance of the cognitions involved and b) the relative number of cognitions standing in dissonant relation to one another' (Zajonc, 1968, p. 361). Certainly, the use of the term 'relative number' evokes the idea of a ratio. However, the form (which is, moreover, mathematically very ambiguous) which Zajonc's discursive text gives to this ratio has nothing to do with the initial ratio. In speaking of cognitions which are dissonant *to one another* (and not with reference to *one* special cognition), the author turns the state of dissonance into an internal property of the cognitive system as a whole. In contrast, in the core theory of 1957 this state is a consequence of the relation between the cognitive system and a special cognition which we have termed the 'generative cognition'. It is self-evident that, on this basis, the propositions which Zajonc advances as explanations of the modes of dissonance reduction (in particular, propositions 7 and 8) simply describe a restoration process which is reminiscent of the 1950s perspective of rationality, that is the psycho-logical rationality which formed the object of the theories of consistency. Indeed, Zajonc's expression 'standing in dissonant relation to one another' points, as we have already seen in the case of Quattrone (1985, chapter 2), towards a lax conception of dissonance, that is a conception which conflates dissonance, imbalance, incongruence, inconsistency and so on. However, if Festinger's theory was no more than a simple theory of consistency, we might well ask by what lucky chance it was able to lead psychosocial research towards paradigms which were so foreign to Heider, Osgood and Tannenbaum, or McGuire, that is towards paradigms in which what is studied is not the subject of knowledge but the subject of action (Beauvois, 1984b).

Thus, the radical theory of dissonance that we are advancing is opposed to the generally prevalent lax conception of dissonance and dissonance reduction. It nevertheless remains in full conformity with Festinger's initial theoretical formulations, even if Festinger himself had not fully considered their implications. Our theory thus includes *all* of the fundamental core of the 1957 theory (and, in particular, the dissonance ratio) as well as the consequences which we have identified:

— the absence of a theoretical equivalence between relations of inconsistency and the state of dissonance
— the primacy of the state of dissonance over the inconsistencies
— the necessity of a generative cognition which is almost always the knowledge of a problematic, counterattitudinal or countermotivational behaviour
— a reduction process whose function is not to eliminate incoherences but simply to eliminate those which involve the generative cognition
— the possibility of new inconsistencies following the reduction of dissonance
— the special status of cognitions of commitment which do no more than characterize the arrival, or lack of it, of the state of dissonance
— the heterogeneous nature of the post-behavioural dissonance reduction process and the processes involved in the causal explanation of behaviour.

It thus seems that the radical theory of dissonance is not a theory of consistency, that is of psycho-logical rationality, but is instead a theory of the rationalization of problematic behaviour. The dissonance reduction process described above does not prepare action but instead simply restores the value of action. We shall return later to the fact that this action is often the result of a state of compliance. However, before doing so we must consider two fields of research which are specifically bound up with the radical theory of dissonance: double forced compliance and act rationalization. This means that we are about to take leave of the largely codified practices of the forced compliance paradigm (nowadays known as induced compliance) and enter a new field of experimental practices which is specific to our investigations and largely unknown in the English-language literature.

This is why, from now on, it seems important to us to provide a more detailed description of the experimental procedures and the results obtained.

Notes

1 In the interpersonal simulations each observer-subject 'simulates' only one real subject. The experimental manipulations are therefore not known to them.
2 It might be argued here that what we have referred to as a 'lax' conception of dissonance theory would in this case, and indeed more generally, have no doubt led to the same expectations as self-perception theory or the theories of self-affirmation. It would have been possible to suggest that the second choice offered to the subject represented an additional source of dissonance which therefore increased both the (uncalculated) 'global' dissonance generated by the situation and, consequently, the magnitude of the attitude change. As we can see, the calculation of the dissonance ratio is indispensible here.

3   If, today, the majority of authors seem to have come to terms with dissonance theory, it is not because it outperforms its rivals in predicting attitude change effects but because of the accumulation of evidence for the arousal properties of the state of dissonance (Jones, 1990, Rajecki, 1990), to such an extent that even Tedeschi has had to introduce a motivational element into his theory of impression management with the concept of social anxiety (Tedeschi 1981).

4   To validate this type of hypothesis it would be necessary to compare internal and external subjects with a control group as part of a before/after experimental structure.

5   Internal causes: I am someone who likes to help; I like to take part in experiments; I am interested in psychology, and so on. External causes: You are obliged to participate in experiments; you have to help one another at a research institute; the experimenter was convincing and so on.

6   It is, in effect, impossible to explain these data in terms of pre-experimental differences. Two facts make this conclusion not only possible but also necessary: (1) the externalization index of the subjects whose performance was *better* than average correlated closely to that of the control group. This would suggest that the situation did not affect their causal theories, whereas it did affect those of the subjects whose performance was below average, these subjects differing very considerably from the control group; (2) although established *post hoc*, the independent variable 'actual performance' gives rise to an excellent distribution of the subjects across the six experimental groups in a 2×3 pattern (see table 4.1). The effect cannot therefore be attributed to the possible existence of a non-orthogonality of the two independent variables.

7. An example is Peter Schönbach who, although accepting our results, criticizes our overly 'mechanical' use of the dissonance ratio (Schönbach, 1993).

Part 2
New Paradigms: Double Forced Compliance and Act Rationalization

Chapter 5

Double forced compliance

The first experiments designed to test the hypotheses derived from cognitive dissonance theory were, in the main, performed within the paradigm of forced compliance. In these experiments the dissonance reduction process appeared as a post-behavioural cognitive process, with subjects adapting their attitudes or motivations *a posteriori* to fit with the behaviour they had been led to perform. In this paradigm, as in the other paradigms implied by Festinger's theory (1957), a single behaviour underlies the dissonance reduction work. All the experiments described in part one of this text, that is the experiments which allowed us to develop our radical theory, were based on this characteristic approach.

However, we have also started (Joule, 1986b, 1991a, and 1991b, Joule and Lebreuilly, 1991, Joule and Girandola, 1992, 1995, Girandola, 1994) to take an interest in cognitive work which is triggered by two behaviours. This concern has led us to propose extending the traditional forced compliance paradigm. We have termed this extension the double forced compliance paradigm, since here the dissonance reduction process is dependent on two behaviours and not just one. This is a new departure for research that represents a quite natural further development of the radical conception of cognitive dissonance theory as a *theory of the rationalization of behaviour*. We may remember that one of the premisses underlying this radical conception is that the cognition which generates a state of dissonance always corresponds to the representation of the subject's actual behaviour. Such a premiss cannot fail to lead researchers to take an interest in situations in which subjects are induced to produce not one but two behaviours.

It is time to explain something of the double forced compliance paradigm. Let us consider a subject who has produced two behaviours, B1 and B2. Naturally, if this subject is to experience a state of dissonance it is necessary and sufficient for one of these behaviours to contradict the subject's attitudes or motivations A. Let us suppose that the discrepant behaviour is B1. If we reason on the basis of behaviour B1 alone then we will consider the subject to be in a classic forced compliance situation. However, if we also consider behaviour B2, we must take account not only of the relations between this new behaviour and the attitudes or motivations A of the subject (inconsistent, consistent or neutral relations), but also of the relations that exist between it and behaviour B1 (inconsistent, consistent or neutral relations). Here, we shall again encounter a theoretical reasoning somewhat similar to the one we applied to the analysis of the effects of arbitrary feedback or argumentation and which allowed us to suggest that the generative cognition is the representation of the problematic behaviour (see chapter 3).

Let us therefore consider all the possible cases. We shall use an unbroken line together with the signs $-$, $+$ or $\bigcirc$ to represent the three types of relation which may exist between any two of the elements B1, B2 and A ($-$ represents inconsistency, $+$ consistency and $\bigcirc$ neutrality or irrelevance).

First, let us consider only the relevant relations that may exist between B1, B2 and A.

If we assume the inconsistent relation between B1 and A to be constant, then logic indicates the presence of four possible cases:

X	X	X	X
$-$ $-$	$-$ $+$	$-$ $+$	$-$ $-$
B1 + B2	B1 $-$ B2	B1 + B2	B1 $-$ B2
case 1	case 2	case 3	case 4

In cases 1 and 4, the two behaviours contradict the attitudes or motivations A, while in cases 2 and 3 only behaviour B1 contradicts A. Moreover, in cases 1 and 3 these two behaviours are consistent with one another, whereas they are mutually contradictory in cases 2 and 4. It can be observed that cases 1 and 2 correspond to what balance theory (Heider, 1958, Flament, 1968) describes as balanced triads $(-,-,+)$ whereas cases 3 and 4 correspond to unbalanced triads $(+,+,-)$ and $(-,-,-)$.

Let us now consider both the relevant and irrelevant relations between B1, B2 and A.

If we once again assume the relation of inconsistency between B1 and A to be constant then logic this time presents us with nine possible cases, namely the four cases presented above and the following five cases:

X	X	X
$-$ $\bigcirc$	$-$ $+$	$-$ $-$
B1 + B2	B1$\bigcirc$B2	B1$\bigcirc$B2
case 5	case 6	case 7

X	X
$-$ $\bigcirc$	$-$ $\bigcirc$
B1$\bigcirc$B2	B1 $-$ B2
case 8	case 9

In cases 5, 6, 8 and 9, only one of the two behaviours contradicts the attitudes or motivations A, while both behaviours contradict A in case 7. In cases 6, 7 and 8 the relation between the two behaviours is one of irrelevance, while the relation is one of consistency in case 5 and inconsistency in case 9.

Of these theoretically possible cases, two have been studied in particular detail. These are cases 1 and 2, which are easier to imagine than the others, possibly because they correspond to balanced triads. In this chapter, we intend to present a number of experimental implementations of these two cases of double compliance and to identify the theoretical implications. Furthermore, we shall demonstrate that whereas the 'radical' theory of cognitive dissonance which we have defended allows us to formulate plausible hypotheses, the same is not true of the 'lax' conceptions of this theory.

Double forced compliance: initial results

We shall start by describing four experiments. The first of these implements case 1, the second case 2 and the third and fourth are simultaneous implementations of cases 1 and 2.

Experiment 18. Effect of performing a boring task on attitude towards this task in the situation used by Festinger and Carlsmith

The logic of this experiment was borrowed from Festinger and Carlsmith (1959). These authors were the first to implement a double forced compliance situation (case 1). However, under the circumstances, they proved to be insufficiently radical to take account of this specificity of the experimental situation they had created. It should be recalled that the subjects of this first experiment had to produce two behaviours before the post-experimental attitude measurement was performed. First, they had to perform a particularly dull task (behaviour B1) and, second, they had to participate in a counterattitudinal role-playing situation in which, in contrast, they emphasized the appeal of the task (behaviour B2). However, Festinger and Carlsmith only took account of the second behaviour in their calculation of the total amount of dissonance, thus ignoring the theoretical status of the first behaviour. It should not be forgotten that, for Festinger, the total amount of dissonance is defined with reference to a particular cognition (which we have called the generative cognition: in this case, this is the representation of behaviour B2) and is obtained by dividing the inconsistent cognitions by the total of the relevant cognitions (inconsistent and consistent). Does this mean that the production of behaviour B1 in no way affects this ratio? Certainly not. The subjects' knowledge that they have themselves already performed the boring task (behaviour B1) is a relevant cognition which fits well with this new behaviour, namely the acceptance of the counterattitudinal role (behaviour B2), with reference to which Festinger and Carlsmith calculated the dissonance ratio.[1] This cognition should therefore reduce the dissonance induced by the counterattitudinal role-playing. If this is genuinely the case, then subjects should exhibit less attitude change in favour of the lie and should, in consequence, find the task less interesting at the post-experimental stage than they would if they had not previously performed the task.

Experiment 18 (Joule and Girandola; experiment 1, 1992) was designed to test this hypothesis.

Dissonance ratio

If we designate the total amount of dissonance experienced by the subjects after producing the counterattitudinal role-playing behaviour (single forced compliance) as T1, and let T2 designate the total amount of dissonance of subjects who performed both the task and the counterattitudinal role-playing (double forced compliance), then, if we follow the reasoning adopted by Festinger and Carlsmith and calculate the dissonance ratio with reference to behaviour B2 (which here corresponds to the generative cognition), we obtain:

Single compliance
counterattitudinal role-playing
$$T1 = X/X + Z$$
since in the single compliance situation:
A→not B2 and Z→B2
and in the double compliance situation:
A→not B2, Z→B2 and B1→B2

Double compliance
task and counterattitudinal role-playing
$$T2 = X/X + Z + B1$$

where:

A represents the subject's attitude towards the task

B1 corresponds to the representation of the behaviour which consists of performing the task

B2 corresponds to the representation of the counterattitudinal role-playing

Z corresponds to a set of cognitions which were not controlled in the experimental situation and which account for the realization of the counterattitudinal role-playing behaviour B2 (to please or help the experimenter, to assist research and so on)

→symbolizes psychological implication.

Subjects

The subjects consisted of male and female first- or second-year literature students at the Université de Provence (Aix-en-Provence, France).

Procedure

We shall investigate four conditions: one condition of double forced compliance (production of both behaviours B1 and B2); two conditions of single forced compliance (production of behaviour B1 only or production of behaviour B2 only) and a control condition (in which neither B1 nor B2 was produced).

The subjects were approached on the university campus and asked to take part in unpaid research lasting for about 20 minutes, nominally concerning the effects of concentration on performance. Those who agreed were asked to go to the laboratory one at a time (individual pass). In all the conditions the experimenter first explained in detail what the concentration task consisted of, namely to spend 13 minutes copying a Finnish text while paying attention to spelling and punctuation and attempting to make as few mistakes as possible. This was therefore a fairly tedious task.

In the double forced compliance condition the subjects performed this tedious task (behaviour B1) before being led, on the pretext of helping the experimenter, to present it positively to a colleague (behaviour B2) with the aim of persuading him or her to perform the task as well. As in Festinger and Carlsmith's experiment, the subjects had to use arguments provided by the experimenter such as, 'it was very enjoyable', 'I had a lot of fun', 'I enjoyed it, it was very interesting', 'it was exciting'.

In one of the single forced compliance situations the subjects simply performed the tedious task (behaviour B1). In the other, they did not perform the task itself but simply took part in the counterattitudinal role-playing (behaviour B2). Finally, in the control condition, the subjects passed directly from the description of the task to the post-experimental questionnaire. When completing the questionnaire, the subjects clearly knew that they would not have to perform the task themselves. This questionnaire made use of the same scales as those employed by Festinger and Carlsmith and, in particular, two 11-point scales (from −5 to +5) designed to measure the subject's attitude towards the task. One of these scales was designed to evaluate the *attraction of the task* and the other the *enjoyment found in performing it*. This questionnaire, which was completed anonymously, was claimed to have been prepared by members of the psychology department, who were anxious to know whether the research work undertaken with the students' help interested them or not so that, if necessary, it could be improved in years to come. The subjects were therefore asked to reply as sincerely as possible to the questionnaire and place it in a box once completed. The object of this procedure was clearly to prevent the subjects from establishing a link between the experiment and the attitude measurement or, at least, to make it more difficult to establish such a link.

Results

The results are presented in table 5.1.

Table 5.1. Effect of performing a boring task on attitude towards this task in the situation used by Festinger and Carlsmith.

	Attraction	Enjoyment
Double compliance (Festinger and Carlsmith's situation)	1·30	0·50
Single compliance (task only)	0·22	−0·27
Single compliance (counterattitudinal role-playing only)	2·17	2·77
Control	−1·02	−1·92

Notes: The figures given represent the mean rating on each scale ($n = 20$ for each condition). The larger the positive numbers, the more attractive or enjoyable the subjects found the task to be. The lower the negative numbers, the less attractive or enjoyable the task was judged to be.

As expected, the subjects who had to perform the task and then present it to a colleague (double forced compliance situation) found it to be significantly less enjoyable (F = 21·15, $p < 0.001$) and marginally less attractive than the subjects who simply had to present it (single forced compliance situation). We may thus conclude that in requiring their subjects to perform the tedious task before playing the counterattitudinal role, Festinger and Carlsmith were involuntarily making it less likely that the expected dissonance effect would occur than if they had directly asked their subjects to take part in the role-playing situation. We may also observe that the classical dissonance reduction effects occur in the two single compliance conditions since the subjects in these two conditions find the task significantly more enjoyable than the subjects in the control condition: task condition vs. control condition (F = 5·46, $p < 0.05$); role-playing condition vs. control condition (F = 44·32, $p < 0.001$).

Experiment 21 can be considered to be an implementation of case 1 in that behaviours B1 and B2 are consonant and that neither B1 nor B2 is consonant with attitude A. In effect, knowing that a task is tedious is inconsistent with the fact of performing it, just as knowing that a task is tedious is inconsistent with the fact that one has, on the contrary, stated in public that it is extremely attractive.

Experiment 19. Effect of attitudinal role-playing in the tedious task situation

Experiment 19 represents an implementation of case 2. To switch from case 1 to case 2 we may retain the same experimental logic and simply ask the subjects to play an attitudinal rather than a tedious task (behaviour B1), they were induced to tell a colleague who was ready to perform it that it was actually very boring (behaviour B2).

This provided an effective implementation of case 2 because only behaviour B1, which consists of performing the task, contradicted the subjects' attitude A (that personally they found the task boring).[2] This is because the fact that the subjects have performed the task themselves (behaviour B1) fits badly with the negative presentation which they are required to make (behaviour B2) and, finally, because this negative presentation is consistent with their attitude A.

Here, therefore, only one behaviour is capable of generating dissonance, namely behaviour B1. The total amount of dissonance should therefore be calculated with reference to this behaviour. In so far as behaviour B2 contradicts B1, the performance of B2 should increase the dissonance induced by B1. In consequence, dissonance reduction should be greater in the subjects who both performed the task and presented it (production of behaviours B1 and B2) than in those who simply performed the task (production of behaviour B1 only). In other words, the subjects who are induced to declare that the task is boring should be the ones who find it the most interesting.

The aim of experiment 19 (Joule and Girandola, experiment 2, 1992) was to test this far-from-insignificant hypothesis.

Dissonance ratio

If we designate the total amount of dissonance experienced by the subjects after performing the task (single forced compliance) as T1, and let T2 designate the total amount of dissonance of subjects who performed both the task and the attitudinal role-playing (double forced compliance) then, if we calculate the dissonance ratio with reference to behaviour B1 (which here corresponds to the generative cognition), we obtain:

Single compliance task   Double compliance task and
                              attitudinal role-playing

$$T1 = X/X + Z \qquad\qquad T2 = X + B2/X + Z + B2$$

since in the single compliance situation:
$A \rightarrow$ not B1 and $Z \rightarrow$ B1
and in the double compliance situation:
$A \rightarrow$ not B1, $B2 \rightarrow$ not B1 and $Z \rightarrow$ B1

where
A represents the subject's attitude towards the task
B1 corresponds to the representation of the behaviour which consists of performing the task
B2 corresponds to the representation of the attitudinal role-playing
Z corresponds to a set of cognitions which were not controlled in the experimental situation and which account for the realization of the task (in order to please or help the experimenter, to assist research and so on).

Subjects
The subjects consisted of female first- or second-year literature students at the Université de Provence (Aix-en-Provence, France).

Procedure
We shall again investigate four conditions: one condition of double forced compliance (production of both behaviours B1 and B2); one condition of single forced compliance (production of behaviour B1 only), one condition of self-persuasion (production of behaviour B2 only) and a control condition (in which neither B1 nor B2 was produced).

The subjects were approached on the university campus. As in the preceding experiment, they were asked to take part in unpaid research which was nominally concerned with the effects of concentration on performance and was said to last for about 20 minutes. The volunteers were asked to go to the laboratory one at a time (individual pass). In all the conditions the experimenter first provided a detailed description of the concentration task. This task was similar to the one used by Festinger and Carlsmith (1959) and consisted of turning 50 knobs fixed to a board a quarter turn to the right, starting with the first and working through the rest in sequence. After reaching the last knob, the subjects were expected, without hesitation, to start again from the beginning. The task was to be performed using one hand only and was to be timed to last 13 minutes.

In the double forced compliance condition, immediately after the subjects had performed this task (behaviour B1) they had to present it negatively to a colleague (behaviour B2) using arguments provided by the experimenter such as, 'it was boring', 'I found it tedious', 'it was tiresome', 'it was uninteresting'. In the single compliance situation the subjects simply performed the task (behaviour B1) but made no presentation of it. In the self-persuasion condition they did not perform the task but simply participated in the attitudinal role-playing (behaviour B2). In the control condition, the subjects performed neither the task nor the attitudinal role-playing.

The post-experimental questionnaire was identical to the one used in the preceding experiment. It was presented in the same way and comprised the same rating scales, one of which was designed to evaluate the attraction of the task and the other the enjoyment found in performing it.

Results
The results are presented in table 5.2.

Table 5.2. Effect of attitudinal role-playing in the tedious task situation.

	Attraction	Enjoyment
Double compliance	1·06	0·42
Single compliance (task)	−0·82	−0·45
Self-persuasion (attitudinal role-playing)	−2·82	−2·52
Control	−1·32	−2·12

Notes: The figures given represent the mean rating on each scale (*n* = 20 for each condition). The larger the positive numbers, the more attractive or enjoyable the subjects found the task to be. The lower the negative numbers, the less attractive or enjoyable the task was judged to be.

These results provide clear confirmation of the tested hypotheses, which had been formulated on the basis of a calculation of the dissonance ratio in conformity with the radical theory: the subjects who both performed the task and took part in the negative presentation of it (double forced compliance) found it significantly more attractive (F = 10·43, $p < 0·01$) and marginally less enjoyable than the subjects who performed but were not called on to present it (single forced compliance).

We also observe that the classical dissonance reduction effect occurs in the single compliance condition, with the subjects in this condition finding the task significantly more enjoyable than those in the control condition: F = 4·60, $p < 0·05$. We also find a fairly classic self-persuasion effect (see Janis and Gilmore, 1965) in the condition in which the subjects have only to take part in the attitudinal role-playing. In contrast with the subjects in the single forced compliance condition, the subjects in this condition judged the task to be significantly less attractive than did those in the control condition: F = 3·99, $p < 0·05$. While, in this condition, attitudinal role-playing leads the subjects to change their attitudes in favour of the arguments that they present, this is not the case in the double compliance condition. In this condition, that is when subjects are in a state of dissonance because they have already performed the tedious task, role-playing has the diametrically opposite effect.

Experiment 20. Counterattitudinal role-playing and attitudinal role-playing in the tedious task situation

Experiment 20 (Joule and Girandola, 1995) implements both cases 1 and 2. In fact, if viewed as a synthesis and replication of the two preceding experiments, it can be said to reproduce the principle underlying them in a 2 × 2 design. The subjects had to make either a positive (behaviour B2) or negative (behaviour B'2) presentation of a tedious task. Some of these subjects had previously performed the task (behaviour B1) whereas others had not. The main hypothesis relates to the comparison of the two situations of double compliance. Our hypothesis was clearly that the subjects who had performed the task and presented it negatively would evaluate it more favourably than those who presented it positively after performing it. In fact, as we have argued, whereas positive presentation fits well with the fact of having performed the task, negative presentation does not. As a consequence, the subjects who have presented the task negatively should have the most dissonance to reduce and should therefore exhibit the greatest attitude change.

Subjects

The subjects consisted of female first- or second-year literature students at the Université de Provence (Aix-en-Provence, France).

Procedure

The subjects were once again approached on the university campus. As in the preceding experiments, they were asked to take part in unpaid research lasting for about 20 minutes, nominally concerning the effects of concentration on performance. Those who agreed were asked to go to the laboratory one at a time (individual pass). In all the conditions the experimenter first explained the task in detail. This was the same task as was used in experiment 19 and which therefore consisted of turning knobs attached to a board for 13 minutes. In the double forced compliance condition the subjects performed this task before being induced to present it either positively (counterattitudinal role-playing) or negatively (attitudinal role-playing) to a colleague using arguments provided by the experimenter ('It was very enjoyable', 'I had a lot of fun' and so on, or, alternatively, 'It was tedious', 'I got bored' and so on). In the single compliance situation the subjects simply performed the counterattitudinal role-playing, while in the self-persuasion condition they simply participated in the attitudinal role-playing.

The post-experimental questionnaire made use of an 11-point scale designed to obtain global information about the interest and enjoyment which the task held for the subjects. This questionnaire was the same as the one used by Festinger and Carlsmith (1959), with subjects replying to the question 'Was the task interesting and enjoyable?' (−5 indicating that the task was extremely monotonous and boring and +5 signifying that it was extremely interesting and enjoyable).

Results

The results are presented in table 5.3.

Table 5.3. Counterattitudinal role-playing and attitudinal role-playing in the tedious task situation.

		Presentation	
		positive	negative
	with	−0·45	1·45
task			
	without	1·42	−1·30

Notes: The figures given correspond to the mean rating ($n = 20$ for each condition). The larger the positive numbers, the more interesting or enjoyable the subjects found the task to be. The lower the negative numbers, the less interesting or enjoyable the task was judged to be.

As expected, in the double forced compliance situations those subjects who presented the task negatively judged it to be significantly more interesting and enjoyable than the subjects who made a positive presentation: $F = 7·32$, $p < 0·01$. In other words, after performing the task, the subjects who declare it to be boring find it more interesting and enjoyable than those who declare it to be extremely attractive. The presentation variable (positive vs. negative presentation) has the opposite effect when the subjects do not have to perform the task themselves. In contrast, in such cases the subjects who present the task positively find it significantly more interesting and enjoyable than those who made a negative presentation: $F = 23·01$, $p < 0·001$. We observe a significant interaction between the two variables under investigation ($F = 11·57$, $p < 0·001$).

In passing, we might note that these results, which the radical theory and, indeed, the fundamental core of Festinger's theory led us to expect, are totally incompatible with Cooper and Fazio's new look (1984). These authors, it should be remembered, consider that the effect of counterattitudinal role-playing, in particular in Festinger and Carlsmith's experiment, is due simply to the anticipation of the aversive consequences to which it may give rise: involving a colleague in a task which the subject knows to be boring. This equating of dissonance with a feeling of responsibility, or even of guilt, which is aroused by an act considered in some way to be unworthy (see Stice, 1992) is based on this interpretation of the status of the consequences of the act. However, in our double compliance situation the subjects who were led to make a negative presentation of the task which they had performed (attitudinal role-playing) experienced more dissonance than the subjects who were induced to present it positively.

If Cooper and Fazio are right in claiming that the effect of counterattitudinal role-playing is linked to the aversive consequences of the act (leading a comrade into a trap), then we should obtain precisely the opposite results. In fact, the attitudinal role-playing, unlike the counterattitudinal role-playing, cannot, to use Cooper and Fazio's terms, have any aversive consequences. That is, unless we are always able to imagine some aversive consequence of any act whatsoever and thereby turn the key concept of the new look into a completely *ad hoc* concept. Even if this were the case, we might still wonder how attitudinal role-playing could have more aversive consequences than counterattitudinal role-playing. To develop the same idea, these results appear to be quite incompatible with any of the reinterpretations of dissonance effects in terms of self-affirmation (Steele, 1988) or related theories. It is difficult to see how warning a colleague that a (tedious) task which you have just performed is, in reality, tedious can constitute a threat to the self, especially since, as we would readily agree, saying the opposite of what you think under these conditions would constitute an act which might well threaten your goodness or worth. Only dissonance theory allows a strict derivation of these two effects, effects which are necessarily contradictory when viewed from the standpoint of the revisionist or alternative theories.

Experiment 21, which was designed as an implementation of cases 2 and 3 of the double compliance paradigm, involves a different behaviour. Our aim in this experiment was to test the same theoretical hypotheses in a different experimental context which exploited a different type of behaviour.

Experiment 21. Effect of pro- or anti-smoking advocacy after agreeing to go without tobacco on the evaluation of the difficulty of abstaining from tobacco
This experiment makes use of two of the most commonly mobilized behaviours in dissonance research: an abstinent behaviour and an essay-writing behaviour. More precisely, the first behaviour, produced by smokers, consisted of refraining from smoking for an evening (behaviour B1) and the second consisted of writing an essay either *against* (behaviour B2) or *in favour of smoking* (behaviour B'2).

What predictions can be made about these two cases? If only the first behaviour is taken into consideration, then it appears that the subjects are in a classic forced compliance situation. In effect, the privative behaviour B1 contradicts A, which, in this experiment, corresponds to a set of cognitions relating to the habits of smokers (needs, motivations and so on). Clearly, a good way for them to reduce their dissonance is to minimize the difficulty of abstaining from tobacco in order to bring their cognitions A into line with their behaviour B1.

However, if we consider both behaviours the question becomes one of determining whether the second behaviour increases or, in contrast, reduces the dissonance induced by the first. When this second behaviour consists of writing an anti-smoking essay the subjects are in a situation that corresponds to case 1. To advance an argument against tobacco (behaviour B2) fits well with the abstinent behaviour (behaviour B1) but contradicts the subject's private cognitions A. If, instead, the second behaviour consists of writing an essay in favour of smoking the subjects find themselves in a situation which corresponds to case 2. To advance a pro-smoking argument (behaviour B'2) does not agree well with the abstinent behaviour (behaviour B1) but fits perfectly with the subject's private cognitions A. If we take as our basis the same theoretical reasoning that we elaborated in the preceding experiments, as well as the reasoning followed in establishing the status of the generative cognition (see chapter 1), then we are in a position to formulate two hypotheses:

If the second behaviour is consonant with the first, as it is when the subjects have to write an anti-smoking essay, it will provide additional consistent cognitions and the total amount of dissonance will be reduced as a result. In contrast, if the second behaviour is not consonant with the first, as is the case when the subjects have to write an essay in favour of smoking, then it will contribute inconsistent cognitions despite the fact that it is in agreement with the subject's private attitude. The total amount of dissonance will therefore increase. We can again assure ourselves of these predictions by calculating the dissonance ratios.

The dissonance ratios

If we designate the total amount of dissonance experienced by the subjects who were induced to abstain from smoking (behaviour B1) as T1, let T2 designate the total amount of dissonance of subjects who went without smoking and wrote an anti-smoking essay (behaviours B1 and B2) and, finally, let T'2 designate the total amount of dissonance of subjects who went without smoking and wrote an essay in favour of tobacco (behaviours B1 and B'2), then, if we calculate the dissonance ratio with reference to behaviour B1 (which here corresponds to the generative cognition), we obtain:

Double compliance abstinence and anti-smoking essay	Single compliance abstinence	Double compliance abstinence and pro-smoking essay
$T2 = X/X + Z + B2$	$< T1 = X/X + Z$	$< T'2 = X + B'2/ X + B'2 + Z$

since in the first double compliance situation:
$A \rightarrow$ not B1 and $Z \rightarrow$ B1 and $B2 \rightarrow$ B1
in the single compliance situation:
$A \rightarrow$ not B1, $Z \rightarrow$ B1
and in the second double compliance situation:
$A \rightarrow$ not B1, $B'2 \rightarrow$ not B1 and $Z \rightarrow$ B1

where:
A represents a set of cognitions held by the subjects relating to the habits of smokers (needs, motivations)
B1 corresponds to the representation of the behaviour which consists of going without smoking
B2 corresponds to the representation of the behaviour which consists of writing an anti-smoking essay
B'2 corresponds to the representation of the behaviour which consists of writing a pro-smoking essay
Z corresponds to a set of cognitions which were not controlled in the experimental

situation and which account for the realization of the task (in order to please or help the experimenter, to assist research and so on)

Therefore, as we hypothesized, the subjects who were induced to write an anti-smoking essay after abstaining from tobacco should have less dissonance to reduce than the subjects who were not called on to advocate this cause. They should therefore minimize the difficulty of going without smoking less. In contrast, the subjects who had to write an essay in favour of smoking after going without it should have more dissonance to reduce than the other subjects. In consequence, they should find abstaining from smoking more difficult. In other words, subjects should find it more difficult to abstain from tobacco after writing an anti-smoking essay than they did beforehand and they should find it easier after writing a pro-smoking essay.

These hypotheses were put to the test in experiment 21 (Joule, 1991a).

Subjects
The subjects were male and female literature students at the Université de Provence (Aix-en-Provence, France).

Procedure
The experiment followed a before/after scheme involving four conditions which we shall present here: two double forced compliance conditions, one single compliance condition and a non-dissonant condition. In the first double forced compliance condition, subjects produced behaviour B1 followed by B2 and, in the second, behaviour B1 followed by B'2. In the single compliance conditions, subjects produced behaviour B1 only, whereas in the non-dissonant condition they produced neither of the behaviours.

In all the conditions the subjects were smokers (consuming more than 18 cigarettes per day) who had been recruited on the university campus to take part in two nominally unrelated pieces of psychological research. The volunteers were then asked to fill in an initial questionnaire (pre-experimental measurement). Among the various questions contained in the questionnaire, the following two questions were posed:

1 How would you find it if you had to stop smoking this instant and not smoke for the next 24 hours? The subjects had to select their response on an 11-point scale ranging from 0 (very easy) to 11 (impossible).
2 At present, for how many hours could you stop smoking without feeling a pressing need? The subjects selected one of 25 responses ranging from 1 hour to more than 24 hours.

Several weeks later, the subjects were invited to the laboratory during the late afternoon in small groups of four or five people, each group being randomly allocated to one of the conditions. To reduce the risks of self-selection to a minimum, a particularly effective influence strategy was used, namely low-ball/*fait accompli*[3] (see Joule, 1987b, Joule, Mugny and Perez, 1988, Joule, Fointiat, Pasquier and Mugny, 1991). On arriving at the laboratory, the subjects in all the conditions were told that as part of an initial piece of research they would have to stop smoking until noon the following day. They were told that this was because the experimenter wanted to compare their performance in concentration tests before and after abstaining from smoking. As might be expected, the subjects were left free to decide whether or not to participate in this initial research. Having made their decision, the subjects performed the first set of concentration tests. It was then as part of what they believed to be the second piece of research, which was conducted by a different experimenter, that the subjects in the double compliance conditions were asked to spend 7 minutes writing as persuasive an essay as possible either against (anti-essay condition) or in favour of (pro-essay condition) smoking. In the *anti-essay* condition, the subjects had to defend the proposition 'Smoking is really very dangerous', whereas in the *pro-essay* they supported the proposition 'Smoking is really not dangerous'. Instead of writing an essay, the subjects in the single compliance condition spent the 7-minute period engaged in a non-verbal task which was unrelated to smoking. In the non-dissonant condition the experimenter did not ask the subjects to refrain from smoking. Instead, they were asked to perform the concentration tests followed, later, by the same non-verbal task that was used in the single compliance situation. Finally, the experimenter asked these subjects to complete a post-experimental questionnaire, for the purpose of which they were to imagine themselves in the place of someone who, in order to take part in the research, had to go without smoking from late afternoon until the following noon. As in the pre-experimental questionnaire, two questions here related to the difficulty of going without smoking:

1 Please estimate how difficult it will be for you not to smoke until tomorrow afternoon (the subjects indicated their response on the same 11-point scale that had been used in the pre-experimental questionnaire).
2 Please estimate how long it will be before you really feel in need of a cigarette (as in the pre-experimental stage, the subjects chose one of 25 possible responses).

The subjects in all three conditions of abstinence from smoking also filled in a post-experimental questionnaire before leaving the laboratory and were 'debriefed' immediately afterwards.[4]

Results:
The results are presented in table 5.4.

The main dependent variables correspond to the difference between the ratings provided by the subjects at the pre- and post-experimental stages in response to the two key questions.

Table 5.4. Effect of arguing for or against smoking after agreeing to go without tobacco on the evaluation of the difficulty of abstinence from smoking.

	Difficulty*	Need**
Double compliance (abstinence and anti-essay)	2·33	4·87
Double compliance (abstinence and pro-essay)	0·06	0·75
Single compliance (abstinence)	1·28	3·26
Non-dissonance	2·87	3·05

Notes: The figures represent the mean of the differences between the pre- and post-experimental ratings. $n = 20$ in each condition.
* the higher the figure, the more difficult going without smoking is.
** the higher the figure the greater the need for smoking is.

Here, again, the results conform to the hypotheses. It was the subjects who had to write an essay *against* tobacco after being induced to refrain from smoking who found it most difficult to go without tobacco, while those who wrote a text *in favour of* smoking found it easiest to go without tobacco. The subjects in the single compliance condition provided an intermediate rating. The two double forced compliance conditions differed significantly from one another ($F = 11·68$, $p < 0·001$) and both differed marginally from the single compliance condition ($F = 2·98$, $p < 0·10$ and $F = 2·59$, $p = 0·10$ respectively). If we look at the number of subjects in each condition who felt refraining from smoking was easier in the post-test than in the pre-test, the same pattern of results is found. Indeed, only 10 per cent of subjects in the *anti-essay* condition of double compliance (two out of 20) reported easier post-test abstinence versus 50 per cent (10 out of 20) in the *pro-essay* double compliance condition: $\chi^2 = 5·33$, $p = 0·02$. This percentage was intermediate in the single compliance condition with post-test abstinence being claimed to be easier in 35 per cent of cases (7 out of 20).

The ratings of the need for tobacco yield the same effects. As expected, it was the subjects who had been required to produce an anti-smoking essay after agreeing to stop smoking who felt the greatest need, whereas subjects who wrote in favour of smoking found abstention the easiest. The subjects in the single compliance condition again produced an intermediate rating. Once again there was a significant difference between the two double compliance conditions ($F = 5·85$, $p < 0·025$) and a marginal difference between them both and the single compliance condition. Finally, we observe that the question relating to the difficulty of abstinence indicates a classic dissonance effect in the single compliance condition, with subjects in this condition finding abstinence easier than subjects in the non-dissonant condition ($F = 3·71$, $0·05 < p < 0·10$).

The results of the four experiments which we have presented in this chapter all point in the same direction. They demonstrate that the total amount of dissonance has to be calculated with reference to a single cognition, a cognition that always represents one of the two behaviours, whether this consists of playing a counterattitudinal role, performing a tedious task or refraining from smoking. We have seen that when the two behaviours harmonize, dissonance reduction (and thus the change of attitude or motivation) is less pronounced than when these two behaviours are contradictory. Since this type of result is not self-evident, we shall now examine the question of calculating the total amount of dissonance in situations of double forced compliance.

Calculating the total amount of dissonance in situations of double forced compliance

Case 1

Dissonance theorists are agreed in considering that the total amount of dissonance $(D/D + C)$ has to be calculated with reference to the most resistant cognition (which we have termed the generative cognition). In situations of single forced compliance this is, of course, the representation of the compliant behaviour. However, whereas the calculation of the total amount of dissonance in situations of single forced compliance is straightforward, it is less so in double forced compliance situations and, in particular, those which represent an implementation of case 1, since these situations mobilize two problematic counterattitudinal or countermotivational behaviours. In such situations, it is essential to know whether the representation of one of these behaviours is more or less resistant than the representation of the other. And on this point, Festinger's theory offers us no assistance. While dissonance theorists speak of resistance to change, they fail to specify the factors which affect this change.

It was, in fact, Kiesler (1971) who specifiied these factors as part of his presentation of his own theory of commitment, of which he rightly considered dissonance theory to be one localized element. In experiment 18, as well as in experiments 20 and 21 which mobilize two behaviours that contradict the attitudes or motivations of the subjects, we have not hesitated in our choice of the behaviour with reference to which the total amount of dissonance should be calculated and, consequently, in our choice of the generative cognition. We have allowed ourselves to be guided by a feeling of self-evidence in choosing the behaviour which Kiesler would have considered to involve the subject in the greatest commitment. In experiments 18 and 20 this behaviour consists of lying to a colleague rather than performing a boring task. This self-evidence is such that Festinger and Carlsmith (1959), as well as the many other researchers who have replicated their experiment, have completely omitted the first behaviour performed by the subject from their theoretical analysis, proceeding as if the fact of having performed a tedious task in no way affects the total amount of dissonance. Allowing ourselves to be led by the same feeling of self-evidence in experiment 21, we chose the behaviour which Kiesler would have viewed as implying the greatest commitment, namely abstaining from tobacco rather than writing an anti-smoking essay. In effect, in experiments 21 and 20 the behaviour which consists of lying and that which involves the performance of a task differ in those very factors which Kiesler considers to be crucial in the generation of commitment. Specifically, they differ in the factors *importance of the task for the subject* (it is more costly to lie than to perform an experimental task, even though tedious, for 13 minutes), *the public nature of the act* (performing the task involves the subject alone whereas the lie involves a colleague) and, finally, in the *degree of volition* (while performing the task forms part of the 'experimental contract', the same is not true of the lie). The same is true of experiment 21 where the abstinent behaviour is again distinguished from the essay-writing behaviour by the main factors of commitment. The two behaviours differ on the dimensions *importance of the task for the subject* (it is clearly more costly to abstain from smoking for an evening than to write an essay against tobacco), *public nature of the act* (going without smoking for an evening at home is a more public action than writing an essay in the laboratory), *degree of volition* (it is easier to refuse an excessive demand — going without smoking — than a more moderate one) and, finally, in the dimension *number of acts performed by the subject* (in some way, subjects repeat their abstinent behaviour each time they feel like lighting a cigarette and refuse to do so. However, the essay writing behaviour is performed only once).

To sum up, in situations of double forced compliance which implement case 1 (that is when the two behaviours, although concordant, contradict the attitudes or motivations of the subject) the total amount of dissonance must be calculated with reference to the behaviour that requires the greatest degree of commitment from the subject. We have seen that producing the behaviour that requires the least commitment, provided that this is consistent, reduces the dissonance induced by the production of the behaviour requiring the higher level of commitment. In such cases, dissonance reduction is less pronounced in situations of double compliance than in single compliance situations.

However, what happens when the two behaviours require an equal level of commitment? In such cases, we must recognize that there is not one but two generative cognitions. Everything suggests that individuals who perform these two behaviours act as if they were subjected to two classic forced compliance situations, one referring to behaviour B1 (B1 is discordant with A) and the other referring to B2 (which is also discordant with A), and that, furthermore, each of these two behaviours possesses sufficient cognitive significance to require rationalization. We can therefore consider each of the two behaviours to possess the status of a generative cognition. We might therefore conclude that the dissonance induced by the two behaviours will act cumulatively. In such cases, the total amount of dissonance should consequently be greater in double compliance situations in which subjects perform two counterattitudinal or countermotivational behaviours than in single compliance situations in which they perform only one of these behaviours.

This hypothesis was tested in experiment 22 (Joule, 1991b).

Experiment 22. Effect of double commitment (to abstinence from smoking and to counterattitudinal role-playing) on the evaluation of the difficulty of abstinence
To this end, this new experiment, which represents a further implementation of case 1, made use of two counterattitudinal or countermotivational behaviours

which were consonant with one another. The first (behaviour B1) consisted, as in the preceding experiment, of refraining from smoking for a period of 18 hours, whereas the second was drawn from experiment 21 and consisted of a counter-attitudinal role-playing situation. More precisely, this second behaviour consisted of telling a colleague that it is easy to go without smoking, in order to persuade him or her to refrain from smoking. This experiment therefore mobilized two behaviours which required considerable commitment on the part of the subjects, some of whom, indeed, refused to comply with the experimenter.[5]

We shall report four experimental conditions: one condition of double forced compliance (production of behaviours B1 and B2), two conditions of single forced compliance (production of behaviour B1 in one condition and production of B2 in the other) and one condition of non-dissonance.

Subjects
The subjects consisted of male and female smokers who were studying literature at the Université de Provence (Aix-en-Provence, France).

Procedure
The experiment followed a before/after scheme.

As in the previous experiment, the volunteer student subjects, who were smokers (consumption higher than 15 cigarettes per day) taken from outside the psychology faculty, were recruited on the campus of the university of Aix-en-Provence. They were told that the objective of the research was to investigate concentration in smokers. The main measurement related to the subjects' response to the question:

1   How would you find it if you had to stop smoking this instant and not smoke for the next 24 hours? The subjects had to select their response on an 11-point scale, ranging from 0 (very easy) to 11 (impossible).

Several weeks later, the subjects were invited one at a time to the laboratory towards the end of the afternoon (individual pass). On arriving at the laboratory, the subjects in the double forced compliance situation were induced to decide to refrain from smoking until the following noon using the same influence strategy (low-ball/*fait accompli*) that had been applied in the preceding experiment. The experimenter again claimed that he wanted to compare subjects' performance in concentration tests administered before and after their abstinence from tobacco. Once they had decided to go without smoking (behaviour B1), the subjects were led to perform a series of non-verbal concentration tests which were claimed to be part of the research. They were then induced to do a favour for the experimenter. This favour consisted of convincing an undecided person (a collaborator) to take part in the research and, consequently, to go without cigarettes for an evening, using arguments such as 'it isn't difficult not to smoke for an evening', 'friends who have done it say that it's no problem', 'it's a very enriching personal experience' (behaviour B2). Once the role-playing behaviour had been concluded, the subjects left the laboratory. They were then intercepted in the corridor by the experimenter, who pretended to have forgotten to ask them to reply to an anonymous questionnaire which, it was said, was intended for the officials of the psychology department who wanted to know what students thought of the experiments which they agreed to take part in.

In one of the single compliance conditions the subjects were induced to decide to refrain from smoking (behaviour B1) but they were not asked to play the counterattitudinal role after performing the concentration tests. In the other condition, the subjects performed the concentration tests without having to make the decision to refrain from smoking. Once they had performed this task, these subjects were asked to play the counterattitudinal role (behaviour B2). Again, in both conditions the subjects were asked to reply to a post-experimental questionnaire in the corridor just after leaving the laboratory.

In the non-dissonant condition the subjects had neither to go without cigarettes nor to perform the counterattitudinal role-playing. They therefore left the laboratory immediately after completing the concentration tests. After intercepting them in the corridor, the experimenter asked them to respond to the questionnaire as if they were someone who, in order to take part in the experiment, had had to stop smoking until the following noon.

The post-experimental questionnaire included the question relating to the difficulty of abstinence:

1 Please estimate how difficult it will be for you not to smoke until tomorrow afternoon. The subjects indicated their response on the same 11-point scale that had been used in the pre-experimental questionnaire.

Results
The results are presented in table 5.5.

The main dependent variable corresponds to the difference between the ratings provided by the subjects at the pre- and post-experimental stages.

Table 5.5. Effect of double commitment (to abstinence from smoking and to counter- attitudinal role-playing) on the evaluation of the difficulty of abstinence.

	Difficulty
Double compliance (abstinence and counterattitudinal role)	$-2 \cdot 33$
Single compliance (abstinence)	$1 \cdot 00$
Single compliance (counterattitudinal role)	$0 \cdot 46$
Control condition	$3 \cdot 46$

Notes: The figures represent the mean of the differences between the pre- and post- experimental ratings ($n = 15$ in each condition). The higher the positive figures, the more difficult abstinence was judged to be. In contrast, the higher the negative figures, the easier it was judged to be.

As expected, it is the subjects in the double forced compliance condition who find abstinence easiest. This condition differs significantly from the single compliance condition in which the subjects are required to go without smoking ($F = 6 \cdot 57$, $p < 0 \cdot 025$), as well as from the condition in which they have to play a counterattitudinal role (F = 5·22, $p < 0.05$). There is no significant difference between the two single compliance conditions. We also observe that, as expected, the three dissonant conditions (the double compliance condition and the two single compliance conditions) differ significantly from the non-dissonant condition, the subjects of which find abstinence more difficult: F = 13·79, $p < 0.001$; F = 4·32, $p < 0.05$ and F = 5·01, $p < 0.05$ with reference to the double compliance condition, the single compliance condition of *abstinence* and the single compliance condition of *counterattitudinal role-playing*, respectively.

A useful distinction

Thus, in situations of double forced compliance that mobilize two counter-attitudinal or countermotivational behaviours (case 1) it is important to distinguish between two types of situation: situations in which the two behaviours both imply a high degree of commitment for the subject, as was the case in the last experiment, and situations in which only one of these behaviours implies such commitment, as in experiments 18, 20 and 21. In situations where both behaviours require a high level of commitment, dissonance is greater after both behaviours have been performed than after the production of either one of them. In contrast, in situations where only one behaviour implies the subject's commitment, the opposite effect is observed. This can be explained by the necessity of calculating two dissonance ratios in the first type of situation, one referring to the first behaviour and the other referring to the second, each behaviour having the status of a generative cognition. In contrast, we need establish only one dissonance ratio in the second type of situation since only the representation of the behaviour which implies the greatest commitment on the part of the subject acts as the generative cognition. Provided that the second behaviour (which implies less commitment) is consistent with the first — and cannot therefore be a generative cognition — then it is theoretically logical for its production to reduce the total amount of dissonance.

Results obtained in a recent experiment (Joule and Azdia, 1994) support this reasoning. In this experiment subjects (students) produced two behaviours which were in contradiction with their attitude A but which were consistent with one another (case 1). Behaviour B1 consisted of writing an essay in favour of the selection of degree students whereas B2 consisted of making a tape recording of a speech also in favour of degree selection. In one condition, as in experiments 20, 21, and 22, the first behaviour aroused a considerable degree of commitment (free choice, non-anonymity, act with consequences) while the second was much less committing (anonymous act without consequences). In another condition, similar this time to experiment 22, both behaviours implied a high level of commitment. Therefore, in the first condition only the representation of the first behaviour has the status of a generative cognition, whereas in the second condition both be-haviours have this status. On the basis of the theoretical option defended above, we clearly expected the total amount of dissonance to be lower following the production of a second behaviour implying a low level of commitment. In contrast, we expected the total amount of dissonance to rise following the production of a second behaviour which required a high degree of commitment. The results confirm these expectations. The subjects exhibited less attitude change (towards a more pro-selection position) after producing a second behaviour which implied less commitment than the first behaviour. In contrast, greater attitude change was observed when the second behaviour required high commitment. This experiment therefore confirms the results of our experiments 18, 20 and 21, in which only one of the behaviours demands a high level of commitment, and experiment 22 in which both behaviours are highly committing.

Taken as a whole, the experiments reported in this chapter lead us to two new conclusions.

Conclusion 5 In situations of double forced compliance involving one counterattitudinal or countermotivational behaviour which requires a high degree of commitment on the part of the subject and one counterattitudinal or countermotivational behaviour which requires a low level of commitment, we consider that only the representation of the highly committing behaviour has the status of a generative cognition. Consequently, only one dissonance ratio is calculated.
Consequence If the two behaviours are consistent with one another then the production of the weakly committing behaviour will provide a new consistency and will therefore reduce the total amount of dissonance.

Conclusion 6 In situations of double forced compliance involving two counterattitudinal or countermotivational behaviours which require a high degree of commitment on the part of the subject, we consider that the representation of each of the behaviours has the status of a generative cognition. Consequently, two dissonance ratios must be calculated, just as if the subject were placed in two situations of single compliance.
Consequence The total amount of dissonance will be greater when both behaviours are produced than when only one of them is produced (provided that the two behaviours are consistent with one another).

Double forced compliance and the radical conception of dissonance theory

The radical conception of dissonance theory (Beauvois and Joule, 1981, Joule, 1986b) predates research into the double forced compliance paradigm. As has been shown, this conception was developed in order to reply to some of the criticisms levelled at Festinger's theory and, in particular, to design much needed tests of the alternative dissonance/self-perception theories (Bem, 1972). We should like to conclude this chapter by showing that this radical conception loses none of its relevance when applied to the double compliance paradigm, in particular when, as was the case in experiments 18, 19, 20 and 21, there is only a single generative cognition.

The proposition that is most characteristic of this radical conception is the idea that the aim of the dissonance reduction process is not to eliminate every cognitive inconsistency but simply to eliminate those inconsistent relations that involve the generative cognition. In other words, the only relations that are taken into account in the calculation of the dissonance ratio are those obtaining between the generative cognition and cognitions which are relevant to it. As we have constantly emphasized, this means that the relations between the relevant cognitions themselves (whether consistent, inconsistent or neutral) are of little importance, since they do not affect the total amount of dissonance (see chapter 2).

The results yielded by the first four experiments presented in this chapter lend support to this proposition. After performing a boring task (behaviour B1), the subjects of experiment 21 were led to present it positively (behaviour B2). Given that the performance of a dull task (behaviour B1) introduces a relation of inconsistency with the subject's attitude A towards this task, one might be tempted to think that someone who had produced both behaviours B1 and B2 would have more dissonance to reduce than someone who had only produced behaviour B2. However, the experiment shows the opposite to be the case. It must therefore be accepted that the relation between B1 (the behaviour which implies less commitment on the part of the subject) and A should not be taken into account in the calculation of the dissonance ratio.

In experiment 19, after the subjects had completed the tedious task (behaviour B1) they were called on to present it negatively (behaviour B2). Since behaviour B2 is consistent with attitude A we might conclude that a subject who had declared the task to be boring would have less dissonance to reduce than one who had made no such statement. Moreover, this prediction agrees with common sense in that we might think that subjects who have had the chance to express their own opinion by stating that the task they have just performed was boring would actually find it more boring than someone who had not been obliged to perform this task. This prediction also conforms to Janis and Gilmore's (1965) theory of self-persuasion, which supposes that subjects persuade themselves when presenting an argument. Again, the results contradict this expectation. In fact, the subjects who stated the task to be tedious found it more interesting than those who did not make this statement. It should therefore be clear that the relation between B2 (the behaviour implying the least commitment on the part of the subjects) and A should not be taken into account in the calculation of the dissonance ratio.

If we turn to experiment 21, we remember that, after deciding not to smoke (behaviour B1), the subjects had to write an essay either against (behaviour B2) or in favour of (behaviour B'2) smoking. In this case, B2 is inconsistent with A, which corresponds to the subjects' attitude towards smoking, whereas B'2 is consistent with A. This might lead to the conclusion that producing B2 would increase the level of dissonance initially aroused by the decision to refrain from smoking and that, in contrast, the production of B′2 would reduce it. Yet again, the experimental results contradict this conclusion and again it must be accepted that the relations between B2 and A, on the one hand, and B′2 and A, on the other, should be omitted from the calculation of the dissonance ratio.

The predictive capabilities of the radical conception of dissonance theory thus continue to function well in situations of double forced compliance. In such situations, as in situations of single forced compliance, it is therefore important to distinguish between relations of inconsistency or consistency involving one (or more) generative cognition and relations of inconsistency or consistency which do not involve this or these cognitions. As hypothesized by the radical conception of dissonance theory — and in contrast to the predictions of a lax conception of dissonance theory — only the first type of relation is involved in the cognitive dynamic which orients the dissonance reduction process and determines its magnitude.

Double compliance: alternative theories

We have already pointed out that it would be very difficult to reinterpret the results obtained in the first four experiments of this chapter, that is to say experiments in which one of the behaviours implies a greater degree of commitment than the other, in terms of the theories which rival cognitive dissonance theory. Our results cannot be explained either by Bem's theory or by the theories of self-presentation or impression management, or indeed by Nuttin's (1975) model of response contagion, to mention only the most famous reinterpretations.

Let us briefly review the results obtained in experiments 18, 19 and 20. In experiments 18 and 20 it is difficult to understand how a subject who has performed a tedious task and then declared that it is interesting can infer that this task is less enjoyable than someone who has performed the same task but has made no presentation of it. On the contrary, presenting the task in a positive light should lead subjects to infer that it is actually more enjoyable than they thought before they presented it. Similarly, in experiments 19 and 20 it is difficult to see how a subject who has performed a genuinely tedious task and then declared it to be boring could infer that this task is more interesting than someone who has performed the same task but has made no presentation of it. Instead, a negative presentation should lead subjects to infer that the task is truly tedious. This inference will clearly not be available to someone who did not make such a presentation.

It is equally difficult to account for the results obtained in experiments 18, 19 and 20 in terms of any of the theories of the self or the model of response contagion. We fail to see how finding less enjoyment in a task which you have just said to be interesting or, alternatively, finding more enjoyment in a task which you have claimed to be tedious can serve the interests of the self or indicate the presence of a response contagion process.

Finally, if we turn to the results provided by experiment 21, we see that they, too, are incapable of reinterpretation in terms of these theories. If we adopt the perspective of self-perception theory, we fail to see why a subject who has decided to refrain from smoking should, after writing an anti-smoking essay, infer that abstinence is more difficult than a subject who has written a pro-smoking text after agreeing to the same abstinent behaviour. If we approach the results from the standpoint of self-presentation and related theories, we again fail to understand how, for a subject who has decided to refrain from smoking, finding this abstinence more difficult after developing an anti-smoking argument or finding it easier after arguing in favour of smoking can help to convey a better self-image to others or can constitute a defence process aimed at preserving self-integrity. Moreover, we might ask whether in experimental situations of abstinence (from drink, food, smoking and so on) the problematic behaviour really constitutes a threat to self-integrity or to the impression that one makes on others. In fact, it would be possible to argue for the opposite position and suggest that the problematic behaviour which requires rationalization is actually more self-affirmative than is its obverse (refusal of abstinence) which, being unproblematic, does not need to be rationalized. Where would an author like Stice (1992) see the scope for guilt in the situation of a subject who, in the cause of science, has agreed to an act which would generally be considered to be courageous and intelligent, namely to stop smoking? Nevertheless, as dissonance theory predicts, this act is indeed rationalized.

Like the forced compliance effects reported in the first part of this work, the effects of double forced compliance presented in this chapter provide further support for the radical conception of dissonance theory and reveal the limitations of the alternative theories.

The final two chapters of this work will concentrate on another field of research which is again specific to the radical conception of dissonance theory. This involves the study of a new mode of dissonance reduction: *act rationalization*.

Notes

1   An anecdote will convince us of the relevance of the first behaviour. A mother who wants her child to eat an unpleasant stew is not satisfied with saying 'it's nice' (behaviour B2). To improve her chances of being believed, she does not hesitate to try the stew herself (behaviour B1). She does so because, for her (and, she thinks, for her child), B1 and B2 fit well. This point can be generalized. A number of past and current researchers into dissonance theory have stated that they do not understand how performing a boring task at the experimenter's request can arouse dissonance or how the fact of having performed this task is consistent with the fact of saying that it is interesting (see, in particular, Schönbach, 1993). We have no response to such researchers apart from to point to

the confirmation of our predictions (including those validated in experiments 1, 2, 3). As for the question of implication, it seems to us that the evidence indicates that 'this task is boring' implies 'I do not do it'. It is true that the tedious task paradigm has little recourse to the key concepts of recent revisions of Festinger's theory (concepts of personal responsibility or aversive consequences). This may explain the problems experienced by the researchers mentioned above.

2   In effect, if I find a task boring and manage to do it all the same then my cognitive universe will contain two discordant elements just like someone who is persuaded to eat a meal he does not like (see Brehm, 1959).

3   Using this strategy, which will be described later (see chapter 6), almost all of the subjects (95 per cent) immediately agreed to go without smoking for 18 hours.

4   While the subjects thought that they really had to stop smoking for 18 hours at the point when the post-experimental measurements were taken, they were, once these measurements had been completed, informed that they were in fact free to carry on smoking.

5   We should point out that the role-playing behaviour was refused as often as the behaviour which consisted of refraining from smoking (5 per cent refusals for each behaviour).

Chapter 6

When a behaviour is rationalized by a new behaviour

In the first part of this work we set out a number of the premises on which the radical theory of dissonance is based. In doing so we remained faithful to the core theory of 1957 and expanded on a number of the theoretical and experimental implications which had hitherto been neglected. In the final two chapters we shall insist on a fundamental assumption of the 1957 theory: the state of dissonance is a drive state. Since 1957, this assumption has given rise to numerous studies. Today these are sufficiently well documented for us not to have to dwell for long on them here (Kiesler and Pallack, 1976, Wicklund and Brehm, 1976, chapter 6, Fazio and Cooper, 1983, Joule, 1987a). Most importantly, it has been shown that dissonance produces familiar drive effects in learning situations: it heightens the general level of activity by provoking the emission of dominant responses; it therefore facilitates non-competitive learning and hinders competitive learning. It has also been shown that dissonance can compete with biological drives (hunger, thirst, pain and so on) and may be accompanied by a modification of certain physiological responses (electrodermal activity in particular) which testify to a state of tension. Finally, it has been shown that dissonance arousal is an undifferentiated state which, like other affects, may give rise to misattribution errors.

However, it is our opinion that one direct implication of Festinger's assumption concerning the motivational properties of dissonance has not yet been shown the attention it merits. This is no doubt because it is liable to run counter to the representations of consistency which have so seriously impaired the understanding of dissonance theory. This implication can be formulated as follows: the adoption of one mode of reducing the drive tension caused by commitment to a problematic act reduces the probability that another mode of reducing this same tension will be observed.

Two paths for rationalizing a problematic behaviour

We know that when subjects commit themselves to a problematic behaviour (one which contradicts their attitudes or motivations), they have to rationalize it. We have defined *rationalization* as a post-behavioural process which renders the problematic behaviour less problematic for the subject who produced it. In effect, subjects realign their cognitions after the production of the behaviour in a way that makes them as predictive as possible of this behaviour. Alongside this classic form of rationalization, which we might term *cognitive rationalization*, which in the type of experiment traditionally conducted in this field is a consequence of the algebraic properties of the dissonance ratio, we have been persuaded of the possibility of another form of rationalization, namely *act rationalization* (Joule, 1986b, Beauvois, Joule and Brunetti, 1993). We have given this name to this new type of rationalization because the problematic behaviour which underlies the generative cognition is rationalized (and thereby rendered less problematic) by the production of a new behaviour rather than by the cognitive realignment which has been the classic object of investigation by dissonance theorists.

We have been led to hypothesize such a process to account for a number of rather puzzling results. These results were obtained in an experiment (Joule, 1986b) which implemented a *gearing situation* (see Joule and Beauvois, 1987, Joule, Mugny and Pérez, 1988, Joule, Fointiat, Pasquier, Mugny, 1991), that is a situation which united a number of compliance procedures (foot-in-the-door: Freedman and Fraser, 1966, low-ball: Cialdini, Basset, Cacioppo and Miller, 1978). In this situation, smokers who had just made the decision to stop smoking for 18 hours showed little resistance in then agreeing to refrain from smoking for a period of 3 days. However, this was not the case with smokers who were allowed time between the decision to go without smoking for 18 hours and the decision to abstain for 3 days.

It might be thought that the first set of subjects, unlike the second set, had lacked the time — and had therefore been unable — to perform the cognitive rationalization of their agreement to go without smoking for 18 hours at the point at which they were asked to abstain from smoking for 3 days. It is therefore not impossible that agreeing to go without smoking for 3 days allows subjects to rationalize the act of abstaining for 18 hours. If this is so, then the agreement to perform a more costly act (3 days' abstinence from smoking) in effect makes the agreement to perform a less costly act (18 hours without smoking) less problematic.

If this is the case, then there are two possible alternative ways of rationalizing a problematic act: a cognitive rationalization, which has been studied in the classic situations of forced compliance and which we have focused on in the preceding chapters, as well as a behavioural rationalization, which has hitherto been ignored by researchers and which is most easily studied in gearing situations.

The experiments presented in this chapter were designed to test this hypothesis.

First, however, let us examine the original experiment conducted by Joule (1986b).

Act rationalization: Joule's original experiment (1986b)

It appears to us to be necessary at this point to present a detailed description of the gearing situation used in this research, especially because the gearing procedures described in the following are directly derived from it.

Recruiting the subjects

The task of the recruiter was to approach male and female students who were alone and smoking. After determining whether or not their daily tobacco consumption exceeded 15 cigarettes, he asked them to take part in a paid experiment: 'At the moment, I have the job of recruiting smokers to take part in some research into concentration. It would take you about an hour and you would be paid 50 francs. The research is due to take place in a fortnight. Would you be interested?' The recruiter asked the volunteers to complete and sign an application form. In fact, this was a questionnaire designed to increase the subject's prior commitment (see Kiesler, 1971).

Inviting the subjects

One week later, the experimenter contacted the subjects by telephone. He explained to them that the experiment would take place in two stages and that they would therefore have to come to the laboratory twice, once at six in the evening (for approximately three-quarters of an hour) and a second time the next day between noon and two in the afternoon (for approximately a quarter of an hour). He then made two appointments with the subjects.

Obtaining 18 hours' abstinence from smoking

The subjects were first induced to refrain from smoking for 18 hours using the low-ball/*fait accompli* technique (Joule, 1987b).

It was only when they arrived at the laboratory that the subjects learned: (1) that they were only to be paid 30 francs and, more importantly, (2) that if they wanted to take part in the research they would have to stop smoking immediately. The experimenter addressed the subject as follows:

First of all, I would like to thank you for coming here. My name is Mister X and I am responsible for the research for which you were recruited. I'm going to tell you just what it involves. First, though, I must tell you that I can't pay you 50 francs as I expected, but only 30 francs... the current economy drive means that the budgets of pretty well all the research programmes have been cut... We are investigating concentration levels in smokers. More precisely, we're looking at the effects of not smoking for a short time (actually 18 hours) on concentration and that's why we've asked you to come to the laboratory twice at an interval of 18 hours, that is from now until noon tomorrow (which is the time when, normally speaking, you should come back to see us at the laboratory). What we want to do is compare your performance in some concentration tests before and after you stop smoking. If you agree to take part in this research, you mustn't smoke a single cigarette until tomorrow so that we can compare the results you turn in today with tomorrow's results. Of course, you're not absolutely bound to take part in this research. Let me remind you that the payment is 30 francs. You must consider yourself entirely free to accept or refuse. It's up to you.

The subjects who agreed to take part were given the chance to smoke a final cigarette and were then immediately asked to sign an undertaking not to smoke until the following noon. This signed undertaking contained the words:

I, the undersigned, promise not to smoke from ... until my return to the laboratory tomorrow at ...

We should point out immediately that the low-ball/*fait accompli* technique (see Joule, 1987b) used to induce the subjects to go without smoking until the following noon was so effective that almost all the interviewees (95 per cent) agreed to abstain for a period of 18 hours.

The final request: three days' abstinence from smoking

After the subjects had performed the concentration tests which had been announced to them, the experimenter gave them the opportunity to take part in a new piece of research which required 3 consecutive days' abstinence from smoking. This time the experimenter phrased his request as follows:

Before you leave the laboratory, I would like to give you some information which might be of interest to you. I'm currently looking for smokers to take part in some more research which is actually part of the same programme but which will mean you have to stop smoking for

for three days. I can pay you 150 francs for it, but it is absolutely essential that you don't smoke a single cigarette during the three days of the experiment. You don't spend much time in the laboratory: 2 hours in all. In fact, you have to come to the laboratory four times: the first time before you stop smoking, then 1 day after, 2 days after and, finally, 3 days after, when the no-smoking period finished so that you can take some concentration tests. This research will take place in a fortnight. If you're interested, I would like you to fill in an application form before you leave. It's up to you to decide whether you want to take part.

In all, 91·67 per cent of the subjects accepted.

A *new rationalized process*

To make sense of this result, let us put ourselves briefly in the position of these subjects.

A fortnight after they have applied to take part in a paid experiment, a researcher telephones them to invite them to the laboratory. On arriving there at the agreed time they are surprised to learn that the payment they will receive will not be the promised 50 francs but only 30 francs and that if they are to take part in the research they must stop smoking immediately and continue to abstain for a period of 18 hours. Certainly, the experimenter tells them they are free to agree or refuse to take part, but he makes sure that they only have a few moments to make their decision. In this situation of *fait accompli*, they agree. Given that under different circumstances[1] they might have refused to take part, we may well imagine that once they had made their decision, these subjects then asked themselves certain questions concerning its justification: 'I have decided not to smoke at all until tomorrow . . . Have I done the right thing or not?' If, before they have had time to answer this question satisfactorily (cognitive rationalizat-ion), the experimenter offers them the opportunity to make their decision appear 'reasonable' by performing an act which involves the same type of behaviour (act rationalization), it is quite understandable that they should take advantage of it. It is not impossible that the request to refrain from smoking for 3 days, coming at the point it did, represented just such an opportunity for the subjects. In fact, to agree voluntarily to take part in an experiment which requires 3 days' abstinence is a way for them to make the agreement, just exacted from them, to stop smoking for 18 hours appear logical, natural, rational, unproblematic; if I am able to (or volunteer to) stop smoking for 3 days, I am most certainly able to (or can volunteer to) stop smoking for 18 hours.

However, if this reasoning, which is based on the concept of act rationalization, is correct, then the subjects should be less inclined to accept the request to refrain from smoking for 3 days if this is proposed later, that is after they have been allowed the time required for the cognitive rationalization of their decision to abstain from smoking for 18 hours (and thus 'to cope' with this decision). The results obtained by Joule (1986b) support this reasoning. In fact, only 39·13 per cent of the subjects agree to stop smoking for 3 days when this request is made 18 hours after the first request, that is at the end of the initial period of abstinence. Nevertheless, in this case we can explain the drop in the level of acceptance of 3 days of abstinence without resorting to a comparison of interpretations in terms of act rationalization or cognitive rationalization. In fact, this fall can be accounted for within the classic framework of the reinforcement theories. After all, we might quite justifiably argue that in a situation where they are asked to agree to a longer period of abstinence at the moment when they are due to commence a shorter period, the subjects do not know how difficult going without smoking is likely to be for them. In contrast, they are well aware of this difficulty in the situation in which they are asked to agree to a longer period of abstinence at the moment when they finish the shorter period. Here, the period of 18 hours spent without smoking has made then realize the discomfort caused by the lack of tobacco. This explanation is quite adequate to account for the fact that in one case the subjects agree to 3 days' abstinence more readily than in the other.

In contrast, the fall in the level of agreement to abstain for 3 days observed by Joule (1986b) in a different situation is less easy to interpret in such terms. The procedure used in this new situation was identical to that of the standard gearing condition except that, in this case, the subjects were informed during the telephone call giving them their appointment (and thus several days before they arrived at the laboratory): (1) of the reduction in the payment from 50 to 30 francs, and (2) of the necessity to go without smoking for 18 hours. More precisely, the experimenter said:

Hello, I'm telephoning you about the research into smoking which you applied to take part in. Before making an appointment, I must tell you that the payment isn't 50 francs, as announced, but only 30 francs... the current economy drive means that the budgets of pretty well all the research programmes have been cut. I should also tell you that the experiment takes place in two stages. If you are still interested you should come to the laboratory twice, the first time at the end of the afternoon (at 6 o'clock) and a second time the following day (between noon and two in the afternoon). The first visit will take about half-an-hour, three-quarters of an hour at the most, and the second visit will take a quarter of an hour. You've got your diary? Oh! before we arrange a time, I must tell you... In this research we are investigating concentration levels in smokers. In fact, we're looking at the effects of going without smoking on concentration. That's why we've asked you to come to the laboratory twice, so that we can study your concentration on the first day, before you stop smoking, and on the second, after you've stopped. That's why for this research we need people who are willing to give up smoking for an evening... as I've said to you, from six in the afternoon until noon the following day. Of course, you're not absolutely bound to take part in this research. Let me remind you that the payment is 30 francs. You must consider yourself entirely free to accept or refuse. It's up to you.

The procedure used to obtain compliance was therefore not a low-ball/*fait accompli* but a classic low-ball approach.

In this situation, the subjects therefore went to the laboratory knowing that they would have to go without cigarettes for 18 hours for a payment of 30 francs. As might be expected, a self-selection phenomenon was observed (see Joule, 1987b). While almost all the subjects (91·1 per cent) contacted by telephone went to the laboratory in the standard condition, that is before being informed of the inconvenience associated with taking part in the research, the same was not true when they were informed as they were here (only 71 per cent arrived at the laboratory). As one might have expected, there was a higher rate of defection among the subjects who were informed at home by telephone of the necessity of going without smoking for an evening than among those who were confronted with the *fait accompli* in the laboratory. Consequently, it might be thought that it was the subjects who from the outset were less troubled by the idea of going without smoking, or those who were most eager to take part in research which would require them to stop smoking, who turned up at the laboratory fully aware of what was expected of them. The situation we have just described is therefore actually prejudicial to the verification of our hypothesis. And yet, the hypothesis was verified.

In fact, when, following completion of the concentration tests the experimenter asked the subjects, as in the standard situation, whether they would like to take part in a new piece of research requiring 3 days' abstinence from smoking, the level of acceptance was only 47·62 per cent. This time the final request was made at the moment when the subjects started the 18-hour period of abstinence and were therefore unaware of the discomfort of going without smoking. It is, therefore, no longer possible to explain the fall in the level of agreement to abstain from tobacco for 3 days (from 91·67 per cent to 47·62 per cent) in terms of the theories of reinforcement. However, an explanation based on the hypothesis of the alternative character of the cognitive and behavioural methods of dissonance reduction remains possible.

It goes without saying that in the situation in which they were informed by telephone that they would have to stop smoking for 18 hours, the subjects had more than enough time (there was an interval of at least 24 hours between the decision to stop smoking for 18 hours and the decision to abstain for 3 days) to find good reasons for agreeing to this period of abstinence: to help a researcher, to test how dependent they are on tobacco, to take the chance to 'give their lungs an airing', to take part in a scientific experiment and so on. Since the cognitive rationalization process had had time to work, we might well expect much of the tension generated by the commitment to go without smoking for 18 hours to have been reduced by the time the subjects were asked to stop smoking for 3 days. If, as we hypothesize, the cognitive and behavioural paths of dissonance reduction do indeed function as alternatives, we can understand why those subjects who were able to make use of the cognitive path were later less inclined to follow the behavioural path than the subjects of the standard condition to whom the cognitive path was not available. In fact, not only were the subjects in the standard condition allowed very little time between their decision to stop smoking for 18 hours and the moment when they were asked to abstain for 3 days (about a quarter of an hour) but, in addition, the concentration tests that they were required to perform during this interval imposed a heavy cognitive burden which deprived them of the intellectual resources necessary for cognitive rationalization. In our opinion, this explains their readiness to adopt the path of act rationalization by agreeing to a new period of abstinence from smoking.

To summarize, this experiment shows that smokers are ready to agree to go without smoking for 3 days provided that the request is made just after they have taken the decision to stop smoking for an 18-hour period (standard condition), but that they are much less likely to do this if they are allowed time between the decision to abstain for 18 hours and the decision relating to the 3-day abstinence. We have considered the possibility that agreeing to stop smoking for 3 days, just after agreeing to stop for 18 hours, may help the subjects to rationalize their first decision. In effect, a very costly act (3 days without cigarettes) may render a less costly act (18 hours without smoking) less problematic. If subjects in the other conditions felt less need to rationalize by means of the behavioural path, it is, we have suggested, because they have been allowed the time to rationalize using the cognitive path. It is for this reason that we have come to support the hypothesis of the alternative character of the cognitive and behavioural paths of reducing the dissonance induced by commitment to a problematic act. This hypothesis is simply one of the consequences of Festinger's assumption, which we feel has been ignored by researchers for far too long, that the state of dissonance possesses all the properties of a drive state. We know that someone who is thirsty and who slakes his thirst by drinking water will subsequently drink less beer than someone who immediately slakes his thirst with beer. If dissonance is indeed a drive state, it is logical to expect that subjects who have already reduced their motivational tension by adopting reduction path A will, immediately afterwards, be less inclined to adopt path B of reducing the same tension than other subjects who make direct use of path B.

As we shall now see, this hypothesis of the alternative nature of the cognitive path (cognitive rationalization) and behavioural path (behavioural rationalization) of dissonance reduction has received substantial empirical support. In the light of the data which are available, it would appear that act rationalization is hindered when cognitive rationalization is promoted and, in contrast, that it is promoted when cognitive rationalization is blocked.

Cognitive rationalization and act rationalization: empirical evidence

The objective of a first set of experiments was to demonstrate that promoting cognitive rationalization makes it less likely that subjects will commit themselves to a more costly act. From our viewpoint, this means that act rationalization is less likely to occur.

Experiment 23. The effect of justifying a short abstinence from smoking on the acceptance of a longer period of abstinence

Experiment 23 (Beauvois, Joule and Brunetti, experiment 1, 1993) was conceived first as a replication of the most important results obtained by Joule (1986b). In the original experiment, the drive associated with dissonance is accompanied by another motivation, namely to earn money. The reader will remember that the subjects attended the first experiment voluntarily, in the belief that they were to be paid 50 francs. They were then informed that the actual payment would only be 30 francs and that they had the opportunity of earning a further 150 francs if they took part in a new experiment. Even if the motivation of the money has the same effect in the different conditions, it still makes a truly 'pure' study of the arousal effects resulting from dissonance impossible. We therefore considered it desirable to test our hypothesis of the alternative character of the cognitive and behavioural modes of rationalization in a context in which money has no role to play either at the moment when the short period of abstinence is requested or when the longer period is proposed. The second, and perhaps most important, reason for designing experiment 23 was to test more directly the inhibitory effect of cognitive rationalization on act rationalization. The experiment again involves smoking subjects who are committed to an 18-hour period of abstinence from smoking. As in Joule's experiment (1986b), some of the subjects arrived at the laboratory ignorant of the fact that they would have to stop smoking immediately and abstain for 18 hours, while other subjects were aware of this. However, in the new experiment, certain subjects had to provide a written justification for their agreement to stop smoking whereas others did not. All the subjects were then offered the chance to take part in a later experiment which required a more extended period of abstinence (6 days). The subjects in the control group were asked immediately if they would agree to the longer period of abstinence.

We expected that the subjects who arrived at the laboratory knowing that they would have to go without smoking for 18 hours and who had therefore had the time to perform cognitive rationalization would be less likely than the unaware subjects to agree to refrain from smoking for 6 days. We also expected that justifying the agreement to the first period of abstinence in cases where the subjects had arrived at the laboratory without knowing that they would have to stop smoking would reduce the likelihood of these subjects agreeing to the second period of abstinence. Since justification promotes cognitive rationalization, these subjects should feel less need to perform act rationalization.

Subjects
The subjects consisted of science students (male and female) at the Université de Provence (Marseille, France), aged between 19 and 23 and smoking more than 15 cigarettes a day.

Procedure
The subjects were seen separately (individual pass).

In the morning, the experimenter contacted a number of students who were smoking alone on the university campus. He asked those who reported smoking more than 15 cigarettes a day to take part in an unpaid experiment, relating to concentration levels in smokers, which was described as taking place in two stages separated by an interval of 18 hours. He then made an appointment with the subjects who agreed for late afternoon of the same day. It was at this point that the first independent variable was manipulated. Once the appointment had been arranged, the experimenter informed half of the subjects that they would have to stop smoking between the two stages of the experiment (*informed condition*). The subjects were therefore exposed to the classic low-ball technique (Cialdini, Basset, Cacioppo and Miller, 1978). The remaining subjects did not receive this information and therefore arrived at the laboratory unaware of the abstinent behaviour that was expected of them (*uninformed condition*).

The subjects arrived singly at the laboratory. There, they were either reminded (*informed condition*) or were told for the first time (*uninformed condition*) that they would have to stop smoking immediately and refrain from cigarettes for a period of 18 hours. The subjects who had not been warned of the necessity of going without smoking were told that they were free to accept or refuse. We know that very few subjects refuse in the face of this type of compliance procedure (low-ball/*fait accompli*, see Joule, 1987b). The subjects then had to perform a first dummy task (paper-and-pencil tests requiring concentration and speed) which lasted 5 minutes. At this point, the second independent variable was manipulated. Half of the subjects were then asked to write down the reasons which had led them to agree to give up smoking for 18 hours (*justified condition*); the other subjects were not asked to provide any such reasons (*unjustified condition*). All the subjects then performed a second dummy task (paper-and-pencil tests similar in nature to the first set). When they had completed this task, they were asked by the experimenter to take part in a second, unpaid experiment, due to take place one month later, which would require them to go without smoking for 6 consecutive days. The volunteers were invited to fill in and sign an application form. The subjects of the control condition were not submitted to the gearing procedure and were immediately asked to give up cigarettes for 6 days.

Results
The percentage of subjects who voluntarily agreed to give up smoking for 6 days in each experimental condition is specified in table 6.1.

Table 6.1. The effect of justifying a short abstinence from smoking on the acceptance of a longer period of abstinence.

informed		
justified (G1)	62.5%	(15/23)
unjustified (G2)	47.8%	(11/23)
uninformed		
justified (G3)	26.1%	(6/23)
unjustified (G4)	82.6%	(19/23)
control	21.7%	(5/23)

Notes: Percentage of subjects agreeing to abstain from smoking for six days after agreeing to a period of abstinence of 18 hours. The actual numbers are given in parentheses.

We can make two comparisons which are directly related to our general hypothesis. The first is between the two groups in the unjustified condition (groups G2 and G4). It appears that being allowed time to perform the cognitive rationalization of the agreement to the first period of abstinence significantly reduces the probability of acceptance of the second ($\chi^2 = 6 \cdot 13$, $p < 0 \cdot 02$). This effect is all the more significant in view of the fact that a self-selection process was operative in group G2, with only 57 per cent of the informed subjects actually coming to the laboratory (compared with 80 per cent of the uninformed subjects). These subjects were therefore the ones who were the least hostile to the idea of going without smoking. Despite this, the level of agreement to the 6-day period of abstinence found in this group was less than that observed in the subjects who, confronted by the *fait accompli*, did not have the time to perform the cognitive rationalization of the decision to deprive themselves of smoking for 18 hours which had just been extracted from them.

The second comparison involves the two uninformed groups (groups G3 and G4). It appears that the requirement to provide a justification for the first period of abstinence significantly reduces the probability that the second period will be accepted ($\chi^2 = 14 \cdot 8$, $p < 0 \cdot 001$). Again, it can be seen that cognitive rationalization reduces the probability of a renewed behavioural commitment to the point where group G3 (uninformed/justified), although subjected to the gearing procedure no longer differs from the control group.

These two comparisons lead us to the same conclusion: irrespective of whether subjects have the time to find their own justifications before coming to the laboratory or whether they are led to seek justifications as part of the experimental procedure, the fact of justifying a costly act (18 hours' abstinence) considerably reduces the probability that the subjects will agree to a behaviour which is more costly still (6 days' abstinence). In contrast, as in Joule's experiment (1986b), it is the subjects who have not had the chance to perform the cognitive rationalization of their first behaviour (because of the limited time available and because of the cognitive burden imposed on them during this period) who are readiest to agree to the second.

This effect of the subjects' verbalization of the reasons justifying the performance of a costly act has been replicated in a number of experiments. We only intend to present one of them here. This experiment mobilized a different countermotivational behaviour (drinking alcohol). In it the subjects were led to do something they did not want to do (drink wine) while in experiment 23 they were led to refrain from doing something they wanted to do (smoke). This new experiment will help us identify more accurately the conditions necessary for the observation of the effect of act rationalization.

We have noted that certain characteristics of the experimental situation are necessary for dissonance arousal and generate cognitions of commitment. Researchers are united in agreeing on the particular importance of the feeling of freedom. In this work (see chapter 3) we have emphasized the importance of the statement of freedom made by the experimenter. This statement helps commit the subject to the compliant behaviour. If, therefore, the statement of freedom is a necessary condition for commitment and, consequently, for dissonance arousal, then subjects who have not been declared free should not feel the need to perform act rationalization in a gearing situation, just as they should not feel the need to perform cognitive rationalization in classic forced compliance situations. If the effect found in experiment 23 were not observed in uncommitted subjects, this would constitute an important argument in support of the value of the concept of act rationalization.

Experiment 24 was designed to test this hypothesis.

Experiment 24. Effect of justifying drinking 20 centilitres of wine on the agreement to drink 30 centilitres
On arriving at the laboratory, the subjects of experiment 24 (Joule and Fointiat, experiment 1, 1992) were induced to drink a glass of wine. The authors of this experiment had already ascertained that even in Provence drinking a glass of wine early in the morning constituted a countermotivational act for young women. Certain subjects were induced to do this in a free-choice condition, whereas the others produced the behaviour in a no-choice condition. Moreover, as in experiment 23, some of the subjects had to produce a written justification of their agreement, while the others did not. Just before drinking the glass, the subjects were asked to take part in a later, unpaid experiment requiring them to drink one-and-a-half glasses of wine.

If the effect of act rationalization is indeed to permit the reduction of the dissonance motivation aroused by the performance of a problematic behaviour, it should only appear under circumstances where this motivation is aroused, that is only in those subjects who have been declared free to agree or refuse to drink a glass of wine. Since the no-choice situations are unable to arouse dissonance motivation, there is no reason why the act rationalization process should be observed. We therefore expected the level of agreement to the request to drink one-and-a-half glasses of wine to be higher in the free choice than in the no-choice condition. Moreover, we hypothesized that when, and only when, dissonance motivation is aroused (free-choice situation), the subjects who had to provide justifications for drinking a glass of wine (cognitive rationalization) would be less inclined than the subjects who provided no justification to agree to drink a larger amount.

Subjects
The subjects consisted of female literature students, aged between 20 and 23, at the University de Provence (Aix-en-Provence, France).

Procedure
The experiment comprised four experimental situations and one control situation. The subjects were seen separately (individual pass).

The subjects were recruited on the university campus in order to take part in an unpaid psychology experiment. They arrived at the laboratory unaware that the experiment required them to drink a glass of wine. The experimenter explained to the subjects that he was involved in research investigating the effect of alcohol on concentration and that in order to take part they would have to drink a glass of wine (20 centilitres) between two concentration tests. At this point, the first independent variable was manipulated, with half of the subjects being induced to take part in the experiment in a context of free-choice and the other half in a no-choice context. In the free choice condition the experimenter made the subjects' freedom to refuse to take part in the experiment extremely clear: 'I understand perfectly well that you might want to refuse . . .it's up to you.' In contrast, the subjects in the no-choice condition received no such opportunity: 'That's how the experiment will be conducted . . .now that you know what you have to do, we'll move on to the first test.'

It was after this first test, and just before the wine was due to be drunk, that the second independent variable was manipulated. Half of the subjects were asked to write down the reasons that had led them to take part in the experiment (justified condition) while the other half were not (unjustified condition). In the latter case, the subjects were occupied for an equivalent period by an irrelevant task (completing a questionnaire on university life). Finally, the experimenter asked all the subjects if they would like to take part in a future piece of research. This research, scheduled for 1 week later, would require the subjects to drink one-and-a-half glasses of wine (30 centilitres). The subjects who agreed to take part were asked to give the experimenter their name and telephone number.

In the control condition, the subjects were immediately asked to take part in the second piece of research.

Results
First, we should point out that almost all of the subjects who came to the laboratory took part in the experiment. The average level of defection did not exceed 5 per cent.

We should also point out that being informed of the requirement to drink a glass of wine did not cause a higher level of defection among the subjects of the free-choice condition than among those of the no-choice condition.

The percentage of subjects who volunteered to drink 30 centilitres of wine in each condition is given in table 6.2.

As expected, the vast majority of the subjects who, in the unjustified condition, were left free to decide whether or not to take part in the first piece of research agreed to take part in the second. The opposite is true of the subjects who were not free to make this decision. The difference between these two levels is statistically highly significant $\chi^2 = 16\cdot94$, $p < 0\cdot001$. The reader will have noted that despite the fact that they were involved in a gearing situation, the subjects who were not left free to decide whether to take part or not were no more ready to drink 30 centilitres of wine than the subjects in the control condition. Since the function of the process of act rationalization, like that of cognitive rationalization, is to reduce the dissonance aroused by a problematic behaviour, it is understandable that this process does not occur when dissonance has not been aroused.

Table 6.2. Effect of justifying drinking 20 centilitres of wine on the agreement to drink 30 centilitres.

free choice		
justified (G1)	35%	(7/20)
unjustified (G2)	85%	(17/20)
no choice		
justified (G3)	35%	(7/20)
unjustified (G4)	20%	(4/20)
control	20%	(4/20)

Notes: Percentage of subjects agreeing to drink 30 centilitres of wine after agreeing to drink 20. The actual numbers are given in parentheses.

In the free-choice condition we again encounter the effect of justification already observed in experiment 23: that providing justifications for taking part in the initial research significantly reduces the probability that subjects will agree to take part in the second. The fall in the level of agreement is again significant: $\chi^2 = 10\cdot41$, $p = 0\cdot001$.

The results obtained in this experiment therefore support those observed in the preceding one. They again show that the function of the process of act rationalization is to reduce the dissonance aroused by the commitment to a problematic act. It seems that agreeing to a new behaviour which is even more costly than the first takes the place of rationalization and forms a substitute for the cognitive process which could not be mobilized. It is self-evident that the cognition, 'I have agreed to drink 30 centilitres of wine' is consistent with the cognition 'I have agreed to drink 20 centilitres of wine', as in experiment 23 the cognition 'I have decided to stop smoking for 6 days' is consistent with the cognition 'I have agreed to stop smoking for 18 hours.'

In the two preceding experiments we either promoted the process of cognitive rationalization by means of explicit instructions (experiments 23 or 24) or we allowed sufficient time for this process to be implemented (experiment 23). We have seen that, in such cases, the process of act rationalization is impeded. In contrast, the general hypothesis of the alternative character of the cognitive and behavioural rationalization paths leads us to think that blocking the process of cognitive rationalization will promote the process of act rationalization. We tested this hypothesis in a new set of experiments.

Experiment 25. The effect of the upgrading vs. downgrading of a costly act (completing a long questionnaire) on the agreement to a more costly act (receiving an interviewer at home)

In this experiment (Beauvois, Joule and Brunetti, experiment 2, 1993) the problematic behaviours involved are again different: the first consisted of replying to a questionnaire in a supermarket car park; and the second, more costly, behaviour consisted of agreeing to be interviewed at home on the same topic as that dealt with in the questionnaire. Just before making the request designed to elicit the second behaviour, the experimenter either downgraded the first behaviour in order to impair its cognitive rationalization or, alternatively, upgraded it in order to facilitate cognitive rationalization. In a third condition the first behaviour was neither downgraded nor upgraded.

We expected agreement to the second behaviour to be more frequent when the first behaviour had been downgraded and less frequent when it had been upgraded.

Subjects

The subjects consisted of (male and female) customers of a large supermarket in Nancy (France).

Procedure

We shall limit ourselves here to reporting the conditions which are relevant to our argument, that is three experimental conditions and a control condition.

The subjects were seen separately (individual pass).

This time, the compliance procedure used to induce agreement to the first problematic behaviour was not the low-ball/*fait accompli* technique but, instead, a foot-in-the-door strategy. The experimenter used either a classic foot-in-the-door approach (see Freedman and Fraser, 1966) consisting of the preliminary extraction of a simple behaviour (here providing information) or a two-feet-in-the-door technique (see Goldman, Creason and McCall, 1981) which required the preliminary extraction of two simple behaviours (here providing information and then fixing a sticker to the windscreen).

The subjects were contacted next to their vehicles on the car park at the moment when they were preparing to leave the supermarket. In order to avoid implicit selection bias, the experimenter approached only single people who parked in one particular bay. After introducing himself, he asked the subjects if they knew of ARC (a well-known French cancer research organization). Then, if the answer was positive (foot-in-the-door), he immediately asked some of them to reply to a five-page questionnaire on cancer research, pointing out that it would take about 10 minutes to complete (50 per cent acceptance). He asked others to fix an ARC sticker to their windscreen (two-feet-in-the-door) before asking them to reply to the questionnaire (69 per cent agreed to display the sticker and, of them, 89 per cent agreed to respond to the questionnaire).

All of those who agreed to reply to the questionnaire were randomly allocated to one of the three experimental conditions. It was at this point that the first independent variable that is of interest to us was manipulated. In one condition, the experimenter informed the subjects that the results of the questionnaire were very unexpected, that the questions were badly formulated and that it might not even be possible to use the results of the inquiry (negative information). In a second condition, he instead informed them that the questions were very well formulated and that the inquiry was proving to be very useful (positive information). In the third condition, the experimenter provided no information regarding the questionnaire (no information). Finally, just before the subjects filled in the questionnaire, the experimenter asked them if they would agree to his visiting them at home a few days later to conduct an interview lasting about half-an-hour. The subjects who agreed were asked to leave their name, address and telephone number. In the control condition, the experimenter directly asked the subjects who said they knew of the ARC whether they were prepared to be interviewed at home.

Results

The percentage of subjects who provided the experimenter with their name, address and telephone number (foot-in-the-door and two-feet-in-the-door conditions combined) prior to the conduct of an interview at their homes is given in table 6.3.

Table 6.3. The effect of the upgrading vs. downgrading of a costly act (completing a long questionnaire) on the agreement to a more costly act (receiving an interviewer at home).

negative information	39·3%	(48/122)
positive information	13%	(14/107)
no information	25·7%	(28/109)
control	10%	(10/100)

Notes: Percentage of subjects agreeing to be interviewed at home after agreeing to complete a questionnaire. The actual numbers are given in parentheses.

As expected, the level of agreement to be interviewed at home was significantly higher in subjects who received the negative information than in those who received no information: $\chi^2 = 4\cdot86$, $p < 0\cdot05$. The opposite is observed in the subjects who received positive information. Only 13 per cent of these subjects agreed to the interview. This level differs significantly from that obtained in the no-information condition: $\chi^2 = 6\cdot61$, $p < 0\cdot01$. Unlike in the other two experimental conditions, the level of agreement in the positive information condition does not differ significantly from that obtained in the control condition. If we accept that the negative information provided by the experimenter prevents subjects from formulating adequate justifications for their agreement to reply to a questionnaire on a supermarket car park, then we must also accept that cognitive rationalization is impeded in these subjects. In effect, it is very difficult for these subjects to find value in the costly behaviour they have just agreed to perform by saying, for example, that they are helping ARC. If, in contrast, we accept that positive information helps subjects to find adequate justifications for their agreement, we will also accept that cognitive rationalization is facilitated in these subjects since it is clearly much easier for them to invest their behaviour with this value. Such subjects are able to tell themselves that they have helped a good cause. As we have just seen, compared with the no-information condition (standard gearing procedure), the level of agreement to the interview at home increases in the negative information condition and falls in the positive information condition. This experiment, therefore, again reveals the alternative nature of the two paths of rationalization, cognitive and behavioural: blocking the cognitive path promotes recourse to the behavioural path whereas facilitation of the cognitive path impedes the behavioural alternative.

These results have been the object of a very recent replication by Brunetti (1994). In this new experiment, a low-ball technique was used to induce super-market customers to spend 5 minutes in the cold listening to a tape through the headphones of a personal stereo in order to help a local radio station. In one condition this behaviour was downgraded, in another it was upgraded and in the third condition it was neither downgraded nor upgraded. Just before the subjects listened to the tape, the experimenter asked them to agree to listen, still outdoors in the cold, to another recording which was considerably longer than the first (about 20 minutes). It was again observed that negative information increases the level of agreement to a second request while positive information reduces this level.

In experiment 25, like that of Brunetti which we have just evoked, the information likely to block (negative information) or, in contrast, promote (positive information) cognitive rationalization was given to the subjects before they performed the problematic act. In the next two experiments this information was supplied *after* the behaviour had been performed.

Experiment 26. The effect of upgrading vs. downgrading a costly act (abstaining from smoking for 24 hours) on agreement to a more costly one (abstaining for 5 days)

In experiment 26 (Joule, 1993, exp. 1) subjects were induced to refrain from smoking for 24 hours to help the experimenter. At the end of this period of absti-nence the experimenter told them either that this abstinence had been useless to him (negative information condition) or, on the contrary, that it had been very useful (positive information condition). Finally, in a no-information condition, he said nothing about the usefulness or lack of it of the abstinent behaviour. In all conditions, he then asked the subjects to help another experimenter by taking part in his research. This new piece of research required the subjects to go without smoking for 5 days. We might imagine that by the time they are asked to take part in this second piece of research the subjects have been able to perform the cognitive rationalization of their first behaviour (they were allowed an interval of 24 hours for this). They should therefore have no need to perform act rationalization by agreeing to this second proposal made by the experimenter unless, that is, a new element intervenes to call the cognitive rationalization into question and reactivate the motivational dynamic. This is certainly the case when negative information is presented. The subjects cannot then say, for example, 'The period of abstinence to which I agreed was useful for the experimenter.' If this undermining of the process of cognitive rationalization is accompanied by renewed dissonance arousal, then the subjects should, in one way or another, take steps to reduce it. Since the cognitive path of dissonance reduction is impeded, our hypothesis is that the behavioural path will be promoted.

What happens, however, when the subjects receive positive information? Since this information is presented after the subjects have had 24 hours to perform the cognitive rationalization of their abstinent behaviour and therefore to reduce their motivational tension, there is no reason to think that it will have any effect on the act rationalization process.

Finally, we expected the level of agreement among the subjects in the negative information condition to be higher than in the standard condition. However, we did not expect that, in this case, the level of agreement in the positive information condition would be lower than in the standard condition.

Subjects

The subjects consisted of male science students, aged between 20 and 24, at the Université de Provence (Marseille, France) with an average daily consumption of more than 15 cigarettes.

Procedure

Experiment 26 comprised three experimental conditions and one control condition. The subjects were seen separately (individual pass).

The experimenter contacted students who were smoking alone on the university campus. He asked those who reported smoking more than 15 cigarettes a day to take part in a very short, unpaid psychology experiment. He then asked the volunteers to accompany him to the laboratory. Once there, the experimenter explained that he was studying the effects of abstinence from smoking on cognitive processes, and in particular on mental speed, and he informed them that if they wanted to take part in the experiment they would have to stop smoking immediately and not smoke again for 24 hours (low-ball/*fait accompli*). He told them that he wanted to compare their performances in a timed test before and after the period of abstinence and left them free to decide whether to take part or not. Once the subjects had agreed (which almost all of them did: further testimony to the effectiveness of the low-ball/*fait accompli* procedure), they performed a timed speed test lasting 3 minutes and left the laboratory after promising not to smoke at all until their return. They returned to the laboratory at the same time the next day. At this point, it should be noted that very few of the subjects had to be eliminated because they did not return or because they had smoked in the intervening period (less than 15 per cent of the total). After ascertaining that the subjects had indeed respected their commitment, the experimenter asked them to perform a second 3-minute speed test. When this was completed, the independent variable was manipulated. In one condition, although in reality the experimenter stopped his watch after 3 minutes, he pretended to have made a mistake in timing the test. Using this as an excuse, he told the subjects that he would be unable to use the results and apologized for having made them go without cigarettes for 24 hours for nothing (*negative information condition*). In another condition he instead informed the subjects that their participation had been of great value. In particular, he told them that the research to which they had just contributed was to be published in a leading international journal (*positive information condition*). In the third condition, the experimenter simply thanked the subjects very politely (*no information condition*).

In all three conditions, the experimenter then asked the subjects if they would be interested in taking part in a new piece of research conducted by a different researcher investigating the link between smoking and memory. This research would require an abstinence from smoking of 5 days. The volunteers were asked to leave their names and telephone numbers.

In a control condition, the subjects were directly asked whether they would be prepared to take part in research requiring them to stop smoking for 5 days.

Results

The percentage of subjects from each condition who were prepared to commit themselves to 5 days' abstinence from smoking is presented in table 6.4.

We again observe the expected effect of negative information; when the experimenter has informed the subjects that he will not be able to use their results the subjects agree more readily to the longer period of abstinence than when they have not received this information (no-information): $\chi 2 = 6 \cdot 48$, $p < 0 \cdot 02$.

Table 6.4. The effect of upgrading vs. downgrading a costly act (abstaining from smoking for 24 hours) on agreement to a more costly one (abstaining for 5 days).

negative information	68·8%	(31/45)
positive information	35·5%	(16/45)
no information	42·2%	(19/45)
control	15·5%	(7/45)

Notes: Percentage of subjects agreeing to stop smoking for five days after a 24-hour period of abstinence. The actual numbers are given in parentheses.

In contrast, the positive information has no effect: when the experimenter informs the subjects that their contribution has been of great value, they are no more inclined than the subjects of the no-information condition to agree to a new period of abstinence.

The level of agreement in the control condition differs significantly from all three experimental conditions.

The results obtained in experiment 26 were replicated in a new experiment.

*Experiment 27. Effect of upgrading vs. downgrading a costly act (missing a meal)
on the agreement to perform a more costly one (missing two meals)*

Experiment 27 (Joule, 1993, exp. 2) involved a different type of problematic behaviour, namely abstinence from food (missing one meal and then missing two). Unlike in the experiments reported so far, agreement to the first and second periods of abstinence was elicited by two different experimenters.

The experiment again comprised three experimental conditions and one control condition.

Subjects
The subjects consisted of male and female literature students, aged 19 to 22, at the Université de Provence (Aix-en-Provence, France).

Procedure
Students who were spotted alone on the university campus were approached in the morning before 11 o'clock. The experimenter asked them to take a general intelligence test as part of a very short piece of unpaid research work. After taking the name, address and telephone number of the volunteers, the experimenter made an appointment with them at the laboratory for two to three in the afternoon of the same day. It was only when this appointment had been made that the experimenter informed the subjects that it was essential for them to skip lunch. He then gave them the chance to confirm or withdraw their participation. The procedure used to induce compliance was therefore a low-ball technique. Once more, this procedure proved to be remarkably effective, with less than 10 per cent of the subjects failing to cooperate. The subjects therefore arrived at the laboratory without having eaten. After ascertaining that this was indeed the case, the experimenter asked them to perform a timed intelligence test lasting 6 minutes. Once this test had been performed, the independent variable was manipulated. In one condition the contrite experimenter, claiming that he had made a timing error, informed the subjects that he would not be able to make use of their results (*negative information condition*). In another condition he was enthusiastic and emphasized the usefulness of their contribution (*positive information condition*). In the third condition, the experimenter did no more than thank the subjects politely (*no information condition*). Just after leaving the experiment, all the subjects were stopped by a second experimenter. Claiming this time to be investigating a different object of research (perception), he asked the subjects if they would be willing in the near future to take part in another piece of research requiring them to miss two meals (breakfast and lunch). Here again, those who agreed were asked to leave their name and telephone number.

In the control condition the second experimenter asked the subjects directly if they would be prepared to take part in research requiring them to miss two meals.

Results
The percentage of subjects who were willing to miss two meals in each of the conditions is given in table 6.5.

Exactly the same result pattern can be observed here as was found in experiment 26.

In the no information condition (standard gearing situation), 45 per cent of the subjects who had missed one meal agreed to miss two. This proportion rose to 77·5 per cent in the negative information condition; the difference between the two conditions was significant: $\chi^2 = 8·90$, $p < 0·01$. The positive information did not affect the probability of the subjects accepting the new period of abstinence. Here, as in the previous experiment, we find a level very close to that of the no information condition: $\chi^2 = 1·31$, $p > 0·10$.

Table 6.5. The effect of upgrading vs. downgrading a costly act (*missing one meal*) on agreement to a more costly one (*missing two meals*).

negative information	77·5%	(31/40)
positive information	37·5%	(15/40)
no information	45%	(18/40)
control	32·5%	(13/40)

Notes: Percentage of subjects agreeing to miss two meals after agreeing to miss one. The actual numbers are given in parentheses.

In the last two experiments (experiments 26 and 27), the request relating to the second behaviour was made just after the first behaviour had been completed. It therefore occurred after the first problematic behaviour had already been cognitively rationalized. In view of the results of these two experiments it would seem that undermining the cognitive rationalization of this first behaviour (negative information condition) means that it has to be re-rationalized. We have seen that, as the path of cognitive rationalization is blocked, subjects rapidly turn to the act rationalization path. These results therefore again support our general hypothesis of the alternative character of the cognitive and behavioural rationalization paths. The fact that we observe no facilitation of cognitive rationalization in the positive information condition in no way contradicts this hypothesis. On the contrary, since the cognitive rationalization process has already had time to operate, it might be thought that the subject is no longer in a state of motivational tension at the point when the experimenter presents the positive information. If all the tension has already been reduced, then this information cannot reduce it further. It is therefore easy to understand that positive information does not affect the level of agreement to the second problematic behaviour as it did in the experiments conducted by Beauvois, Joule and Brunetti (1993) and by Brunetti (unpublished). If someone who has just drunk two large glasses of water is no longer really thirsty, then he or she will not immediately drink the glass of beer that is offered to them. If the same person has drunk three large glasses of water, when two would have been quite adequate to quench their thirst, they will similarly refuse the glass of beer which is offered to them. This analogy accounts for the fact that positive information has no effect in experiments 26 and 27.

So far, the request for agreement to the second problematic behaviour has constituted an explicit demand on the part of the experimenter. A number of results obtained in the foot-in-the-door paradigm lead us to think that it is not necessarily essential that this request is made. We may recall that researchers have used the foot-in-the-door technique to increase the probability that one subject will help another to pick up pamphlets that the other has just dropped, or to indicate the loss of an object to another, or to make a spontaneous interjection in a conversation in order to correct an error which may be damaging to one of the interlocutors and so on (for a summary, see, in particular, Dejong, 1976 and Joule, 1987c; for particularly illustrative research, see Uranowitz, 1975). In such research, experimenters simply create a context that gives the subjects the opportunity to produce the behaviour that is expected of them: someone pretends, clumsily, to drop a pile of pamphlets, to lose an object, to give misleading information to someone else and so on. If such foot-in-the-door effects can be obtained without any explicit request, there is every reason to think that it should also be possible to obtain gearing effects without an explicit request being made. We know that the gearing procedure is based on the linking of a variety of compliance procedures, the last of which is always the foot-in-the-door procedure. For example, in all our experiments the most costly request is always preceded by one that is less so — this is indeed the basic principle of the foot-in-the-door technique.

The aim of experiment 28 was again to test the effect of undermining the cognitive rationalization of a problematic behaviour which had just been performed. However, this time the second problematic behaviour was not solicited by an explicit request. We may therefore term the paradigm governing this experiment *gearing with implicit request*.

Experiment 28. *Effect of downgrading abstinence from smoking on later consumption*

The subjects in this experiment (Joule, 1991d) stopped smoking for 18 hours. Following this period of abstinence, the process of cognitive rationalization was blocked in some of the subjects, but not in others, by minimizing the dangers of smoking. The dependent variable relates to the subjects' subsequent consumption of tobacco. We hypothesized that consumption would be less in subjects whose cognitive rationalization had been impeded than in the others. In effect, reducing tobacco consumption is a way for subjects to rationalize the 18-hours' abstinence which they have just accepted and which, in this way, they turn to their own advantage. This behavioural mode of rationalization should be more readily grasped by subjects whose cognitive rationalization has been impeded than by those in whom it is allowed to function normally.

Subjects

The subjects consisted of male and female literature students, aged between 20 and 22, at the Université de Provence (Aix-en-Provence, France) whose daily tobacco consumption exceeded 15 cigarettes.

Procedure

Experiment 28 included two experimental conditions.

The subjects were recruited individually on the university campus in order to take part in unpaid research investigating concentration in smokers. Their average daily tobacco consumption was recorded. The research took place in two stages and the volunteers were asked to visit the laboratory twice, once at six in the afternoon and a second time at noon the following day. Between five and six subjects were asked to the laboratory on the same day (group pass). Once they had arrived, the experimenter informed them that they could not smoke until the following noon (that is for 18 hours) and left them free to agree to or refuse this period of abstinence. Those who agreed (again nearly 90 per cent) performed an initial set of concentration tests lasting approximately a quarter of an hour before promising not to smoke in the intervening period and leaving the laboratory. These subjects returned to the laboratory at noon the next day (less than 20 per cent had to be eliminated because they had smoked or because they did not come back to the laboratory). After having conducted the second set of tests, the experimenter pretended to have left a document in his office and left the room for a few minutes.

While the experimenter was absent the independent variable was manipulated. One of the subjects (in fact, a colleague who had been present the day before) then struck up a conversation with the others. He told some (*negative information condition*) that his family doctor had recently told him that the link between smoking and cancer had not yet been scientifically proved. He then gave the example of his grandfather, an 83-year-old farmer whom he had never seen without a cigarette in his mouth, who was in rude good health. He therefore concluded that what was important was to live in a healthy environment, to eat good food and to avoid stress; and that smoking or not smoking was something irrelevant which did not really affect life expectancy. With other subjects (*no information condition*), he spent the same length of time talking about something unrelated to smoking. Instead, he spoke about the difficulty of finding accommodation in Aix-en-Provence as a student. On his return, the experimenter asked the subjects to perform a final task and then allowed those who so wished to smoke a first cigarette. Before the subjects left the laboratory, the experimenter told them that he would contact them during the following evening to find out how many cigarettes they had smoked, thus giving them the opportunity to perform act rationalization. They were then asked to count the number of cigarettes they smoked in the wake of their abstinence. In fact, the experimenter contacted the subjects three times, once the next day as announced, then 3 days later and finally 8 days later. In the last two calls, made without warning, the experimenter asked the subjects to estimate the number of cigarettes they had smoked during the past 24 hours.

Results

The subjects' average consumption is given in table 6.6.

The main measures represent the mean number of cigarettes smoked in the 30 hours following the end of the period of abstinence (second column).

Table 6.6. Effect of downgrading abstinence from smoking on subsequent consumption.

	before	1 day after	3 days after	8 days after
negative information	20·9	5·94	11·3	11·6
	(n = 23)	(n = 19)	(n = 17)	(n = 17)
no information	17·8	14·45	15·3	16·3
	(n = 24)	(n = 18)	(n = 17)	(n = 15)

Notes: Tobacco consumption before and after an 18-hour period of abstinence.

In the negative information condition the subjects smoked an average 20.9 cigarettes a day. During the 30 hours following the end of the period of abstinence, they smoked an average of only 5·94 (that is about 15 cigarettes fewer than before the experiment). This difference is significant ($p < 0.001$).

The subjects in the no information condition smoked an average 17·8 cigarettes a day prior to the experiment. During the day following the experiment they smoked an average 14·45 cigarettes (that is only three cigarettes fewer than before taking part in the experiment). This difference is only marginally significant ($p < 0.10$).

Three days later, the subjects in the negative information condition continued to smoke significantly fewer cigarettes than before participating in the experiment (11·1 cigarettes on average, $p < 0.01$). The same was true of these subjects eight days after the experiment (average 11·6 cigarettes, $p < 0.01$). In contrast, while the subjects of the no information condition continued to exhibit a marginally significant drop in consumption after 3 days (average 15·3 cigarettes, $p < 0.10$), this was no longer observed on the eighth day (average 16·3 cigarettes, $p > 0.10$).

Thus, everything in the negative information condition suggests that smoking less represents the behavioural rationalization of an abstinence whose cognitive rationalization has been undermined. It would therefore appear that, unlike the others, the subjects who were exposed to the argument minimizing the dangers of tobacco were in some way constrained to reconsider their cognitive rationalization of their 18 hours of abstinence from cigarettes. No doubt during their abstinence (which we know to be difficult and costly) these subjects told themselves that it could only do them good, that it was beneficial to their health and so on. The words of their colleague thus created a problem for the subjects of this condition where none had existed before, in that they introduced an inconsistency capable of reactivating the motivational dynamic. The cognition 'smoking is not dangerous for the health' does not fit well with the cognition 'I have just agreed to go without smoking.' It is precisely the arousal of this drive state that causes subjects whose cognitive rationalization has been undermined to perform act rationalization; the cognition 'I am managing to cut down my consumption of tobacco' fits perfectly with the cognition 'I have just agreed to go without smoking.'

Experiment 28 showed us that the process of act rationalization can take place even when the behaviour that helps the subject to rationalize a prior act is not elicited by a direct request. In the experiments that follow, the behaviour which allows us to study the process of act rationalization is explicitly requested of the subjects.

Experiments 29 and 30, which we are going to present in the next chapter, again test the hypothesis of the alternative nature of the cognitive and behavioural rationalization paths. However, this time the hypothesis is tested within a new paradigm, namely that of misattribution (see Fazio and Cooper, 1983, Joule 1987a for reviews). These experiments therefore bring us back to one of the now traditional areas of dissonance research.

However, before moving on to the next chapter we should like to draw another general conclusion:

Conclusion 7 *The adoption of one mode of reducing the drive tension resulting from commitment to a problematic act diminishes the likelihood that another mode will be observed. Conversely, if it is impossible to adopt a particular mode of reducing this tension, then the probability increases that a different mode will be adopted.*
Consequence *If the drive tension can be reduced using the cognitive path, then it will not have to be reduced behaviourally. Conversely, if the tension cannot be reduced cognitively, then the behavioural path may be adopted.*

Notes

1   We should point out that only 12·5 per cent of the subjects in a control condition agreed to stop smoking for 18 hours. In this condition the request to perform the abstinent behaviour was formulated in the same way but was made directly on the university campus by the experimenter.

Chapter 7

Misattribution paradigm and act rationalization

Research conducted within the framework of the misattribution paradigm shows that subjects who are able to attribute their arousal to an external source do not change their attitude after performing a problematic act. These results clearly conform with Festinger's assumption that the state of dissonance is an emotional state. In the wake of Schachter's work (1964, 1966, Schachter and Singer, 1962) we know that an emotion is, in effect, a combination of physiological arousal and cognitive labelling, with subjects being able, for example, to appear angry or happy simply as a result of the cognitive labelling they perform (see Cotton, 1981, for a review of the idea of the misattribution of arousal in Schachter).

For example, Storms and Nisbett (1970), whose study was a direct descendant of Schachter's work, showed that insomniacs sleep better if they are able to attribute their physiological arousal to some external cause (in their work this consisted of a pill likely to make the subjects feel tense). If dissonance is arousing, then Schacter's theory of emotion would lead us to expect it to be affected by the use of external labels, like the physiological arousal of insomniacs in the research carried out by Storms and Nisbett. Researchers have consequently adopted the following hypothesis: if subjects who have been aroused by dissonance are able to attribute their arousal to an external cause, they should show less of a need to change their attitude as a means of reducing dissonance (see Zanna and Cooper, 1974). And, in fact, when subjects are in the presence of a potential source of tension, classic attitude change effects are no longer observed. Researchers have used a wide variety of tension-inducing sources; administering a supposedly stimulating pill (see Zanna and Cooper, 1974), erotic photographs, or pictures of war, accidents or surgical operations (Drachman and Worchel, 1976), fluorescent lamps declared to be uncomfortable to the eye (Gonzalez and Cooper, 1976), comic strips (Cooper, Fazio and Rhodewald, 1978) and so on. In none of this research into misattribution do we observe the classic dissonance effects.

Most authors explain these results (absence of attitude change) by proposing that subjects are not in a state of dissonance at the point when the post-experimental attitude measurement is taken. Others are less categorical in their approach and think that the misattribution process may only temporarily reduce the dissonance. This is particularly true of Drachman and Worchel (1976), who believe that subjects can avoid focusing on inconsistent cognitions (dissonance between behaviour and attitude) if they are able to suppose that their arousal is due to a specific external source of tension. This is certainly the case when the post-experimental attitude measurements are made, since the external source of tension is still salient at this point. During this period, but for no longer, subjects will not experience dissonance arousal as such. Since this has been suppressed or, more precisely, made unavailable for processing, the subjects have no reason to modify their cognitions.

While using psychophysiological techniques to examine the misattribution process, Croyle (1985) was able to show that less physiological stimulation was observed in subjects who were able to attribute the tension they experienced to an external source than in those who were unable to do so. In particular, Croyle demonstrated that electrodermal activity changes less in misattribution situations than in standard situations. In an analysis of these results, he suggests that the absence of a dissonance effect in the misattribution paradigm could be due to an attenuation of the physiological stimulation which is no longer sufficient to trigger the cognitive work required for attitude change. That may be so. However, we still have to ask whether, in situations of misattribution, the production of the problematic behaviour fails to arouse dissonance or whether dissonance arousal is simply suppressed or rendered unavailable for processing for a limited period.

The hypotheses that we are able to formulate within the gearing paradigm clearly depend on the way we answer this question.

Let us summarize:

The absence of attitude change, and therefore of cognitive rationalization, in misattribution situations might lead one to think that the subjects are not in a state of dissonance, that they never have been and that their external attributions will allow them to avoid being so in the future. If this is indeed the case then they should also fail to perform act rationalization when the chance is offered to them.

However, it is also possible that external attributions simply block the process of cognitive rationalization and that the dissonance remains present, ready to re-emerge should the subjects be induced to refocus on their problematic behaviour, for example if they are asked to perform a new problematic act. If cognitive rationalization has indeed been blocked by the external attribution then, following this refocusing, dissonance should be reduced through act rationalization since the cognitive and behavioural rationalization paths function as alternatives.

We are inclined to support this second mode of reasoning. Two experiments were designed to test it.

Misattribution and dissonance arousal

Experiment 29. Effect of the misattribution of dissonance arousal generated by an uncostly act (drinking a glass of wine) on the agreement to perform a more costly one (drinking two glasses of wine)

In this experiment (Joule and Fointiat, 1992, experiment 2), as in experiment 24, the subjects were induced to decide to drink a large glass of wine immediately. The walls of the laboratory in which the experiment was conducted were either covered with photographs likely to lead to a misattribution (photo condition) or were left blank (no-photo condition). Just before the subjects drank the glass of wine, the experimenter asked them if they would be prepared to take part in a future experiment requiring them to drink two glasses of wine. On the basis of the reasoning suggested above, we expected subjects to agree more readily to drink two glasses of wine in the misattribution condition, that is when in the presence of photographs having arousal properties.

Subjects
The subjects consisted of male and female humanities students, aged between 20 and 22, at the Université de Provence (Aix-en-Provence, France).

Procedure
We shall present three experimental conditions here, two with photographs and one without. The subjects were seen in small groups of four to five people (group pass).

The subjects were recruited one at a time on the university campus in order to participate in an unpaid psychology experiment. The subjects were invited to the laboratory in groups of five. They arrived at the laboratory unaware that they were to be asked to decide whether or not to drink a large glass of wine. Some of the groups were also surprised to find the walls of the laboratory covered with photographs. These were either large, particularly provocative photographs of naked women or equally large photographs of war injuries or surgical operations. The experimenter explained the presence of these photographs by saying that he was temporarily sharing the room with a researcher investigating the representation of women in the erotic press (or the representation of pain) and that he had been asked not to move anything. In the standard condition (no photographs) the walls of the laboratory were left blank. Apart from this single difference (with photographs vs. without photographs), the procedure used in the three conditions was identical. The experimenter explained to the subjects that as his research investigated the effect of alcohol on concentration they would, if they agreed to take part, have to drink a glass of wine between two concentration tests. The subjects were then persuaded, within a context of free choice, to take part in the research. The procedure used to obtain compliance was therefore again the low-ball/*fait accompli* technique which guarantees an acceptance level close to 90 per cent. After the first test and just before they were due to drink, the subjects were asked by the experimenter if they would like to take part in his next piece of research. This experiment, which was scheduled to take place the following week, was presented as a continuation of the first in which the subjects would have to drink two glasses of wine. In the conditions with photographs the experimenter also specified that the research would take place in his own room and that there would therefore not be any photographs on the wall. The subjects who wanted to take part were asked to leave their names and telephone numbers on a sheet of paper.

The subjects in the control condition were immediately asked if they would take part in the second piece of research.

Results

The percentage of subjects ready, in each condition, to drink two glasses of wine is presented in table 7.1.

We should note first of all that the classic gearing effect is observed in the standard condition (without photographs), with the level of agreement in this condition being significantly higher than in the control condition: $\chi^2 = 10\cdot79$, $p < 0\cdot001$. We also note that this gearing effect is even more pronounced in the conditions with photographs. In fact, irrespective of the nature of the photographs, far more of the subjects in these conditions agreed to drink two glasses of wine than in the standard condition. The rate of agreement rises to $95\cdot8$ per cent in the condition with pictures of naked women and $94\cdot7$ per cent in the condition with photographs of war or surgical operations. These two levels differ from the no-photograph condition at $\chi^2 = 4\cdot45$, $p < 0\cdot05$ and $\chi^2 = 3\cdot24$, $p = 0\cdot06$ respectively.

Table 7.1. Effect of the misattribution of dissonance arousal generated by an uncostly act (drinking a glass of wine) on the agreement to perform a more costly one (drinking two glasses of wine).

with photographs of women	95·8%	(23/24)
with photographs of war and surgery	94·7%	(18/19)
without photographs	73·9%	(17/23)
control	22%	(4/18)

Notes: The percentage of subjects who agreed to drink two glasses of wine after agreeing to drink one. The actual numbers are given in parentheses.

As expected, it was indeed the subjects whose opportunity to perform cognitive rationalization had been limited — here by the sight of particularly provocative or shocking pictures — who were more inclined to perform act rationalization.

Experiment 30. Effect of the misattribution of dissonance arousal generated by an uncostly act (drinking 20 centilitres) on the agreement to perform a more costly one (drinking half a litre)

This effect has been replicated (Joule and Fointiat, 1992, experiment 3) in another experiment which elicited the wine-drinking behaviour. After being induced to drink a glass of wine, the subjects of this experiment were asked to drink half a litre. The quantity of wine involved in this experiment had been increased to ensure that the level of agreement would be less than in the standard condition (without photographs) in order to avoid a ceiling effect preventing us from verifying our hypothesis. Clearly, we expected to observe a higher level of agreement to drinking the half litre of wine in the presence of photographs than in the standard condition.

Subjects
The subjects were all female humanities students, aged between 18 and 23, at the Université de Provence (Aix-en-Provence, France).

Procedure
Since the procedure was identical to that applied in the preceding experiment, with the exception that the subjects were this time seen separately (individual pass), we shall not describe it here. This experiment made use of only one condition with photographs, the laboratory walls being covered with the same pictures of naked women that had been used in the earlier experiment.

Results
The percentage of subjects prepared, in each condition, to drink half a litre of wine is presented in table 7.2. We shall limit ourselves here to presenting the results obtained in the experimental conditions which were necessary for the testing of our hypothesis.

Table 7.2. Effect of the misattribution of dissonance arousal generated by an uncostly act (drinking 20 centilitres) on the agreement to perform a more costly one (drinking half a litre).

with photographs	75%	(15/20)
without photographs	40%	(8/20)
control	10%	(2/20)

Notes: The percentage of subjects who agreed to drink half a litre of wine after agreeing to drink 20 centilitres. The actual numbers are given in parentheses.

We again observe the classic gearing effect in the standard condition (without photographs) where the level of agreement is significantly higher than in the control condition: $\chi^2 = 4 \cdot 8$, $p < 0 \cdot 05$. Moreover, as in the preceding experiment significantly more of the subjects in the condition with photographs than in the no-photograph condition agreed to take part in the research requiring them to drink half a litre of wine: $\chi^2 = 5 \cdot 01$, $p < 0 \cdot 03$. Thus, the hypothesis which we constructed on the basis of the alternative nature of the cognitive and behavioural rationalization paths is again confirmed.

The results obtained in experiments 29 and 30 therefore lead us to believe that the effects traditionally obtained within the misattribution paradigm are better explained in terms of the suppression of the possibility of cognitive rationalization than by the absence of motivational tension or its elimination by misattribution. It would otherwise be difficult to explain why in experiments 29 and 30 the subjects in the condition with photographs were more inclined than those in the no-photograph condition to agree to drink the extra wine and thereby to perform act rationalization. It would appear that the request to perform the second problematic behaviour (to drink two glasses of wine or to drink half a litre) refocuses · subjects on the contradiction between their initial problematic behaviour (drinking a glass of wine) and their motivations (I do not want to drink wine) and in some way reactivates the motivational dynamic which had been temporarily held in abeyance as a result of the misattribution. Once this dynamic is reactivated, the subjects experience the need to rationalize their first problematic behaviour (the now imminent drinking of a glass of wine to which they have been led to agree). If, as Drachman and Worchel (1976) have shown, the path of cognitive rationalization is impeded in the condition with photographs, then subjects in this condition should be readier to perform act rationalization than the subjects of the no-photograph condition in which cognitive rationalization is not blocked. This is exactly what we observe in experiments 29 and 30.

As we shall see, the results obtained in the last two experiments are complemented by those of a new experiment. This new experiment was performed using the bogus pipeline paradigm first engineered by Jones and Sigall (1971) and later adopted by Tedeschi to test his interpretation of dissonance effects in the light of his impression management theory.

Bogus pipeline and dissonance arousal

Tedeschi (1981) has reinterpreted the attitude change following the production of a problematic behaviour observed in dissonance research. He suggests that subjects simply lie to the experimenter, assuming an attitude which they do not hold in order to avoid showing that they have behaved in a way which is inconsistent with their beliefs. Tedeschi and his colleagues (Gaes, Kalle and Tedeschi, 1978, Reiss, Kalle and Tedeschi, 1981; for a synthesis of this work, see Tedeschi, 1981) report evidence supporting this interpretation. When subjects know that they cannot be found out (which is the case under normal experimental conditions), the usual dissonance effect is obtained, that is they exhibit an attitude change oriented towards rationalization. In contrast, when they know they risk being exposed, no attitude change is observed. Such a situation is obtained when the subjects are monitored by the bogus pipeline equipment. According to Tedeschi it is only in these circumstances that subjects report their true beliefs. In effect, it is less uncomfortable for the image they are going to present of themselves to be thought of as inconsistent than to be considered a liar.

Stults, Messe and Kerr (1984) have suggested that the results obtained by Tedeschi and his colleagues can equally well be interpreted within the framework of research on dissonance arousal attribution. They argue that the bogus pipeline equipment used in the impression management studies may have the same effects as external sources of tension in situations of misattribution. In effect, subjects may attribute their state of tension to the presence of the lie detector, just as in other experiments they attribute it to photographs, pills, fluorescent lamps and so on. These authors conducted an experiment comprising three experimental conditions. In the first condition the subjects wrote a counterattitudinal essay similar to those typically employed in counterattitudinal advocacy studies (standard condition). In another condition the subjects wrote the essay after being monitored by the bogus pipeline equipment (bogus pipeline nonhabituation condition). The third condition was identical to the second with the exception that the subjects had already been familiarized with the bogus pipeline equipment in order to ensure that it could not give rise to any misattribution effect (bogus pipeline habituation condition). Stults et al. expected to obtain the classic dissonance effect in the standard condition and in the condition in which the subjects were habituated to the bogus pipeline equipment but not in the condition where habituation had not taken place. The results provided strong confirmation of this hypothesis and consequently revealed the limitations of reinterpreting dissonance effects in terms of Tedeschi's impression management theory.

The experiment conducted by Stults et al. (1984) provided the principle on which experiment 31 was based.

Experiment 31. *The attitudinal and behavioural effect of misattribution in a bogus pipeline situation*

This new experiment (Fointiat, 1994) deployed three gearing conditions, the first being a standard condition, that is with no bogus pipeline, the second a condition of bogus pipeline non-habituation and the third a bogus pipeline habituation condition. After they had made the decision to drink a glass of wine, the subjects in this experiment were invited to drink half a litre. Given the reasoning we advocated above (experiments 29 and 30), it was expected that the subjects in the condition of non-habituation to the bogus pipeline, whose cognitive rationalization is blocked (misattribution), would be more likely to perform act rationalization than the subjects in the other two experimental conditions for whom cognitive rationalization was unimpaired.

Subjects

The subjects were female humanities students, aged 18 to 23, at the Université de Provence (Aix-en-Provence, France).

Procedure

Once they had been induced to decide to drink a glass of wine using a low-ball/*fait accompli* technique, the subjects were allocated to one of the three experimental conditions.

The standard gearing condition (no bogus pipeline) is, with one exception, identical to the no-photograph condition of experiment 30. The difference was that in this new experiment the subjects were led to reply to a very short questionnaire during the interval which followed the first test. One of the questions made it possible to identify the arousal of dissonance. This question related to the personal benefit to the subjects of taking part in the experiment which was to be rated on an 11-point scale ranging from 0 (no benefit) to 10 (enormous benefit). It was following this interval, and just before the subjects were due to drink that the experimenter asked them to take part in the research requiring them to drink half a litre of wine.

The bogus pipeline non-habituation condition differed from the standard condition in one respect: when replying to the questionnaire, the subjects were connected by two electrodes attached to their temples to a bogus pipeline which was claimed to be very reliable. The experimenter justified the use of a lie detector by saying he had noticed that without it students did not give sincere replies to the questionnaire. In the bogus pipeline habituation condition, the subjects did not respond to the questionnaire immediately after being connected to the lie detector. Instead, they filled in an irrelevant form relating to alcohol. They were told that this form was designed to help them relax so that they would be less disturbed by the presence of the detector and would therefore provide more reliable answers.

In the control condition, the subjects were not asked to take part in an experiment requiring them to drink wine. Instead, the experiment was described to them and they were then asked to reply to the questionnaire as if they had taken part. They were then immediately invited to take part in the experiment requiring them to consume half a litre of wine.

Results

The mean post-experimental attitude of the subjects towards the benefit to them of the experiment as well as the percentage of subjects agreeing to drink half a litre of wine is given in table 7.3.

Table 7.3. *The attitudinal and behavioural effects of misattribution in a bogus pipeline setting: attitude towards the personal benefit of the experiment(1)* and percentage of subjects agreeing to drink half a litre of wine after agreeing to drink a glass(2).***

	(1)	(2)	
without bogus pipeline	5·72	25%	(5/20)
with bogus pipeline nonhabituation	4·40	70%	(14/20)
with bogus pipeline habituation	5·60	20%	(4/20)
control	3·95	10%	(2/20)

Notes: *The higher the figure, the more important the personal benefit is judged to be.
**The actual numbers are given in parentheses.

Let us consider for a moment the attitude of the subjects towards the experiment. In the condition containing no bogus pipeline (standard condition), the personal benefit to the subjects is judged to be significantly higher than in the control condition: $F = 6·81$, $p < 0·02$. We are therefore again in the presence of a classic dissonance effect, with the subjects who are induced to decide to take part in a piece of research which is costly for them finding that it is more rewarding for them than the subjects who have not been led to make any such decision. This dissonance effect is diminished in the bogus pipeline non-habituation condition in which subjects are able to attribute their arousal to the lie detector. It should be noted that while this condition differs significantly from the condition without bogus pipeline ($F = 4 \cdot 71$, $p < 0 \cdot 05$), it does not differ significantly from the control condition. The dissonance effect reappears in the condition in which the subjects are habituated to the bogus pipeline. Once the subjects of this condition have habituated to the lie detector, they are no longer able to perform a misattribution of arousal. This condition differs significantly from both the non-habituation condition and the control condition, yielding the values ($F = 4 \cdot 62$, $p < 0 \cdot 05$ and $F = 6 \cdot 86$, $p < 0 \cdot 02$ respectively.)

The results relating to the subjects' attitudes are therefore similar to those reported by Stults, Messe and Kerr (1984).

What happens at the behavioural level? As expected, act rationalization is more frequent in the condition in which cognitive rationalization is unable to occur, that is in the condition of non-habituation to the bogus pipeline. Many more of the subjects in this condition declare themselves to be prepared to drink half a litre of wine than in the other two experimental conditions: 70 per cent vs. 25 per cent when compared with the condition without bogus pipeline ($\chi^2 = 8 \cdot 12$, $p < 0 \cdot 01$) and 70 per cent vs. 20 per cent in the bogus pipeline habituation condition ($\chi^2 = 10 \cdot 10$, $p < 0 \cdot 01$).

Thus, the results obtained in this experiment reinforce those obtained in the misattribution contexts implemented in experiments 26 and 27. They consequently provide additional evidence in favour of the hypothesis of the alternative character of the cognitive and behavioural paths.

When behaviour is derogated

Such results might lead us to believe that act rationalization can be observed whenever cognitive rationalization is absent, as is the case, for example, in the misattribution studies that we have presented above. However, it is clear that this can only be the case when rationalization of the first problematic behaviour is essential. If, in contrast, such rationalization is not indispensable, we have no reason to suppose that act rationalization will replace cognitive rationalization. Here we are thinking of situations where, even if they do not go so far as to deny their problematic behaviour, subjects minimize its importance or its repercussions. This is probably what happens in situations that mobilize an attitude that is particularly accessible and is available to the subject at the onset of the forced compliance procedure. We might equally well imagine that the same occurs in situations that focus subjects on themselves or their internal universe. We are thinking in particular of the situation engineered by Scheier and Carver (1980) in which subjects are positioned in front of a mirror. It is known that in such situations subjects do not change their attitude, which has probably been made extremely salient by the sight of their own reflection. In the light of this, it is possible to understand why a potentially problematic behaviour which has been derogated by the subject no longer needs to be rationalized. This can not be observed in a classic gearing situation. But this can be observed in a gearing situation which have been designed to encourage subjects to derogate their behaviour, by minimizing its importance or its repercussions, rather than to rationalize it. We expect act rationalization to be less pronounced in this second situation than in the first since the absence of the classic attitude change in the second situation is not explained by the blocking of the cognitive rationalization path but by the fact that subjects do not have to rationalize behaviours which they have probably derogated.

This hypothesis was tested in experiment 32.

Experiment 32. The effect of derogating a counterattitudinal behaviour (anti-smoking essay) in front of a mirror on agreement to a problematic behaviour (agreement to refrain from smoking)

In this experiment (Joule, 1991d), smokers who had written a counterattitudinal essay against smoking as part of a first study were asked, as part of a second study, to refrain from smoking for 48 hours. Some of the subjects were seated in front of a mirror to write their essays while others were not. It was expected that subjects would be less likely to agree to stop smoking for 48 hours when confronted by the mirror than when the mirror was absent.

Subjects

The subjects were female literature students, aged 20 to 23, at the Université de Provence (Aix-en-Provence, France) with a daily consumption of more than 15 cigarettes.

Procedure

Here we shall report two experimental conditions (gearing with mirror and gearing without mirror) and a control condition. The subjects were seen separately (individual pass).

The subjects of the experiment were recruited on the university campus, where they were asked to take part in an unpaid psychology experiment scheduled to last no more than 10 minutes. The volunteers went to the laboratory. Some of them (gearing condition with mirror) were then asked to sit opposite a large mirror (2 m × 1 m). The writing desk was positioned such that the subject was seated 50 cm from the mirror. The experimenter justified the presence of the mirror by saying that he had been lent the room, which was not his usual one and which was being used for another experiment, on condition that nothing was moved. The other subjects sat at the same desk but after the mirror had been removed (gearing condition without mirror).

The subjects in both experimental conditions were immediately led to write a signed text, arguing as persuasively as possible for the proposition 'smoking is worthless', as part of what was described as a public awareness study. The subjects were left free to agree or to refuse to write the essay. As expected, almost all of them agreed. Once they had finished writing the essay, the experimenter asked them to take part in a new piece of research. This was said to be scheduled to take place three weeks later and was described as an investigation of the relationship between smoking and memory, which would require the subjects to abstain from tobacco for a period of 48 hours. The volunteers were asked to leave their name and telephone number.

In the control condition, the subjects were immediately asked to take part in the research requiring them to stop smoking for 48 hours.

Results

The percentage of subjects from each condition who were prepared to commit themselves to 48 hours without smoking is presented in table 7.4.

Table 7.4. *The effect of derogating a counterattitudinal behaviour (anti-smoking essay) in front of a mirror on agreement to a problematic behaviour (agreement to refrain from smoking).*

gearing with mirror	55%	(22/40)
gearing without mirror	77·5%	(31/40)
control	35%	(14/40)

Notes: Level of agreement to abstain from smoking for 48 hours after writing an anti-tobacco essay. The actual numbers are given in parentheses.

As predicted, fewer subjects in the gearing condition with the mirror than in the gearing condition without the mirror agreed to go without smoking for 48 hours: $\chi^2 = 4\cdot52$, $p < 0\cdot02$. We know that subjects who are seated opposite a mirror tend to minimize the force of their arguments and believe their essays to be considerably less effective than subjects who are not placed in front of a mirror (see Scheier and Carver, 1980). Ultimately, this type of strategy amounts to a failure to recognize the problematic nature of the behaviour that has been produced. It is therefore no surprise that the subjects who employ this strategy have less need than the others to rationalize (cognitively or behaviourally) their essay-writing behaviour. In contrast, in the gearing condition without a mirror the effect of the essay-writing behaviour is not minimized and the act, which remains problematic, has to be rationalized. The results show that it is indeed in this condition that the greatest rationalization (here, act rationalization) is observed.

This experiment is valuable in that it shows that the absence of cognitive rationalization does not necessarily result in a higher level of act rationalization. In fact, the failure to perform the rationalization of a problematic act may signify one of two things. On the one hand, it may simply mean that the procedures for cognitive rationalization are blocked. In this case other dissonance reduction procedures will have to be deployed in accordance with the principle of hydraulic relationships (see, in particular, experiments 29, 30 and 31 above). However, the failure to rationalize a problematic behaviour may also indicate that the behaviour has not generated any dissonance, either because the subject is not committed to the behaviour (for instance absence of personal responsibility, see Wicklund and Brehm, 1976, Cooper and Fazio, 1984) or because, after its completion, the behaviour is rejected by the subject (see Scheier and Carver, 1980), which ultimately comes to the same thing. In this case, subjects do not find themselves in a state of dissonance motivation and consequently do not need to rationalize their act either cognitively or behaviourally (see the results of the no-choice condition in experiment 24 and those of the gearing condition with mirror in experiment 32 above).

In both the present chapter and the last, we have defended the idea that a problematic behaviour can be rationalized by the production of a second behaviour of the same type, especially if this second behaviour is more costly than the first (as it is in the various experiments presented here). All the evidence that we have reported supports this idea. As we have seen, facilitating the cognitive rationalization of a problematic behaviour makes it less likely that act rationalization will be performed. In contrast, impeding subjects' ability to perform cognitive rationalization makes it more likely that act rationalization will occur. However, we have so far provided only indirect proof.

Let us now follow our reasoning through to its logical conclusion. If agreeing to the second problematic behaviour really makes it possible to rationalize the first, then subjects who have agreed to produce this second behaviour should feel less need to perform the cognitive rationalization of their first behaviour than subjects who have refused to produce it. This leads us to some extremely counterintuitive hypotheses. Let us imagine, as an example, subjects who have freely given their agreement to refrain from smoking for 24 hours. At the end of this period of abstinence they are asked to agree to a second, longer period without smoking (5 days). They can accept or refuse. For those who agree, acceptance will constitute a cognition that is consonant with their first period of abstinence (the cognition 'I have agreed to go without cigarettes for 5 days' fits well with the cognition 'I have just gone without smoking'). If these subjects are then asked to rate the difficulty they experienced in refraining from cigarettes for 24 hours, they should consider the task more difficult than they would have done if the question had been posed before they were asked to agree to the longer period of abstinence. Since they have less dissonance to reduce they should consequently have less need to change their attitude in a way that favours rationalization. However, for those subjects who do not agree to the extended period of abstinence, refusal will constitute a cognition which is dissonant with the initial period of abstinence. Since these subjects have more dissonance to reduce, they should simultaneously exhibit more attitude change and find abstinence easier. In other words, the subjects who agree to the long period of abstinence should find the shorter period more difficult than subjects who have refused the longer one.

This hypothesis was put to the test in a final experiment.

Experiment 33. The effect of agreeing to a very costly behaviour (5 days without smoking) on the rating of the difficulty of a less costly one (24 hours without smoking)

Subjects

The subjects consisted of male science students, aged 20 to 24, at the Université de Provence (Marseille, France) with a daily tobacco consumption of more than 15 cigarettes.

Procedure

Here, we shall report two experimental conditions and two control conditions.

Since the conduction of this experiment (Joule, 1993, exp. 3) was broadly similar to that of experiment 23 (see above), we shall restrict ourselves here to describing the differences, which relate to attitude measurement. In the experimental conditions, the subjects' attitude towards the short period of abstinence was measured either before or after the request to agree to the longer period.

A low-ball/*fait accompli* technique was used to induce the subjects in the experimental conditions to refrain from smoking for 24 hours as part of an unpaid, psychological study. The subjects returned to the laboratory at the end of the period of abstinence. The experimenter then informed half of them ('attitude before' condition) that it was usual for the psychology department to request subjects' opinions of the experiments in which they had just taken part, in particular in order to ascertain whether they had found it difficult or not. The subjects were then asked to rate the difficulty of the task on an 11-point scale ranging from -5 (very difficult) to $+5$ (very easy). Once these measurements had been taken, the experimenter asked the subjects to take part in a new piece of unpaid research which would require them to go without cigarettes for 5 consecutive days. The volunteers were asked to leave their names and telephone numbers with the experimenter. The attitude of the other half of the subjects ('attitude after' condition) was measured after they had been asked to take part in the second piece of research and therefore after they had made their decision to participate or not.

In one control condition the subjects were not asked to stop smoking before their attitude towards a 24-hour no-smoking period was measured. Instead, in this condition, they were asked to imagine themselves in the position of someone who had had to go without cigarettes for 24 hours. The subjects in this condition were then asked to take part in the research requiring them to stop smoking for 5 days. In another control condition the subjects were first asked to take part in the research associated with the 5 days' abstinence. It was only when they had either agreed to or refused this request that their attitude towards a 24-hour period of abstinence was measured. Again, the subjects were asked to imagine themselves in the position of someone who had been obliged to stop smoking for 24 hours.

Results

The mean rating in each condition is presented in table 7.5. The subjects of the 'attitude before' conditions were allocated to one of two groups following the attitude measurement depending on whether they agreed to or refused the 5-day period of abstinence.

Table 7.5. *The effect of agreeing to a very costly behaviour (5 days without smoking) on the rating of the difficulty of a less costly one (24 hours without smoking).*

		5-day abstinence			
		agreed		refused	
experimental conditions	attitude before	$-0 \cdot 4$	$(n = 20)$	$-0 \cdot 24$	$(n = 25)$
	attitude after	$-2 \cdot 69$	$(n = 26)$	$1 \cdot 21$	$(n = 19)$
control conditions	attitude before	$-1 \cdot 00$	$(n = 9)$	$-2 \cdot 41$	$(n = 36)$
	attitude after	$-1 \cdot 71$	$(n = 7)$	$-2 \cdot 18$	$(n = 38)$

Notes: 11-point rating scale ranging from -5 (very difficult) to +5 (very easy). The actual numbers are given in parentheses.

As expected, subjects who accepted the 5-day deprivation found the 24-hour period of abstinence which they had just completed more difficult than the subjects who refused this more extended period: $t = 8 \cdot 17$, $p < 0 \cdot 001$. In contrast, in the 'attitude before' condition, no difference is observed between the attitudes of the subjects who, a few seconds later, were to agree to the prolonged period of abstinence and those who were to reject it. If we turn to the attitude of the subjects who agreed to stop smoking for 5 days, we note that the 24-hour period of abstinence is judged to be more difficult when attitude is measured after the request to take part in the 5-day experiment than when it is measured before this request: $t = 4 \cdot 87$, $p < 0 \cdot 001$. In contrast, when subjects refuse to take part in the 5-day experiment, they consider that the 24-hour period of abstinence is easier when their attitude is measured after the request for the longer commitment than when it is measured before. In this case, however, the results only tend towards statistical significance ($t = 1 \cdot 87$, $p < 0 \cdot 10$).

These results seem to us to be particularly important from the theoretical viewpoint. In effect, they provide us with direct proof that we are justified in our support of the hypothesis defended in the last two chapters, namely that a problematic behaviour can be rationalized by the production of another problematic behaviour of the same type. We have just seen that the subjects who agreed to the long period of abstinence from smoking find the shorter period more difficult than subjects who refused to take part in the more prolonged experiment. We have also seen that subjects find the 24-hour period more difficult after agreeing to the longer period than before agreeing to it.

It must therefore be accepted that agreeing to the long period of abstinence makes it possible to reduce the dissonance which has been generated by the shorter period.

The results obtained in the control conditions are completely different. When the subjects are not in a state of dissonance, their behaviour appears to be derived perfectly from their attitude. Very logically, in effect, those who consider the 24-hour period of abstinence to be easy agree to stop smoking for 5 days, whereas those who consider the short period difficult refuse the longer period: − 1 vs. − 2·41 ($t = 3·81$, $p < 0·001$). Moreover, when attitude is measured after the decision to agree to or refuse the 5-day period of abstinence, the subjects who agree, unlike those of the experimental condition, do not find stopping smoking for 24 hours any more difficult than those who refuse. If anything, we observe the opposite tendency: − 1·71 vs. − 2·18 (not significant). This conforms more closely to what we intuitively expect of the link between attitude and behaviour or, in this case, between behaviour and attitude.

The results obtained in this last experiment enable us to draw a further conclusion:

Conclusion 8 *A problematic behaviour can be rationalized by the production of a second behaviour which is similar in nature to the first (act rationalization).*
Consequence *In this case, the cognitive rationalization of an initial problematic behaviour will be less pronounced following the production of a second problematic behaviour of the same nature as the first.*

The act rationalization process

Three observations will help us detail more precisely what is involved in the act rationalization process.

1 Taken in their entirety, the experiments that we have presented in the last two chapters show that the phenomenon of act rationalization may occur in a variety of contexts (in the laboratory, of course, but also under more natural conditions — for example, in a supermarket car park) and may relate to behaviours as different as abstinence from smoking, drinking alcohol, going without food, participating in an inquiry and so on. These experiments also show that this phenomenon may occur even when the second problematic behaviour is not elicited by the agent who obtained the first (see experiment 27) and even if it is not the object of an explicit request (experiment 28). They also demonstrate that the first problematic behaviour may be obtained using a variety of techniques of compliance without pressure, whether this is a low-ball procedure, a low-ball/*fait accompli* technique, or a foot-in-the-door or two-feet-in-the-door approach. All that matters is that the first problematic behaviour implies a commitment on the part of the subject and that it therefore generates a state of dissonance arousal.
2 In all our experiments, act rationalization was identified through the articulation of intended behaviour: subjects declared themselves to be prepared or not to take part in a piece of subsequent research. It should be noted that such a declaration is not simply a formality. In fact, almost all

the subjects who were later telephoned confirmed their participation, the level of defection varying from 5 per cent (supermarket customers who had agreed to be interviewed at home) to 16 per cent (of students who had decided to stop smoking for 5 days). This is a measure of how ready the subjects were to perform the costly problematic behaviour which enabled them to rationalize their earlier act.

3 Our third observation, which relates to the possible reinterpretations of the phenomenon of act rationalization, requires rather more extensive consideration.

If we only possessed the data relating to the experiments testing the effects of the upgrading versus downgrading of the first problematic behaviour, we could equally well interpret our results in terms of the idea of attitude/behaviour consistency without needing to invoke the act rationalization process. For example, negative feedback functions as a cognition which is dissonant with the initial behaviour. Thus subjects who have received this sort of feedback should experience a higher total amount of dissonance than subjects who have received no such feedback. These subjects should therefore exhibit more attitude change in line with the initial behaviour, namely a change that increases the value of this behaviour or that reduces its cost (see our experiments 1, 2 and 3 on the effect of arbitrary feedback). If this behaviour has acquired more value, or has become less costly in the eyes of the subject, it is understandable that he or she should be more inclined to produce subsequent behaviours which are similar to the first.

Moreover, the attitude measurements taken in these experiments are unambiguous. They show that negative feedback does indeed lead subjects to modify their representation of the initial behaviour in a way that permits rationalization (see the results of experiments 1, 2 and 3). For example, in experiment 27 (Joule, 1992) the subjects who learned that their results were useless to the experimenter due to an error in timing found the period of abstinence from food which they had completed (missing one meal) easier than subjects in a similar condition who had received no such feedback. We can therefore explain the greater willingness of the subjects who had received negative feedback to submit to a renewed period of abstinence in terms of their more favourable post-experimental attitude towards abstinence. What is more, we can propose this interpretation without stepping outside the strict framework of Festinger's theory.

However, we know of other results that are not compatible with an explanation that is based on the idea of attitude/behaviour consistency. These results yield attitude measurements which would sometimes lead one to expect behavioural effects which are the complete opposite of those observed. This is particularly true of research performed in the misattribution paradigm. We have seen that, in such research, act rationalization (agreeing to drink more wine) is more pronounced in subjects placed in a situation of misattribution (presence of photographs, use of a lie detector). And yet, the post-behavioural attitude of these subjects is no more favourable to alcohol than that of the others. Indeed, if anything, the opposite is the case since these subjects do not change their attitude (or change it less) in a way that will allow them to rationalize their initial behaviour (typical misattribution effect). For example, in experiment 29 (Joule and Fointiat, 1992), subjects confronted with erotic pictures found drinking alcohol more difficult than the subjects who were not confronted with this type of picture. However, this did not stop more of them agreeing to drink half a litre of wine. In the same way, the attitude of the subjects who are connected to a lie detector (non-habituation condition) is no more favourable than that of the subjects who are not connected to it. Again, they even tend to find it more difficult to drink alcohol. And yet, it is these subjects who are the most ready to agree to drink alcohol later.

Experiment 33 certainly provides the best illustration yet, since the subjects who agreed not to smoke for a period of 5 days find the period of abstinence of 24 hours which they have just completed more difficult than those who refuse to undergo this new period of abstinence. Our intuitions concerning attitude/behaviour consistency would have led us to expect the opposite phenomenon. While it is easy to see how a negative attitude towards abstinence will lead someone to refuse a new period of abstinence, it is not so easy to understand why such an attitude should result in agreement to this new abstinence.

It is therefore not possible in these experiments to explain the occurrence of act rationalization by pointing to the emergence of a process of attitude/behaviour consistency. In this work we have repeatedly emphasized the fact that rationalization, whether behavioural or cognitive in nature, has no other objective than to reduce the tension that follows the production of a problematic behaviour. However, it is self-evident that, when this tension has been reduced, other processes may arise including, in particular, processes aimed at producing consistency. Nevertheless, during the period necessary for the reduction of tension, the dissonance reduction process takes precedence over the others. We have seen that in certain cases this process can tolerate the presence of inconsistencies between attitudes (see chapter 2) or inconsistencies between the cognitive and behavioural registers (as described in the current chapter). These inconsistencies, which may arise during the period necessary for rationalization, are not incompatible with cognitive dissonance theory, which is not a theory of cognitive consistency but rather a theory of the rationalization of behaviour.

We have demonstrated (see chapters 1 and 2) that the sole aim of the dissonance reduction process is to reduce inconsistencies which involve the behaviour. However, while certain inconsistencies are compatible with Festinger's theory, they are, as we have frequently reiterated, incompatible with the major reinterpretations of dissonance effects, and in particular those which are based on the concepts of self-perception and self-presentation/impression management. In effect, the notion of consistency is a prerequisite for the operation of these reinterpretations.[1] As we have already discussed this point (see chapter 4), we shall resist returning to it here. It is not therefore surprising that theories such as those proposed by Bem or Baumeister or like those advanced by Tedeschi or by Steele and Liu are no more able to account for the behavioural effects reported here than they were able to explain the cognitive effects reported elsewhere.

Notes

1 Admittedly, the advocates of self-affirmation theory (see, in particular, Steele, 1988) are willing to accept the idea that subjects are perfectly able to tolerate cognitive inconsistencies as such. Indeed, this claim forms a particularly important part of their criticism of dissonance theory. However, at the same time, they feel it necessary to add that this inconsistency represents a threat to self-integrity and that it is for this reason that it generates dissonance effects.

Conclusion

Forced compliance, rationalization and agentic status

In the preceding chapters we have attempted to show that the fundamental core of the theory of dissonance proposed by Festinger in 1957 deserves to be fully revived in view of the fact that many of its implications have received inadequate debate and empirical exploration. In truth, this core theory simply requires the addition of the idea of commitment (Kiesler and Sakumura, 1966, Kiesler, 1971, 1977) if it is to be capable of explaining the effects observed in forced compliance situations and of generating the new hypotheses which have been proposed and experimentally validated by us and our colleagues. The revival of this core theory, the awareness of all its implications and the integration of the notions of commitment (and of commitment to compliance) constitute what we term the 'radical' conception of dissonance theory or, in short, the radical theory of dissonance.

Is the radical theory of dissonance useful?

In fact, this conception implies nothing very new from the theoretical point of view. A number of colleagues who have appraised our articles have spoken of the high degree of conformity between our hypotheses and what they know of the initial theory. They have even suggested that we abandon the term 'radical' since it could give the impression that our theory does not in some way conform entirely with the original theory. Yet, the fact that we insist on taking *all* the implications of the dissonance ratio into consideration and advance these as propositions of dissonance theory may sometimes appear to be an infidelity to the original theory which, for the majority of theorists, remains a theory of cognitive consistency, with its roots definitively sunk in what we have termed 'the 1950s perspective of rationality'. This is no doubt why yet other colleagues, performing the same role of appraisal, have gone so far as to suggest to us that in order to avoid any misunderstanding we use a designation other than 'dissonance theory'. Festinger himself once said to Serge Moscovici that the principal hypothesis of our experiment 5 seemed very strange to him (finding arguments in favour of the defended counterattitudinal position reduces dissonance and therefore diminishes the likelihood of a change in the initial attitude). He did not accept that it could be the subjects who had not yet started the counterattitudinal essay who exhibited the greatest attitude change. All humility aside, we believe that we have remained extremely faithful, if not to Festinger who we never met, then at least to his theory which we consider to be one of the finest creations of experimental psychology.

However, is there a use for this radical conception of dissonance theory which we have elaborated in the first part of this volume and whose experimental basis we have attempted to demonstrate? We think that there are at least three reasons for replying positively to this question. These three reasons will be recalled only briefly here since they have also been presented in the various chapters of this work. To these three reasons, we shall add two more. The first relates to certain practical implications of the radical theory. As the aims of this volume are primarily theoretical in nature, we shall limit ourselves to a brief examination of this point. The second reason relates to the integration of the paradigmatic situation of forced compliance, which has been amply explored in this work, within a wider theoretical framework, namely that of the social relation of obedience. We consider that this second argument in favour of the usefulness of the radical theory will open up new avenues of research which have hitherto been neglected. We shall therefore deal with it in greater detail.

1   Although the radical theory conforms rigorously to Festinger's *theoretical* statements, it has allowed us to establish new, frequently counterintuitive, hypotheses within a family of situations (forced compliance situations as well as compliance without pressure situations). These are situations that social psychology had largely neglected for many years due, no doubt, to the absence of any conceptual revival on a scale which might permit the implementation of new independent variables. Admittedly, it may appear strange from the scientific point of view that such a revival should be based on the almost literal restatement of a theory which is now some 40 years old, and on the disputing of the various 'revisions' (in fact, dilutions) of this theory. However, in our opinion, the origins of this strangeness can be traced as far back as Festinger's *metatheoretical* position. As a theorist, Festinger does not appear to have examined in full all the consequences of his theory. In binding his theory to the dominant paradigm of cognitive consistency, he has even suggested that this should not be done. He has thus opened the door to a number of rather biased reformulations (such as Zajonc's, which appeared as early as 1968) as well as to a series of increasingly anodyne revisions which present the subject described by dissonance theory as someone who performs the cognitive management of the personal responsibility implied by his freedom to act in order to satisfy his own ego (Wicklund and Brehm, 1976, Cooper and Fazio, 1984).

2   We feel able to assert that the radical conception allows us,

unambiguously in our opinion, to resolve in favour of dissonance theory the debates which have pitted it against its main rivals: Bem's (1966, 1972) self-perception theory and the numerous theories which we have grouped together here (self-presentation theory, Baumeister, 1982; self-affirmation theory, Steele and Liu, 1983, Steele 1988; impression management theory, Tedeschi, 1981). We have seen that this is not the least important contribution of the radical conception in view of the fact that Festinger himself seems to have abandoned the defence of the specificity of his own theory (Jones, 1990). Most of the effects reported in this volume cannot be reinterpreted in terms of the competing theories. It is, of course, true that here we are more interested in the irrelevance of the processes of self-perception than in that of the processes of self-presentation, impression management or related theories. This is because the evocation of the self-perception processes has led us to discuss an important problem, namely the status that should be attributed to the processes of causal explanation in forced compliance situations and in the interpretation of the effects that are observed in such situations. Nevertheless, we should not lose sight of the fact that in the majority of cases where self-perception theory has proved to be totally ineffective, it is because the experimental effects under discussion are contradictory to intuitions of attitude–behaviour consistency (see, in particular, experiments 1, 2, 3, 4, 5, 6, 7, 11 and 12). Yet, it is on such intuitions of consistency that the self-perceptual inferences postulated by Bem are founded.

In consequence, everything suggests that because the predictive functioning of the self-presentation and related theories necessarily implies that the subject has recourse to these same intuitions of consistency (are they not in fact based on the social and/or personal desirability of consistency between a subject's attitude and behaviour?), these theories are similarly unable to account for these inconsistency effects. Generally speaking, the acceptability of the theories which are in competition with dissonance theory is bound up with the validity or the normativity of intuitions of consistency which are articulated and endorsed by common sense. When experimental results run contrary to such intuitions, these theories lose all their effectiveness. In contrast, the (radical) theory of dissonance allows us to make direct predictions of inconsistency between relevant cognitions in the experimental situation, on the one hand, and between post-experimental attitudes and the produced behaviour on the other.

3   We note that, unlike previous revisions of Festinger's theory, the radical conception has successfully promoted the exploration of two new types of theoretically comprehensible experimental effects (in fact, two new experimental situations); double forced compliance effects (see chapter 5) and act rationalization effects (see chapters 6 and 7). It is the insistence on the necessity of antecedent behaviour and on the importance of the

generative cognition in the core theory of 1957 that has led us to study situations in which subjects are induced to produce not one but two behaviours as is the case in double forced compliance situations. It is on this same basis that it has been possible to formulate the hypothesis that producing a more costly behaviour can make it possible to rationalize an earlier, less costly one (act rationalization effect). The investigation of these two new types of effect tends, at the very least, to demonstrate the heuristic virtues of our 'radicalism'. The main contribution of the revisions of the past has been to permit the reinterpretation of the classic effects by proposing a number of new hypotheses relating to the conditions of production of these effects.

We can therefore provide three reasons underlining the usefulness of our radical conception. They are based on the theoretical arguments which we have attempted to detail earlier and which have been supported by the experimental data at our disposal.

4 Alongside these theoretical reasons which we have advanced for the usefulness of the radical theory, we should not fail to point out that the specificity of the rationalization process may have practical implications that run contrary to certain tendencies which are spontaneously manifested by certain types of practitioner. However, we shall limit ourselves to the two practical implications which are most closely bound up with the theoretical arguments which we have defended in the preceding chapters.

4a The first type of practical implication relates to the status of causal explanations in the dissonance reduction process. As we have seen, subjects who possess an explanation, whether external or internal, for their problematic behaviour rationalize this behaviour less. In other words, they attribute less significance to it. However, the implications of this fact run counter to what appears to be a spontaneous tendency of managers, teachers and even certain psychotherapists or social workers, all of whom frequently need to elicit some form of problematic behaviour (learning behaviour, conduct at work, new modes of behaviour in social or interpersonal relations and so on. Such actors may be tempted to provide explanations which are generally internal in nature when attempting to elicit such behaviour ('You see that you are perfectly capable of doing this task: You see that you find this job rewarding: You see that you have finally decided to face up to your responsibilities, to get on with it . . . '). In providing cognitions that are consistent with the problematic act, such comments may reduce the amount of rationalization performed by the subject and may consequently negate some of the educational or therapeutic benefits (cognitive or evaluative) associated with the subject's agreement to perform the act in question. While such explanations may be useful later in facilitating the internalization process (see below), their occurrence during the dissonance reduction period may block the process through which individuals attribute values to their acts (rationalization). It is one thing to be led to think (rationalization) that 'there is a point in doing what one has done' (grilled grasshoppers really aren't as bad as all that). However, it is quite another to say that what one has done is the result of an internal causality ('I like tasting disgusting food'). The radical theory therefore suggests that we focus on the specificity of the rationalization process and distinguish it from other processes which may compromise its benefits. As a result, we would strenuously recommend that practitioners wait until the rationalization process has terminated before providing their subjects with explanations which enable them to deal with their behaviour in personalized terms.

4b The concept of act rationalization also carries a number of practical implications. This is the only concept within the radical theory that allows us to make behavioural predictions. In particular, it defines the optimum conditions for obtaining increasingly costly acts. It may therefore prove to be of use to practitioners interested in behavioural change. Given that we consider act rationalization to be an alternative process to cognitive rationalization, then this concept should again dissuade us from helping subjects find good reasons for doing what they have done (cognitive rationalization) since such reasons reduce their motivational tension and remove the necessity for performing act rationalization. Let us recall the example of a smoker who has agreed to go without tobacco for a short period. We have seen that a good way of subsequently obtaining the subject's agreement to a more extensive period of abstinence (act rationalization) consists of suppressing any possibility of cognitive rationalization (for example, by not giving the subject time to find good reasons for agreeing to the initial period of abstinence or by informing the subject that this short period of abstinence is actually of little use). It can be seen that the implications of the concept of act rationalization again run counter to the spontaneous tendencies of teachers or other care or aid workers. When eliciting a problematic act from a client, it is, of course, 'natural' to add a comment such as 'You see how well you're getting on . . . You see it's not really difficult . . .' However, because such comments encourage subjects to perform cognitive rationalization, they reduce the probability that individuals will turn to a new problematic act as a mode of rationalization. Indeed, the radical theory suggests the very opposite, namely that it is better to disable cognitive rationalization by emphasizing the meagre value of the first problematic behaviour.

Thus, the radical theory may contradict a number of common intuitions. Nevertheless, we should emphasize that the radical theory is purely and simply a theory of the rationalization of behaviour. We therefore in no way exclude the possibility that these common intuitions may prove to be useful once the motivational tension induced by the problematic behaviour (state of dissonance) has been reduced. They may indeed prove to be extremely desirable for the triggering of other processes such as the process of internalization (see below).

Finally, there is a fifth reason for the usefulness of our radical theory and it is with this argument that we wish to conclude this volume. We have kept it until the conclusion because it leads us to contemplate propositions which are undeniably of a more speculative nature than those put forward so far. The radical theory prompts a revision of the paradigmatic status of dissonance theory which carries us far away from the '1950s perspective of rationality'. Given the somewhat speculative nature of this revision,[1] we shall leave the reader to judge its necessity.

Forced compliance and agentic status

In our opinion, the experimental study of the forced compliance situation, conducted on the basis of the statements of the radical theory of cognitive dissonance, enables us to formulate more precise definitions both of the paradigmatic status of this situation and, *a fortiori*, of the crucial contribution of our theory. Let us start by summarizing the points which will aid us in our discussion.

1 The forced compliance paradigm requires that an agent who is endowed with a certain authority, even if only symbolic (when the agent is simply a researcher), elicits from a subject *a behaviour which is said to be problematic because its principle is in contradiction with the attitudes or motivations of this subject*.

2 The level of refusals to perform the problematic act encountered in the totality of experiments into forced compliance reported here[2] is lower, when the subjects are declared to be free, than 5 per cent. It is frequently 0 per cent. It seems to us that the implications of this fact, which is encountered in the entire body of forced compliance literature, have yet to be exhausted.

3 When re-evaluated from our 'radical' point of view, the dissonance reduction process appears to be not a process for restoring cognitive consistency but, instead, a rationalization process, that is a process for restoring by cognitive or behavioural means the value of problematic behaviour performed under conditions of commitment. In fact, we have shown that when this process is mediated by the cognitive path, it in no way leads to the elimination of all the inconsistencies which may arise in the cognitive universe after the production of a problematic behaviour. Instead, it entails only the modification of those cognitions which would have implied a different (unproblematic) behaviour, that is cognitions that are generally derived from what is known as the evaluative

component of attitude and that are entered in the numerator of the dissonance ratio. We have also noted that making the subjects' initial attitude salient, doubtless because it focuses subjects on their own values and attitudes (see the mirror effect in Scheier and Carver, 1980), changes the situation and leads subjects to downgrade their behaviour rather than to rationalize it.

4 *The subject's commitment is generally obtained by means of a statement of freedom which is **emphasized** by the agent who exerts the pressure* which leads to compliance. However, this commitment may also have its roots in other characteristics of the situation (consequences of the act, public nature of the act . . .), or in cognitions present in the subject (private beliefs). When commitment is established on the basis of a statement of freedom, this is the freedom to comply or not to comply and not the freedom to do one thing rather than another.

5 We have also been able to show that the *dissonance reduction process, or the rationalization process, is a specific process which cannot be compounded with other cognitive processes* which may arise after the production of a problematic behaviour, notably the processes for the causal explanation of behaviour or processes for restoring attitudinal or cognitive consistency.

The forced compliance situation as a situation of obedience

Let us imagine that we are looking for subjects to take part in an experiment requiring them to inflict violent electric shocks on a colleague (this scenario was inspired by a piece of work conducted by Glass, 1964). We may proceed in two ways:

First situation: simple request We approach students on the campus and immediately make the following request: I am looking for students who will agree to inflict electric shocks of 150 volts on one of their colleagues to punish him for any mistakes he might make in a fairly difficult verbal learning task. Would you agree to be one of these students? Everything would lead us to expect that the number of refusals in such a situation would be very high. We know that the majority of students detest this type of experiment which involves causing pain to someone and have, indeed, made this opinion known on occasions.

Second situation: low-ball and participation in an experiment The students are asked to act as subjects in a psychology experiment investigating the role of punishment in learning. They arrive at the laboratory to learn that they have to inflict electric shocks of 150 volts on a 'pupil' each time he makes a mistake in learning a list of words. The experimenter ostensibly declares them to be free to agree or refuse to take part in the experiment (that is to say, to stay or to leave). We know that in this type of situation the refusal level is very low.

When the experimenter makes the statement of freedom in the second situation, the students are clearly already committed to their position as experimental subjects. They have agreed to take part in an experiment, made an appointment and come to the laboratory. They have probably arrived at the laboratory knowing that they will have to do what they are asked to do and that this will not necessarily be pleasant. They have not come to enjoy themselves. Like the subjects of Milgram's famous experiments (1974), they have come to obey. Does the statement of freedom inspire the individual to escape from the role of an experimental subject ready to obey instructions? Does it allow him to free himself from the necessity of performing a counterattitudinal or countermotivational act which he would very probably have refused in a situation of non-dependence?

Nearly half a century of experimental research into forced compliance forces us to give a negative response to these questions. Somehow or other the statement of freedom comes too late. Almost systematically, subjects who have been declared free behave in exactly the same way as those for whom the constraints have been made salient, at least with regard to agreement to the situation in which they are asked to take part and the behaviour which they will be required to produce. In similar proportions to constrained subjects, subjects who have been declared free have agreed to advocate causes contradictory to their assumed initial attitude, to go without water or tobacco, to perform tedious, frankly disgusting or sometimes quite simply immoral tasks. Far from inciting individuals to escape from their position of compliant subjects, this statement of freedom instead leads them to *attribute value* to the behaviour which they will have to perform and which forms part of their compliance, that is it leads them to rationalize this behaviour.

It is precisely this process of rationalization that is described by cognitive dissonance theory. It shows us how an individual who, although declared to be free, is subjected to an agent who is invested with authority comes to attribute a value to what this agent causes him to do. These observations enable us to understand better why the experimenter/subject relationship has sometimes appeared to be so determining a factor in the dissonance reduction process (see experiments 3, 11, 12 and 13).

It thus appears that the forced compliance situation should be thought of primarily as implementing a relationship between the subjects and a figure who is representative of authority, and that the dissonance reduction process (rationalization process) should be considered to be an implication of a certain type of power relationship characterized by *both* a request for obedience *and* a declaration of freedom. Joule (1986b) has used the expression 'freely given compliance' to provide a better characterization of this relation to authority. This freely given compliance is not mediated by an evocation of the beliefs and attitudes of the subject. If this were the case, we might suppose that dissonance reduction would frequently be achieved more easily through the derogation of the behaviour than through its reduction. Although research exists that shows that subjects can change attitudes which are very important to them (Chris and Woodyard, 1973; Shaffer, 1974), we may join Bem and McConnell (1970) in accepting that this does not prove that such attitudes were truly salient for the subjects at the point where they gave their consent. We are also able to accept that in cases where this initial attitude is extremely salient, rationalization takes other paths (Scheier and Carver, 1980). The consent given by subjects is therefore probably not based on their processing of their attitudes and values. Instead it is probably only an optional element of a script which permits subjects to manage their relationship with the experimenter.

Before touching on this point, let us summarize:

Conclusion 9 *The forced compliance situation studied by social psychologists is a situation in which subjects adopt a position of obedience to an authority (the experimenter) and are thus induced to perform problematic acts.*
Consequence *The theory of dissonance describes the process by which obedient agents, who have been declared free, rationalize the acts required by their obedience and therefore attribute enough value to these acts to be able to justify their production.*

The script of obedience

One question should preoccupy democratic, humanist researchers such as us. How can it happen that individuals so easily agree to perform problematic acts in a position of freely given compliance to an authority which is sometimes no more than symbolic or moral in nature?

The response to this question does not seem to be very mysterious. Before formulating it, it is important to note the remarkable structural similarity between the forced compliance situation as we have described it here and the situations of adult–child interaction which Hoffman (1970, 1983) refers to as *disciplinary encounters*. Hoffman defines the disciplinary encounter as an adult–child interaction in which the adult knowingly expects the child to do something different from what he or she really wants to do, that is that the adult expects the child to renounce an internal egoistic tendency in order to satisfy an external social requirement. The illustrative statistics gathered by Hoffman show that such encounters occur with extreme frequency in a child's life (one disciplinary encounter every 6 to 7 minutes in the home life of a child aged between 3 and 7 years). The same statistics also show that a large majority of these encounters result in obedience on the part of the child.

Thus, the pupil who is told by 'a gentleman' introduced by the teacher not to play with a magnificent robot which has been left in his or her physical proximity is not confronted by a particularly exceptional situation. In fact, it is simply one more disciplinary encounter. The fact that the child refrains from playing with the robot even when the adult has made no formal threat (Aronson and Carlsmith, 1963, Freedman, 1965) should therefore not really surprise us. The child will certainly have constructed a sort of *script* which implies obedience to an adult who is invested with a certain degree of legitimate authority. And it must again be this script which is called up in situations of forced compliance even when the subjects consist of adolescents or adults. In brief, the forced compliance situation simply reproduces a model of interaction with authority which was scripted long beforehand.

The study of such disciplinary practices actually reveals that the success of a disciplinary encounter (the child does what is demanded) is relatively independent of the way it is handled by the adult, even though the cognitive consequences of the encounter may differ considerably depending on the type of pedagogic procedure utilized by the adult. It even appears that the feature of the encounter which has the greatest impact on its cognitive consequences is the degree of salience of the affirmation of power (which is an essential precondition for such an encounter). It turns out that the more liberal processes are also far more efficient in their effect on the processes of internalization. This, too, should be no surprise to us. The study of forced compliance has shown us that the likelihood that a problematic act will be rationalized increases with the commitment of the individual who performs it, a statement of freedom being particularly effective, and that, in contrast, the salience of an external constraint eliminates any rationalization procedure. It is therefore perfectly natural that the study of forced compliance effects in children, in particular the famous 'forbidden toy' situation, has been incorporated in the study of the internalization of values (see Jones and Gerard, 1967, Amerio, Bosotti and Amione, 1978, Lepper, 1983).

Rationalization and internalization

However, it seems that there is a certain theoretical imprecision in the contribution made by theorists of cognitive dissonance. Theorists have failed to distinguish adequately between the actual rationalization of the behaviour and the internalization of the social value (or social utility) of this behaviour (see Beauvois, 1994).

The rationalization process consists of conferring value on the act performed in the situation of freely given compliance. This process is well described by dissonance theory. It enables the individual to say in some way 'it is not totally stupid to do what I have done'; 'I had reasons to do what I did' and so on. It in no way precludes subjects from feeling that they have been constrained in some way (Steiner, 1980). Individuals are not cut off from reality: they know full well that they are subjected to an external requirement. While the rationalization process is undeniably an important aspect of the cognitive dynamic which accompanies the development of the acquisition of values and other useful social aptitudes, it does not on its own furnish a sufficient explanation for this development:

Cognitive changes induced by the forced compliance situation are extremely specific in nature (see experiments 6, 7 and 8 conducted by Pavin and experiment 9 conducted by Channouf).

There is nothing to lead us to expect more consistency between the attitude (new) and the behaviour (future) than might be deduced from the long tradition of research into the prediction of behaviour from attitude (Wicker, 1969).

It is therefore important that the rationalization process which we have described here gives way to other processes.

The internalization process, properly speaking, should result in subjects having the feeling that their behaviour is a product of their own psychological reality: not only is it not stupid to do what I have done (rationalization process), but also, if I have done it, then it is because there was something in me which drove me to do it (internalization process). In fact, many theorists of moral development have attempted to show that an altruistic behaviour elicited from a child by straightforward exhortation or by modelling is more likely to be reproduced and, above all, generalized if it is explained in dispositional terms, if necessary by the adult (see, in particular, Grusec, 1983). While the rationalization process may generate behavioural values (it is good to do this), the internalization process must permit the *naturalization* of these values (this corresponds to what I am, to my psychological nature). There can be no doubt that this process is facilitated by the child's acquisition of a social norm, namely the social norm of internality which implies that the explanations of psychological events (behaviours and reinforcements) which are socially most desirable are those which emphasize the causal significance of the actor (Beauvois, 1984a, 1994, Beauvois and Le Poultier, 1986, Beauvois and Dubois, 1988, 1991, Dubois, 1987, 1994).

Position of obedience and position of autonomy

The reader will now understand better why we have insisted on discussing at such length the status of the processes of causal explanation in the forced compliance situation. This discussion has led us to two conclusions and these conclusions may appear to be somewhat at odds with the picture we have just sketched, albeit rapidly, of the processes of rationalization and internalization:

1 It is unlikely that adult subjects who are committed to the forced compliance situation spontaneously seek causal inferences concerning their behaviour in this situation.

2 If they should do so, the causal explanation of the problematic behaviour brings cognitions which are likely to reduce the dissonance they feel (in the case of internal explanations) or suppress their commitment (in the case of external explanations).

If we content ourselves with these conclusions, we might be tempted to think that the processes of rationalization and internalization pull in opposite directions. In dealing with this apparent contradiction we shall be led to make a number of statements which are, we have to admit, purely speculative since our research into the relations capable of linking dissonance reduction and causal explanations in a child involved in a disciplinary encounter has only just begun.

Let us turn to the curious effect of the actual performance of the subjects considered by Beauvois and Rainis (experiment 3, table 1.3) on the causal theories exhibited by the subjects at the conclusion of the experiment. We may recall that while the arbitrary feedback provided by the experimenter dramatically affected the rating of the task (rationalization effect), actual performance produced an equally dramatic effect on the causal theories, with the subjects who performed the worst shifting towards more internal conceptions of psychological causality during the course of the experiment. We have suggested that the fact that the subjects have been able to minimize the implications of the contract of forced compliance which binds them to the experimenter probably foregrounds the private cognitions these subjects may hold concerning the degree of control they exercise in such a situation. Although they have respected the terms of the contract which implies their obedience, although they have therefore adopted the position of a compliant agent, it is possible that these subjects have introduced strategies which allow the expression of what we are quite happy to join Milgram in calling an autonomous state. The definitions provided by Milgram and others suggest that the internality of causal explanations may arise as a consequence of this intrusion of an autonomous state in the experimental situation (Milgram, 1974, p. 133, Ibanez, 1989, p. 38). It is clear that, for us, this autonomous state is unable to account for the classic effect of dissonance reduction which we associate with its precise antithesis, namely the position of a compliant agent who has been declared to be free. However, there is nothing to exclude a priori that a subject may in one and the same situation adopt both positions. The first (the position of agent) consists of respecting the contract which binds the subject to the experimenter (such subjects have actually performed the task and have, like the others, also rationalized the task by ultimately finding it interesting). The second (position of autonomy) consists of the private management of the contract (by investing less effort in the task than might otherwise have been possible). If there is any validity in these considerations then we are led to associate two elements: (1) the intrusion, in the forced compliance situation, of an optional autonomous state in the management of the contract of forced compliance; and (2) the availability of internal beliefs in the search for psychological explanations.

A second result that we should take into consideration here is the one obtained from the uncommitted subjects of Beauvois, Michel, Py, Rainis and Somat who had to respond to a questionnaire which had been designed to make theoretical internal explanations of their compliance salient ('internal' questionnaire: experiment 14, table 4.2). The reader may recall that these subjects were the only uncommitted subjects (in fact, the subjects who had not been declared free) to exhibit a post-experimental attitude which implied that they found the copying task more interesting than any of the other uncommitted subjects. We interpret this result by suggesting that the salience of the theoretical internal explanations in some way took the place of a statement of freedom in committing the subjects to compliance. These data again tend to support the suggestions that, in this case, a new type of commitment would no longer depend on what the experimenter said about the situation but on the emergence of self-generated internal causal explanations.

Thus, because the forced compliance situation reproduces a model of interaction with power scripted many years previously in the course of the disciplinary encounters experienced by the child, it places the subjects in a position of obedience or, to use Milgram's concept, the position of an agent. The addition of a statement of freedom on the part of the agent who exerts the pressure does not change this position. Instead, it acts as a factor of commitment and thereby clears the way for the rationalization of the demanded behaviour by the compliant agent. However, this agentic state in no way precludes an optional state of autonomy, the determinants of which remain to be studied. The position of autonomy seems to be associated with a heightened availability of the internal register of causal explanations. On this basis, the effects of autonomy may seem to be contradictory. On the one hand, it makes it more likely that the behaviour of the agent will be rationalized since it facilitates commitment to compliance. On the other, it reduces the magnitude of this rationalization since it provides explanations which are consistent with the problematic act. Despite this contradiction, the advantages of autonomy become clear as soon as we turn our attention to the lengthy processes which, in the child, lead to the realization of values or behavioural utilities. Learning these positions of autonomy maintains the context of commitment within which the child experiences disciplinary encounters on the one hand, while, on the other, it prompts the practice of the internal causal explanations which seem to be necessary for the reproduction and generalization of the behaviours produced within the framework of these encounters. To summarize:

Conclusion 10 Because it is accompanied by internal attributions, the possibility of an optional position of autonomy in the forced compliance situation maintains the subject's commitment to compliance and permits the internalization of the value (or social utility) of the problematic behaviour elicited.
Consequence Even if it reduces rationalization effects, the position of autonomy makes it possible to maintain the values and behavioural utilities acquired in the agentic state.

These propositions are again highly speculative.[3] It is for this reason that we have insisted on reserving them for the conclusion of this work. They are, nevertheless, entirely compatible with the data obtained in forced compliance situations involving both adults and children, as well as with the experimental data collected in studies of the internalization of values (see Beauvois, 1994). An experimental programme which has just commenced should permit us to evaluate both the validity and the heuristic value of these ideas.

Notes

1   In the following we insist on the speculative nature of the propositions concerning the paradigmatic status of dissonance theory. However, it should not be forgotten that there is no reason to consider the radical theory of dissonance itself to be particularly speculative since its statements are derived from Festinger's propositions which have been amply validated since 1957.

2   We therefore exclude from this calculation certain situations which are appropriately described as compliance without pressure (foot-in-the-door, gearing).

3   However, the contrast we have drawn here between the agentic state and the state of autonomy seems to be in conformity with certain theories of the initiation and regulation of behaviour (for instance, Deci and Ryan, 1985, 1987) as well as with the vast body of literature concerning objective self-awareness (Duval and Wicklund, 1972) or behavioural self-regulation (Scheier and Carver, 1988). In terms of the model of behavioural self-regulation, the state of autonomy would be characterized by the implementation of a comparator whose function is to check the correspondence between what the subject is doing and what he/she is intending to do. In contrast, the agentic state would be characterized by the non-implementation of this comparator. This distinction also makes it possible to revisit, as Milgram envisaged, the theoretical problems posed by responsibility in situations of organizational obedience (see Hamilton and Sanders, 1992). These authors focus on how authority frames the situation in such a way that subordinates do not engage in individualistic calculus. Thus they present these problems in terms which are entirely compatible with our formulations.

Bibliography

ABELSON, R. P. and REICH, C. M. (1969). 'Implicational molecules: a method for extracting meaning from input sentences', in WALKER, D. E. and NORTON, L. M. (Eds) *Proceedings of the International Joint Conference on Artificial Intelligence*, Tbilissi, Georgia.

ABELSON, R. P. and ROSENBERG, M. J. (1958) 'A symbolic psycho-logic: a model of attitudinal cognition', *Behavioral Science*, 3, pp. 1–13.

AJZEN, I. (1977). 'Intuitive theories of events and the effect of baserate information on prediction', *Journal of Personality and Social Psychology*, 35, pp. 303–14.

AMERIO, P., BOSOTTI, E. and AMIONE, F. (1978) 'Cognitive dissonance and internalization of social norms: effects of threat severity on children', *International Journal of Behavioral Development*, 1, pp. 355–62.

APFELBAUM, E. (1966) 'Etudes expérimentales du conflit: les jeux expérimentaux', *L'Année Psychologique*, 66, pp. 599–621.

ARONSON, E. (1968) 'Dissonance theory: progress and problems', in ABELSON, R. P., ARONSON, E., McGUIRE, W. J., NEWCOMB, T. M., ROSENBERG, M. J. and TANNENBAUM, P. H. (Eds) *Theories of Cognitive Consistency: A Sourcebook*, Chicago: Rand McNally.

ARONSON, E. (1969) 'The theory of cognitive dissonance: a current perspective', in BERKOWITZ, L. (Ed.) *Advances in Experimental Social Psychology*, 4, New York: Academic Press.

ARONSON, E. (1992) *The Social Amimal*, San Francisco: Freeman, (6th Edn).

ARONSON, E. and CARLSMITH, J. M. (1963) 'Effect of severity of threat on the valuation of a forbidden behavior, *Journal of Abnormal and Social Psychology*, 66, pp. 584–8.

BAUMEISTER, R. F. (1982) 'A self-presentional view of social phenomena', *Psychological Bulletin*, 91, pp. 3–26.

BEAUVOIS, J. L. (1984a) *La Psychologie Quotidienne*, Paris, Presses Universitaires de France.

BEAUVOIS, J. L. (1984b) 'Sujet de la connaissance et sujet de l'action: pour un néo-cognitivisme en psychologie sociale', *Cahiers de Psychologie Cognitive*, 4, 385–400.

BEAUVOIS, J. L. (1990) 'L'acceptabilité sociale et la connaissance évaluative', *Connexions*, 56, pp. 7–16.

BEAUVOIS, J.L. (1994) *Traité de la Servitude Libérale. Une Analyse de la Soumission*, Paris: Dunod.

BEAUVOIS, J. L., BUNGERT, M. and MARIETTE, P. (1995) 'Forced compliance: commitment to compliance and commitment to activity', *European Journal of Social Psychology*, 25, 17–26.

BEAUVOIS, J.L., BUNGERT, M., RAINIS, N. and TORNIOR, L. (1993) *Rationalisation, Explication Causale et Position d'agent dans la Situation de Soumission Forcée*, in BEAUVOIS, J. L., JOULE, R. V. and MONTEIL, J. M. (Eds) *Perspectives cognitives et conduites sociales, 4*, Neuchâtel: Delachaux et Niestlé.

BEAUVOIS, J. L. and DUBOIS, N. (1988) 'The norm of internality in the explanation of psychological events', *European Journal of Social Psychology*, 18, 299–316.

Bibliography

BEAUVOIS, J.L. and DUBOIS, N. (1991) 'Internal/external orientations and psychological information processing', *CPC- European Bulletin of Cognitive Psychology*, **11**, 193–212.

BEAUVOIS, J.L., GHIGLIONE, R. and JOULE, R.V. (1976) 'Quelques limites des réinterprétations commodes des effets de dissonance', *Bulletin de Psychologie*, **29**, 758–65.

BEAUVOIS, J.L. and JOULE, R.V. (1981) *Soumission et idéologies. Psychosociologie de la rationalisation*, Paris: Presses Universitaires de France.

BEAUVOIS, J.L. and JOULE, R.V. (1982) 'Dissonance versus self-perception theories: A radical conception of Festinger's theory', *Journal of Social Psychology*, **117**, pp. 99–113.

BEAUVOIS, J.L., JOULE, R.V. and BRUNETTI, F. (1993) 'Cognitive rationalization and act rationalization in an escalation of commitment', *Basic and Applied Social Psychology*, **14**, pp. 1–17.

BEAUVOIS, J.L., JOULE, R.V. and MONTEIL, J.M. (1987) *Perspectives cognitives et conduites sociales*, **1**, Cousset: DelVal.

BEAUVOIS, J.L. and LE POULTIER, F. (1986) 'Norme d'internalité et pouvoir social en psychologie quotidienne', *Psychologie Française*, **31**, pp. 100–8.

BEAUVOIS, J.L., MICHEL, S., PY, J., RAINIS, N. and SOMAT, A. (1996) 'Activation d'explications internes et externes du comportement problématique dans la situation de soumission forcée, in BEAUVOIS, J.L., JOULE, R.V., MONTEIL, J.M. (Eds), *Perspectives Cognitives et Conduites Sociales*, **5**, Neuchâtel: Delachaux et Niestlé.

BEAUVOIS, J.L. and RAINIS, N. (1993a) 'Dissonance reduction and causal explanation in a forced compliance situation', *European Journal of Social Psychology*, **23**, pp. 103–107.

BEAUVOIS, J.L. and RAINIS, N. (1993b) 'Activation d'explications internes et externes dans la situation de soumission forcée', Communication at the 5th Meeting of *Cognitions et conduites sociales*, Genève.

BEM, D.J. (1967) 'Self-perception: an alternative interpretation of cognitive dissonance phenomena', *Psychological Review*, **74**, pp. 183–200

BEM, D.J. (1972) 'Self-perception theory', in BERKOWITZ, L. (Ed.) *Advances in Experimental Social Psychology*, **6**, New York: Academic Press.

BEM, D.J. and MCCONNELL, H.K. (1970) 'Testing the self-perception explanation of dissonance phenomena: on the salience of premanipulation attitudes', *Journal of Personality and Social Psychology*, **14**, pp. 23–31.

BERKOWITZ, L. and DEVINE, P.G. (1989) 'Research traditions, analysis, and synthesis in social psychological theories: the case of dissonance theory', *Personality and Social Psychology Bulletin*, **15**, pp. 493–507.

BREHM, J.W. (1959) 'Increasing cognitive dissonance by a fait-accompli', *Journal of Abnormal and Social Psychology*, **58**, pp. 379–382.

BREHM, J.W. (1962) 'Motivational effects of cognitive dissonance', in JONES, M.R. (Ed.) *Nebraska Symposium on Motivation*. Lincoln: University of Nebraska Press.

BREHM, J.W. and COHEN, A.R. (1962) *Explorations in Cognitive Dissonance*, New York: Wiley.

BREHM, J.W. and CROCKER, J.C. (1962) 'An experiment on hunger', in BREHM, J.W. and COHEN A.R., (Eds) *Explorations in Cognitive Dissonance*, New York: Wiley.

BROCK, T.C. (1962) 'Cognitive restructuring and attitude change', *Journal of Abnormal and Social Psychology*, **64**, pp. 264–71.

BRUNER, J.S. (1957) 'Discussion on L. Festinger, the relationship between behavior and cognition', In BRUNER, J.S. (Ed.) *Contemporary Approaches to Cognition*. Cambridge: Harvard University Press.

BRUNETTI, F. (1994) 'Effet de la valorisation vs. dévalorisation d'un comportement problématique sur sa rationalisation en acte', Communication at the ADRIPS junior-meeting, June, Aix-en-Provence.

BRUNSWIK, E. (1956) *Perception and the Representative Design of Experiments*, Berkeley: University of California Press.

CALDER, B. J., ROSS, M. and INSKO, C. A. (1973) 'Attitude change and attribution: effect of incentive, choice and consequences', *Journal of Personality and Social Psychology*, **25**, pp. 95–99.

CARLSMITH, J. M., COLLINS, B. E. and HELMREICH, R. K. (1966) 'Studies in forced compliance: 1. The effect of pressure for compliance on attitude change produced by face to face role playing and anonymous essay writing', *Journal of Personality and Social Psychology*, **4**, pp. 1–13.

CARTWRIGHT, D. and HARARY, F. (1956) 'Structural balance: a generalization of Heider's theory', *Psychological Review*, **63**, pp. 277–93.

CHANDLER, T. A. and SPIES, C. J. (1984) 'Semantic differential placement of attributions and dimensions in four different groups', *Journal of Educational Psychology*, **76**, pp. 1119—27.

CHANNOUF, A. (1990) Antécédents et Effets Cognitifs et Comportementaux des Conduites de Soumission: de l'Internalité à la Consistance, Doctoral dissertation, Grenoble: Université Pierre Mendès France.

CHANNOUF, A. (1991) 'Activation du modèle explicatif des conduites et des renforcements et acceptation d'un acte coûteux', in BEAUVOIS, J. L., JOULE, R. V. and MONTEIL, J. M. (Eds), *Perspectives Cognitives et Conduites Sociales*, **3**, Cousset (Fribourg) DelVal.

CHANNOUF, A., LE MANIO, P. Y., PY, J. and SOMAT, A (1993) 'Internality, normative clearsightedness and temporal persistence of the effects of dissonance. *Revue Internationale de Psychologie Sociale*, **6**, pp. 69–84.

CHANNOUF, A., PY, J. and SOMAT, A. (1991) 'Internalité, clairvoyance normative et dissonance', communication at the 4th meeting *Cognitions et Conduites Sociales*, Grenoble.

CHRIS, S. A. and WOODYARD, H. D. (1973) 'Self-perception and characteristics of premanipulations attitudes: a test of Bem's theory', *Memory and Cognition*, **1**, pp. 229–335.

CIALDINI, R. B., BASSET, R., CACIOPPO, J. T. and MILLER, J. A. (1978) 'Low-ball procedure for producing compliance: commitment then cost', *Journal of Personality and Social Psychology*, **36**, pp. 463–76.

CLÉMENCE, A. (1987) *Efficacité de l'Exercice du Pouvoir: une Lecture Psychosociologique du Phénomène de Dissonance Cognitive*, Doctoral dissertation, Lausanne: Université de Lausanne.

CLÉMENCE, A. (1991). 'Les théories de la dissonance cognitive', *Information sur les Sciences Sociales*, **30**, pp. 55–79.

CLÉMENCE, A. and DESCHAMPS, J. C. (1989) 'Effet de la dissonance consécutive à la justification d'une notation', in BEAUVOIS, J. L., JOULE, R. V. and MONTEIL, J. M. (Eds) *Perspectives cognitives et conduites sociales*, **2**, Cousset (Fribourg): DelVal.

COHEN, A. R. (1959) 'An experiment on small rewards for discrepant compliance and attitude change', In BREHM, J. W. and COHEN, A. R. (1962, Eds), *Exploration in Cognitive Dissonance*. New York: Wiley.

COHEN, A. R., BREHM, J. W. and LATANÉ, B. (1959) 'Choice of strategy and voluntary exposure to information under public and private conditions', *Journal of Personality*, **27**, pp. 63–73.

COOPER, J. and CROYLE, R. T. (1984) 'Attitudes and attitude change', *Annual Review of Psychology*, **35**, pp. 395–426

COOPER, J. and FAZIO, R. H. (1984) 'A new look at dissonance theory. In BERKOWITZ, L. (Ed) *Advances in Experimental Social Psychology*, **17**, pp. 229–66, New York: Academic Press.

COOPER, J., FAZIO, R. H. and RHODEWALD, F. (1978) 'Dissonance and Humor: evidence for the undifferentiated nature of dissonance arousal', *Journal of Personality and Social Psychology*, **36**, pp. 280–5.

COOPER, J. and MACKIE, D. (1983) 'Cognitive dissonance in an intergroup context', *Journal of Personality and Social Psychology*, **44**, pp. 536–44.

COOPER, J. and WORCHEL, S. (1970) 'Role of undesired consequences in arousing cognitive dissonance', *Journal of Personality and Social Psychology*, **16**, pp. 199–206.

COOPER, J., ZANNA, M. P. and GOETHALS, G. R. (1974) 'Mistreatment of an esteemed other as a consequence afiecting dissonance reduction', *Journal of Experimental Social Psychology*, **10**, pp. 224–33.

COTTON, J. L. (1981) 'A review of research on Schachter's theory of emotion and the misattribution of arousal', *European Journal of Social Psychology*, **11**, pp. 365–97.

CROYLE, R. T. (1985) 'Cognitive dissonance and misattribution: a psychological examination', *Dissertation Abstracts International*, **45** (12–B,Pt1), 3993.

DECI, E. L. and RYAN, R. M. (1985) *Intrinsic motivation and self-determination in human behavior*. New York: Plenum Press

DECI, E. L. and RYAN, R. M. (1987) 'The support of autonomy and the control of behavior', *Journal of Personality and Social Psychology*, **53**, pp. 1024–37

DEJONG, W. (1976) 'An examination of self-perception mediation of the foot-in-the-door effect', *Journal of Personality and Social Psychology*, **37**, pp. 2221–39.

DESCHAMPS, J. C. and CLMENCE, A. (1990) *L'explication quotidienne. Perspectives Psychosociologiques*, Cousset: Del Val.

DRACHMAN, D. L. and WORCHEL, S. (1976) 'Misattribution of arousal as a means of dissonance reduction', *Sociometry*, **39**, pp. 53–9.

DUBOIS, N. (1987) *La Psychologie du Contrôle. Les Croyances Internes et Externes*, Grenoble: Presses Universitaires de Grenoble.

DUBOIS, N. (1994) *La Norme d'Internalité et le Libéralisme*, Grenoble: Presses Universitaires de Grenoble.

DUVAL, S. and WICKLUND, R. A. (1972) *A Theory of Objective Self-awareness*. New York: Academic Press.

FAZIO R. H. and COOPER, J. (1983) 'Arousal in the dissonance process', in CACIOPPO, J. T. and PETTY, R. E. (Eds) *Social Psychophysiology: a Sourcebook*. New York: Guilford.

FAZIO, R. H., ZANNA, M. P. and COOPER, J. (1977) 'Dissonance and self-perception: an integrative view of each theory's proper domain of application', *Journal of Experimental Social Psychology*, **13**, pp. 464–79.

FESTINGER, L. (1950) 'Informal social communication', *Psychological Review*, **57**, pp. 271–82.

FESTINGER, L. (1957a) *A Theory of Cognitive Dissonance*, Stanford: Standford University Press.

FESTINGER, L. (1957b) 'The relation between behavior and cognition', In BRUNER, J. S. (Ed) *Contemporary Approaches to Cognition*, Cambridge: Harvard University Press.

FESTINGER, L. and CARLSMITH, J. M. (1959) 'Cognitive consequences of forced compliance', *Journal of Abnormal and Social Psychology*, **58**, pp. 203–10.

FLAMENT, C. (1968) *Théorie des Graphes et Structures Sociales*, Paris: Gauthier-Villars.

FOINTIAT, V. (1994) *Rationalisation en Acte dans le Paradigme de la Fausse Attribution*, Doctoral dissertation, Aix-en-Provence: Université de Provence.

FREEMAN, J. L. (1965) 'Long-term behavioral effect of cognitive dissonance', *Journal of Experimental Social Psychology*, **1**, pp. 145–55.

FREEMAN, J. L. and FRASER, S. C. (1966) 'Compliance without pressure: the foot-in-the-door technique', *Journal of Personality and Social Psychology*, **4**, pp. 195–202.

GAES, G. G., KALLE, R. J. and TEDESCHI, J. T. (1978) 'Impression management in the forced compliance situation: Two studies using the bogus pipeline', *Journal of Experimental and Social Psychology*, **14**, pp. 493–510.

GIRANDOLA, F. (1994) *Le Paradigme de la Double Soumission Induite: un Nouveau Regard sur l'expérience de Festinger et Carlsmith, 1959*, Doctoral dissertation, Aix-en-Provence, Université de Provence.

GLASS, D. C. (1964) 'Change in liking as means of reducing cognitive discrepancies between self-esteem and agression. *Journal of Personality*, **32**, pp. 531–49.

GOLDMAN, M. , CREASON, C. R. and McCALL, C. G. (1981) 'Compliance employing a two-feet-in-the-door procedure', *Journal of Social Psychology*, **114**, pp. 259–65.

GONZALEZ, A. E. and COOPER, J. (1976), 'What to do with leftover dissonance: blame it on the lights', Reported in ZANNA, M. P. and COOPER, J., 'Dissonance and the attribution process', in HARVEY, J. H., ICKES, W. J. and KIDD, R. F. (Eds) *New Directions in Attribution Research*, **1**, Hillsdale, Erlbaum.

GREENWALD, A. G. and RONIS, D. L. (1978) 'Twenty years of cognitive dissonance: case study of the evolution of a theory', *Psychological Review*, **85**, pp. 53–7.

GRUSEC, J. E. (1983) 'The internalization of altruistic dispositions: a cognitive analysis', in HIGGINS, E. T., RUBLE, D. N. and HARTUP, W. W. (Eds) *Social Cognition and Social Development. A Sociocultural Perspective*, Cambridge: Cambridge University Press.

HAMILTON, V. L. and SANDERS, J. (1992) 'Responsability and risk in organizational crimes of obedience', in STAW, B. M. CUMMINGS, L. L. (Eds) *Research in Organizational Behavior*, **14**, Greenwich: JAI Press

HAMMOND, K. R. (1955) 'Probabilistic functioning and the clinical method', *Psychological Review*, **62**, pp. 255–62.

HEIDER, F. (1958) *The Psychology of Interpersonal Relations*, New York: Wiley.

HELMREICH, R. K. and COLLINS, B. E. (1968) 'Studies in forced compliance: commitment and magnitude of inducement to comply as determinants of opinion change', *Journal of Personality and Social Psychology*, **10**, pp. 75–81.

HOFFMAN, M. L. (1970) 'Moral development', in MUSSEN, P. H. (Ed) *Carmichael's Manual of Child Psychology*, New York: Wiley.

HOFFMAN, M. L. (1983) 'Affective and cognitive processes in moral internalization', in HIGGINS, E. T., RUBLE, D., and HARTUP, W. W. (Eds) *Social Cognition and Social Development. A Sociocultural Perspective*, Cambridge: Cambridge University Press.

HOLMES, J. G. and STRICKLAND, L. H. (1970) 'Choice freedom and confirmation of incentive expectancy as determinants of attitude change', *Journal of Personality and Social Psychology*, **14**, pp. 39–45.

IBANEZ, T. (1989) 'Faire et croire', in BEAUVOIS, J. L., JOULE, R. V. and MONTEIL, J. M. (Eds) *Perspectives Cognitives et Conduites Sociale*, **3**, Cousset (Fribourg): DelVal.

JANIS, I. L. and GILMORE, J. B. (1966) 'The influence of incentive conditions on the success of role playing in modifying attitudes', *Journal of Personality and Social Psychology*, **1**, pp. 17–27.

JELLISON, J. M. and GREEN, J. (1981) 'A self-presentation approach to the fundamental attribution error: the norm of internality', *Journal of Personality and Social Psychology*, **40**, pp. 643–9.

JONES, E. E. (1990) *Interpersonal perception*, New York, Freeman.

JONES, E. E. and GERARD, H. B. (1967) *Foundations of Social Psychology*, New York: Wiley.

JONES, E. E. and SIGALL, H. (1971) 'The bogus pipeline: a new paradigm for measuring affect and attitudes', *Psychological Bulletin*, **76**, pp. 349–64.

JORDAN, N. (1953) 'Behavioral forces that are function of attitudes and of cognitive organization', *Human Relations*, **6**, pp. 273–87.

JOULE, R. V. (1986a) 'Twenty five years on: yet another version of cognitive dissonance theory?', *European Journal of Social Psychology*, **16**, pp. 65–78.

JOULE, R. V. (1986b) *Rationalisation et Engagement dans la Soumission Librement Consentie*, Doctoral dissertation, Grenoble: Université Pierre Mendès France.

JOULE, R. V. (1987a) 'La dissonance cognitive: un état de motivation?', *L'Année Psychologique*, **87**, pp. 273–90.

JOULE, R. V. (1987b) 'Tobacco deprivation: the foot-in-the door technique versus the low-ball technique', *European Journal of Social Psychology*, **17**, pp. 361–5.

JOULE, R. V. (1987c) 'Le pied-dans-la-porte: un paradigme à la recherche d'une théorie', *Psychologie Française*, **32**, pp. 301–6.

JOULE, R. V. (1991a) 'Practising and arguing for abstinence from smoking: a test of the double forced compliance paradigm', *European Journal of Social Psychology*, **21**, pp. 119–29.

JOULE, R. V. (1991b) 'Double forced compliance: a new paradigm in cognitive dissonance theory', *Journal of Social Psychology*, **131**, pp. 839–45.

JOULE, R. V. (1991c) 'Dissonance cognitive, privation de tabac et motivation', *Psychologie Française*, **36**, pp. 5–11.

JOULE, R. V. (1991d) *Dissonance Cognitive et Rationalisation en Acte*, communication at the French Psychological Society, Clermont-Ferrand.

JOULE, R. V. (1993) *Privation de Tabac dans le Paradigme de la Rationalisation en Acte: Test d'une Hypothse Limite*, communication at the 5th meeting *Cognitions et Conduites Sociales*, Genève.

JOULE, R. V. and AZDIA, T. (1994) 'Engagement fort versus faible dans une situation de double soumission forcée', Université de Provence (unpublished manuscript).

JOULE, R. V. and BEAUVOIS, J. L. (1987) *Petit Traité de Manipulation à l'Usage des Honnetes Gens*, Grenoble: Presses Universitaires de Grenoble.

JOULE, R. V. and FOINTIAT, V. (1992) *Act Rationalization*, European meeting *Structuring Conflict*, Valencia.

JOULE, R. V. and FOINTIAT, V. (1992) *Rationalisation en Acte et Fausse Attribution*, communication at the meeting *Structuring Conflict*, Valencia.

JOULE, R. V., FOINTIAT, V. PASQUIER, C. and MUGNY, G. (1991) 'Behavioral conversion in a compliance paradigm: a replication and a refinement', *European Journal of Social Psychology*, **21**, pp. 365–369.

JOULE, R. V. and GIRANDOLA, F. (1992) *La Théorie de la Dissonance Cognitive: Nouveaux Paradigmes*, communication at the 25th International Congress of Psychology, Brussels.

JOULE, R. V. and GIRANDOLA, F. (1995) 'Tâche fastidieuse et jeu de rôle dans le paradigme de la double soumission', *Revue Internationale de Psychologie Sociale*, **8**, pp. 101–116.

JOULE, R. V. and LEBREUILLY, J. (1991) 'Privation de boisson anchois et gateaux dans le paradigme de la double soumission forcée', in BEAUVOIS, J. L., JOULE, R. V. and MONTEIL, J. M. (Eds) *Perspectives Cognitives et Conduites Sociales*, **3**, pp. 121–34, Cousset: Del Val.

JOULE, R. V. and LÉVÈQUE, L. (1994) 'Effets de la durée de l'argumentation contre-attitudi-nelle sur le changement d'attitude', Laboratoire de Psychologie Sociale, Université de Provence at Aix-en-Provence.

JOULE, R. V., MUGNY, G. and PEREZ, J.-A. (1988) 'When a compliance without pressure strategy fails due to a minority dissenter: a case of "behavioral conversion"', *European Journal of Social Psychology*, **18**, pp. 531–5.

KAHNEMAN, D. and TVERSKY, A. (1973) 'On the psychology of prediction', *Psychological Review*, **80**, pp. 237–251.

KATZ, D. and STOTLAND, E. (1959) 'A preliminary statement to a theory of attitude structure and change', in KOCH, S. (Ed) *Psychology, a study of a science*, **3**, New York: McGraw Hill.

KELLEY, H. H. (1967) 'Attribution theory in social psychology', in DEVINE, D. (Ed.) *Nebraska Symposium on Motivation*, **15**, Lincoln: Nebraska University Press.

KELLY, G. A. (1955) *The Psychology of Personal Constructs*. New York: Norton.

KIESLER, C. A. (1971) *The Psychology of Commitment. Experiments Linking Behavior to Belief*, New York: Academic Press.

KIESLER, C. A. (1977) 'Commitment, hope, and despondency', *Humanitas*, **13**, pp. 327–38.

KIESLER, C. A. and PALLACK, M. S. (1976) 'Arousal properties of dissonance manipulat-ions', *Psychological Bulletin*, **83**, pp. 1014–25.

KIESLER, C. A. and SAKUMURA, J. (1966) 'A test of a model for commitment', *Journal of Personality and Social Psychology*, 3, pp. 349–353.

KRUGLANSKI, A. W., FRIEDLAND, N. and FARKASH, E. (1984) 'Lay persons' sensitivity to statistical information: the case of high perceived applicability', *Journal of Personality and Social Psychology*, 46, pp. 503–18.

LANGER, E. (1978) 'Rethinking the role of thought in social interaction', in HARVEY, J. H., ICKES, W. J., and KIDD, R. F. (Eds) *New Direction in Attribution Research*, 2, Hillsdale: Erlbaum.

LEDLEY, R. S. and LUSTED, L. B. (1959) 'Reasoning foundations of medical diagnosis', *Science*, 130, pp. 9–21.

LEPPER, M. R. (1973) 'Dissonance, self-perception and honesty in children', *Journal of Personality and Social Psychology*, 25, pp. 65–74.

LEPPER, M. R. (1983) 'Social-control processes and the internalization of social values: an attributional perspective', in HIGGINS, E. T., RUBLE, D. and HARTUP, W. W. (Eds) *Social cognition and social development. A sociocultural perspective*, Cambridge: Cambridge University Press.

LINDER, D. E., COOPER, J. and JONES, E. E. (1967) 'Decision freedom as determinant of the role of incentive magnitude in attitude change', *Journal of Personality and Social Psychology*, 6, pp. 245–54.

MARCH, J. G. and SIMON, H. A. (1958) *Organizations*, New York: Wiley.

MCGUIRE, W. J. (1960) 'A syllogistic analysis of cognitive relationships', in ROSENBERG, M. J., HOVLAND, C. I., MCGUIRE, W. J., ABELSON, R. P. and BREHM, J. W. (Eds) *Attitude Organization and Change. An Analysis of Consistency among Attitude Components*, New Haven: Yale University Press.

MCGUIRE, W. J. (1966) 'The current status of cognitive consistency theories', in FELDMAN, S. (Ed.) *Cognitive consistency. Motivational Antecedents and Behavioral Consequents*, New York: Academic Press.

MCGUIRE, W. J. (1968) 'Theory of the structure of human thought', in ABELSON, R. P. et al. (Eds) *Theory of Cognitive Consistency: a Sourcebook*, Chicago: Rand McNally.

MILGRAM, S. (1974) *Obedience to Authority*, London: Tavistock Publications.

MILLS, J. and O'NEAL, E. (1971) 'Anticipated choice, attention, and the halo effect', *Psychonomic Science*, 22, pp. 231–3

NEUMANN, J. VON. and MORGENSTERN, O. (1944) *Theory of Games and Economic Behavior*, Princeton: Princeton University Press.

NEWCOMB, T. M. (1953) 'An approach to the study of communicative acts', *Psychological Review*, 60, pp. 393–404.

NICHOLS, M. P. and DUKE, M. P. (1977) 'Cognitive dissonance and locus of control: interface of two paradigms', *Journal of Social Psychology*, 11, pp. 291–7

NUTTIN, J. M. (1975) *The illusion of Attitude Change. Towards a Response Contagion Theory of Persuasion*. London: Academic Press

O'NEAL, E. (1971) 'Influence of future choice importance and arousal upon the halo effect', *Journal of Personality and Social Psychology*, 19, pp. 334–40.

OSGOOD, C. E. and TANNENBAUM, P. H. (1955) 'The principle of congruity in the prediction of attitude chang', *Psychological Review*, 62, pp. 42–55.

PAVIN, C. (1991a). ' Persistance du changement d'attitude et de l'argumentation chez des enfants placés en situation de soumission forcée', in BEAUVOIS, J. L., JOULE, R. V. and MONTEIL, J. M. (Eds) *Perspectives Cognitives et Conduites Sociales*, 3. Cousset (Fribourg): DelVal.

PAVIN, C. (1991b) 'La situation de soumission forcée: modifications cognitives à long terme', annual meeting of the Société française de Psychology, Clermont-Ferrand

PAVIN, C. (1992) *Le Paradigme des Grandes Vacances*. Doctoral dissertation, Grenoble: Université Pierre Mendès, France

PAVIN, C. (1993) 'La réduction de la dissonance génératrice de déséquibre entre soi et autrui', *Revue Internationale de Psychologie Sociale*, 6, pp. 85–104.

PEPITONE, A. (1966) 'Some conceptual and empirical problems of consistency models', in FELDMAN, S. (Ed.) *Cognitive Consistency. Motivational Antecedents and Behavioral Consequents*, New York: Academic Press.

PLON, M. (1967) 'Problèmes théoriques et expérimentaux posés par l'emploi, des "jeux" dans l'étude des conflits interpersonnels', *Bulletin du C.E.R.P.*, 17, pp. 393-433.

POITOU, J. P. (1974) *La Dissonance Cognitive*, Paris: Colin.

PRATKANIS, A.R. and GREENWALD, A.G. (1989) ' A sociocognitive model of attitude structure and function', in L. BERKOWITZ, L. *Advances in Experimental Social Psychology*, 22, pp. 245-85, New York: Academic Press.

QUATTRONE, G.A. (1985) 'On the congruity between internal states and action', *Psychological Review*, 98, pp. 3-40.

RABBIE, J.M., BREHM, J.W. and COHEN, A.R. (1959) 'Verbalization and reactions to cognitive dissonance', *Journal of Personality*, 27, pp. 407-17

RAJECKI, D. W. (1990) *Attitudes*, Sunderland: Sinauer

RAPOPORT, A. and ORWART, C. (1962) 'Experimental games: a review', *Behavioral Science*, 7, pp. 1-37

REISS, M., KALLE, R.J. and TEDESCHI, J.T. (1981) 'Bogus pipeline attitude assessment, impression management and misattribution in induced compliance settings', *Journal of Social Psychology*, 115, pp. 247-58.

ROSENBERG, M.J. (1960) 'An analysis of affective-cognitive consistency', in ROSENBERG, M.J., HOVLAND, C.I., MCGUIRE, W.J., ABELSON, R.P. and BREHM, J.W. (Eds) *Attitude Organization and Change. An Analysis of Consistency among Attitude Components*, New Haven: Yale University Press.

ROSENBERG, M.J. (1966) 'Some limits of dissonance: toward a differentiated view of counter-attitudinal performance', in FELDMAN, S. (Ed.) *Cognitive Consistency. Motivational Antecedents and Behavioral Consequents*, New York: Academic Press.

SAVAGE, L. (1954) *The Foundations of Statistics*, New York: Wiley.

SCHACHTER, S. (1964) 'The interaction of cognitive and physiological determinants of emotional state', in BERKOWITZ, L. (Ed.) *Advances in Experimental Social Psychology*, pp. 48-81, New York: Academic Press.

SCHACHTER, S. (1966) 'The interaction of cognitive and physiological determinants of emotional state', in SPIELBERGER, C.D. (Ed.) *Anxiety and Behavior*, pp. 193-224, New York: Academic Press.

SCHACHTER, S. and SINGER, J.E. (1962) 'Cognitive, social and physiological determinants of emotional state', *Psychological Review*, 69, pp. 379-99.

SCHEIER, M.F. and CARVER, C.S. (1980) 'Private and public self-attention, resistance to change and dissonance reduction', *Journal of Personality and Social Psychology*, 39, pp. 390-405.

SCHEIER, M.F. and CARVER, C.S. (1988) 'A model of behavioral self-regulation: translating intention into action', in. BERKOVITZ, L. (Ed.) *Advances in Experimental Social Psychology*, 21, pp. 303-46, New York: Academic Press.

SCHLAIFER, R. (1959) *Probability and Statistics for Business Decisions*. New York: McGraw-Hill.

SCHÖNBACH, P. (1993) 'Commentaires sur quatre études', in BEAUVOIS, J.L., JOULE, R.V. and MONTEIL, J.M. (Eds) *Perspectives Cognitives et Conduites Sociales*, 4, Neuchâtel: Delachaux et Niestlé.

SHAFFER, D.R. (1974) 'Attitude extremity as a determinant of change in the forced-compliance experiment', *Bulletin of the Psychonomic Society*, 3, pp. 51-3.

SHERMAN, S.J. (1973) 'Internal-external control and its relationship to attitude change under different social influence techniques', *Journal of Personality and Social Psychology*, 26, pp. 23-9.

SINGER, J.E. (1966) 'Motivation for consistency', in Feldman, S. (Ed.) *Cognitive Consistency. Motivational Antecedents and Behavioral Consequents*, New York: Academic Press.

SLOVIC, P. and LICHTENSTEIN, S. (1973) 'Comparison of Bayesian and regression approaches to the study of information processing in judgement', in RAPPOPORT, L. and SUMMERS, D. A. (Eds) *Human Judgment and Social Interaction*. New York: Holt, Rinehart & Winston.

SOGIN, S. R. and PALLACK, M. S. (1976) 'Bad decisions, responsibility and attitude change: effects of volition, foreseeability and locus of causality of negative consequences', *Journal of Personality and Social Psychology*, 33, pp. 300–6.

STEELE, C. M. (1988) 'The psychology of self-affirmation: sustaining the integrity of the self', in BERKOVITZ, L. (Ed.) *Advances in Experimental Social Psychology*, 21, pp. 261–302, New York: Academic Press.

STEELE, C. M. and LIU, T. J. (1983) 'Dissonance processes as self-affirmation', *Journal of Personality and Social Psychology*, 45, p. 5.19.

STEINER, I. D. (1980) 'Attribution of choice', in FISHBEIN, M. (Ed.) *Progress in Social Psychology*, 1, Hillsdale: Erlbaum.

STICE, E. (1992) 'The similarities between cognitive dissonance and guilt: confession as a relief of dissonance', *Current Psychology: research, reviews*, 11, pp. 69–77

STORMS, M. D. and NISBETT, R. E. (1970) 'Insomnia and the attribution process', *Journal of Personality and Social Psychology*, 16, pp. 319–28.

STULTS, D. M., MESSE, L. A. and KERR, N. L. (1984) 'Belief discrepant behavior and the bogus pipeline: impression management or arousal attribution?', *Journal of Experimental Social Psychology*, 20, pp. 47–54.

TEDESCHI, J. T. (1981) *Impression Management Theory and Social Psychological Research*, New York: Academic Press.

URANOWITZ, S. (1975) 'Helping and self-attributions: a field experiment', *Journal of Personality and Social Psychology*, 31, pp. 852–4.

VISSCHER, P. DE (1991) *Us, Avatars et Métamorphoses de la Dynamique des Groupes*, Grenoble: Presses Universitaires de Grenoble.

WICKER, A. W. (1969) 'Attitudes versus actions: the relationship of verbal and overt behavioral responses to attitude object', *Journal of Social Issues*, 25, pp. 41–78.

WICKLUND, R. A. and BREHM, J. W. (1976) *Perspectives on Cognitive Dissonance*, New York: Wiley.

ZAJONC, R. B. (1968) 'Cognitive theories in social psychology', in LINDZEY, G., and ARONSON, E. (Eds) *Handbook of social psychology*, 1, Reading: Addison-Wesley.

ZANNA, M. P. and COOPER, J. (1974) 'Dissonance and the pill: an attribution approach to studying the arousal properties of dissonance', *Journal of Personality and Social Psychology*, 29, pp. 703–9.

ZANNA, M. P. and COOPER, J. (1976) 'Dissonance and the attribution processes', in HARVEY, J. H., ICKES, W. J. and KIDD, R. F. (Eds) *New Directions in Attribution Research*, 1, Hillsdale: Erlbaum.

ZIMBARDO, P. G. (1969) *The Cognitive Control of Motivation. The Consequences of Choice and Dissonance*, Glenview: Scott, Foresman.

Index

Abelson, R. P. ix, xi, 155
abstinence behaviour 83–88, 89–93, 96, 99–109, 114–122, 134–137, 139
act rationalization 96, 99–122, 123–140, 143–145
agentic status 141–154
Ajzen, I. xi, 155
Amerio, P. 150, 155
Amione, F. 150, 155
Apfelbaum, E. viii, x, 155
argument time effects 13–20
Aronson, E. xiv, xx, xxi, 3, 149, 155
attitude 54–55, 77
  -behaviour consistency 51, 52, 54–55, 137–139, 143
  change 7–21, 23–33, 39, 57–66, 123, 124, 128, 136, 138
  consistency 25–30
  measurement 77, 135
  stability 26–30
attitudinal role-playing 78–83
attribution theory xxiii
authority 150, 153
autonomy 151–154
aversive consequences of behaviour 36, 82–83
Azdia, T. 92, 160

Basset, R. 99, 107, 157
Baumeister, R. F. 51, 143, 155
Bayesian models viii
Beauvois, J. L. xii, xxiv, 10, 11, 12, 14, 16, 19, 24, 32, 44, 46, 50, 53, 55, 56, 57, 60, 64, 67, 93, 99, 106, 112, 118, 150, 151, 153, 155, 156, 160
behaviour
  -attitude consistency 51, 52, 54–55, 137–139, 143
  cognition 6–21, 24–25, 30–32, 35, 45
  derogation 131–137

behaviour (*continued*)
  downgrading 20, 112–122
  organizational vii
  predictions 145
  upgrading 112–119
behavioural rationalization 73, 99–122
Bem, D. J. 19, 41, 51, 93, 143, 148, 156
Berkowitz, L. xxiii, 156
binary relations 2
bogus pipeline 128–131
boring task 9–10, 75–83, 94–95
Bosotti, E. 150, 155
Brehm, J. W. xiii, xiv, xx, xxii, 3, 6, 7, 16, 34, 35, 40, 48, 97, 98, 133, 142, 156, 157, 162, 163
Brock, T. C. 40, 41, 156
Bruner, J. S. 156
Brunetti, F. 99, 106, 112, 114, 118, 156
Brunswik, E. viii, 156
Bungert, M. 44, 46, 55, 155

Cacioppo, J. T. 99, 107, 157
Calder, B. J. 34, 50, 156
Carlsmith, J. M. xiii, xiv, xix, xx, 3, 5, 14, 16, 34, 35, 75, 79, 82, 149, 155, 156, 158
Cartwright, D. xviii, 157
Carver, C. S. 20, 131, 133, 134, 147, 149, 154, 162
causal explanation 56–69, 143, 144, 151, 152
  effects 60–63
  processes 56–66
Chandler, T. A. 64, 157
Channouf, A. 19, 26, 30, 32, 33, 56, 57, 60, 62, 63, 157
Chris, S. A. 148, 157
Cialdini, R. B. 99, 107, 157
Clemence, A. xxiii, 20, 47, 157, 158

Index

Index